The Celebrated Pet:
How Americans Memorialize Their Animal Friends

by

Gay L. Balliet-Perkins

This is a work of nonfiction. Most names, characters, locales, dates, businesses, events, incidences, organizations, and establishments are real. The author has been given permission to use people's and organizations' real names throughout the work and their photos on her website.

The Celebrated Pet
How Americans Memorialize Their Animal Friends

Cover Art by *The Wild Rose Press, Inc.*

The Wild Rose Press, Inc.
PO Box 708
Adams Basin, NY 14410-0708
Visit us at www.thewildrosepress.com

Publishing History
First Edition, 2020
Print ISBN 978-1-5092-3052-5
Digital ISBN 978-1-5092-3053-2

Published in the United States of America

Rob and his fellow travelers arrived in Tibet on July 2, 2007. At Jokang, the oldest Buddhist monastery in Lhasa, the capital of Tibet and most revered Buddhist holy site, Rob opened his knapsack, took out Diane's face mask jar, which at one time had held exfoliation cream, and unscrewed the lid. He shook some dust into the palm of his hand, then flicked it into the air, where a light breeze carried it away. "Be free, here, Wools. Let your spirit be free. You're in a good place here."

The culmination of the trip was climbing to Mount Everest's base camp. There Rob said a prayer for his friend Bill and laid the old man's photo in the snow. Then, while the others were photographing Her Snowy Highness, Rob walked back to his sack and took out Diane's jar. Holding an eight-by-ten photo of Wools, Rob walked over to a rocky outcropping punctuated by scores of pink and yellow wildflowers. He gathered snow from the mountain into a pile. Then he opened the jar. Sifting Wools' ashes between his fingers, and looking up at Everest, he spread them over the pile of snow. "We made it, Wools—you and me—together. This is the highest hike we've ever done, ya know? Seventeen thousand feet we climbed." Rob placed the rest of Wools' ashes atop a pile of snow with her picture next to them.

Rob's trip to Tibet with Wools riding in his knapsack sealed his decision to quit his Irish pub and begin life anew at Ron's pet crematory. He had witnessed a simpler, purer, and more honest life in Tibet—one reflective of Wools herself. Wools had found fulfillment simply by sharing life with her human companions. She hadn't needed material things to be happy; she simply had been content to *be*.

Praise for Gay L. Balliet-Perkins and...

Touched By All Creatures **(1999):**
"Eminently readable. Will be welcomed by everyone who enjoyed James Herriot's efforts."

~Booklist

"The wonders of animals and the earthy, humane details of doctoring them shines through."

~Publishers Weekly

"Every bit as eccentric, loveable and heart-tugging as [James Herriot's] Yorkshire chronicles."

~Sunday Tribune Review

***

Lowell: The True Story of an Existential Pig **(2000):**
"...another delectable trough's worth of vets-at-home and vets-on-the-road anecdotes..."

~Publisher's Weekly

"Like James Herriot's books, Balliet's *Lowell* reads more like a riveting novel than a 'pigography.'"

~Sunday Star-Ledger

Dedication

In Memory of all my animal friends—
Someday we'll meet again.
Cats: Beverly Ann, Timmy Lee, Brian, Sticky Bun,
Starvin' Marvin, Sophie, Little Sophie, Gadney,
Broccoli, Allen, Hailey, Susan, Lyle, Lyla, Marshall,
Blackie, Blackie II, Blackie III, Robert, Heidi, Bruce,
Milton, Jean, Willis, Timmy Timster, Kramer, Annie,
Missy, Jessie, Mindy, Irazu, Poas, Arenal, Spittin' Po,
Robin, Terry, Louise, Stevie I, Spike, Lucy, Ricky,
Wendy "Wrinky Nose," Conrad, Willis, Tiger Lily,
Mort, Spinny, Stevie, Mort & Pat Eckensberger,
Purrlicue, Ralphie, and Spittin' Broccoli,
Seanie on the Lehigh, Elaine, Whitey, Tony, Wendy,
Ricky, Elliot, Curly.
Horses: Nicholas, Merry, Fax, Lillie, Fancy, Julie,
Timmy, Lucy.
Pigs: Lowell, Lucille, Ivy Mae, Skippy, Miss Piggy,
Sniffer, Ashley, Grunt, Sally, Big Will, Wilbur, Annie
Louise.
Pea fowl: Fred and Ethel
Chickens: Big Red, Silver Talker, Nutty, Blackie.
Dogs: Pal, Heidi, Greta, Daphne, Abby, Diane, Lady.
Llamas: Larry, Autumn, Seamus
Scotch Highland steer: Scotty
Finally, I dedicate this book to all the forgotten
farm animals who suffered to fill human bellies.
May your offspring secure a more peaceful, content life
and a more humane end.

In Memory of
Lucy Perelson
(1997-2006)
Port Elizabeth, South Africa

Lucy, a pig adopted out of the African bush by the Perelson family, delighted people with her loving, kind nature and her mischievousness: from rearranging the living room furniture to raiding the refrigerator to sharing her family's beds to romping through the waves at the beach. Lucy was a special pig-person, a true character, and a cherished member of the family.

Lucy is sadly missed and lovingly remembered by her family and friends. This poem is dedicated to the memory of Lucy, who, through numerous emails from her mother, Ivanhoe Perelson, I came to know, love, and consider one of my own.

My Lucy

Wanting to meet Lucy,
Lucy the Great,
Your Highness Lucy.
But South Africa worlds from Pennsylvania.
Grew to love Lucy
Through photographs
Through emails.

Lucy
Wearing two pigtails
in   in
her her
hair hair

Breakfast mash
on her   smile.
     morning

      Playing
        the
in   waves,

      Rolling
        the
in   waves.

A pet bird
On her back
   riding.

In her people's bed
bbbblllllaaaannnnkkkkeeeettt
   peeking.

    S   S
    I   I
    D   by   D
    E   E

Dog Emily   Lucy Pig.

Sharing a world,
far apart yet close
Ivanhoe,
Lucy,
Gay.

"We need another and a wiser and perhaps a more mystical concept of animals....We patronize them for their incompleteness, for their tragic fate of having taken form so far below ourselves. And therein we err, and greatly err. For the animal shall not be measured by man. In a world older and more complete than ours they move finished and complete, gifted with extensions of the senses we have lost or never attained, living by voices we shall never hear. They are not brethren, they are not underlings; they are other nations, caught with ourselves in the net of life and time, fellow prisoners of the splendour and travail of the earth."

From "The Outermost House" by Henry Beston (1928)

***

Please Note: Readers are welcome to access photos to accompany the following chapters by going to the author's website, www.gayballiet.net, where pictures for each chapter can be viewed.

Introduction

When I was five years old, Thomas died.

I had enjoyed a mock tea party with my mother beneath the boughs of the budding apricot tree and dressed myself as Roy Rogers' bride, complete with cowgirl hat and boots. I ran toward the flowering crabapple tree and scooted on my scaly knees next to my dime-store turtle, who was enjoying an afternoon in the sun. I'd brought him a few crumbs from our tea and part of a worm, just in case he didn't like cookies. But when I bent down and offered him the treat, he didn't move. He lay motionless in the grass.

A week earlier on a sojourn with my mother to the local Woolworth store, I had plucked Thomas from an aquarium piled high with at least a hundred black-and-orange squirming, wriggling turtles, all the size of a child's palm. I was wildly excited to have a new friend to take home.

Back in the fifties and sixties, variety stores sold these helpless creatures with no concern for how their new owners, mostly kids under the age of twelve, would be able to feed them and keep them alive. To the child being towed in hand by a parent toward the light bulb or vacuum cleaner bag department, the pet section with its colorful array of dyed chicks, guinea pigs, turtles, baby crocodiles, and fish was wonderfully appealing. These unassuming creatures were sold not only in the local Woolworths and five-and-dimes but also in hardware stores and the town's general store. No specialty turtle food or instructions on how to raise a turtle were sent home with the doomed pets. In fact, store managers never expected the turtles to survive beyond a few days at most, but the kids who bought them did. The stores became outlets for selling critters whose life span was as short as it took to starve the animal to death.

The afternoon I knelt beside my immobile turtle was one of the saddest in my life. I didn't understand why its orange legs and neck, longer than I'd ever seen them, hung limp from his shell. I tried to flip an eyelid open with my chubby fingers but couldn't get a grip. The eyes remained tightly shut. As a five-year-old I didn't know much about life and nothing about death—no one I knew had ever died, and I'd never attended a funeral—so I just waited and waited and waited for my turtle to wake up. The afternoon seemed endless.

My mother came out onto the porch. "What are you doing out there? You've been under that tree all afternoon. Do you feel okay?"

"Thomas won't move, Mommy. I guess he's asleep, but I can't get him to wake up."

With that my mother wiped her hands on her royal-blue apron and walked over. She squatted next to me, her dress and apron between her legs, and took the turtle in her hands. Then she looked at me with sad eyes. "Thomas is dead, sweetie."

"What do you mean—dead?" I took him from her hands. I held him and tried to open his lids again.

"Don't do that, dear. He's gone."

"Gone *where*? Where *is* he?" I wasn't referring to

the physical turtle who for a week had been my constant companion. I meant his personality, the part of Thomas that lay inside him, that made him blink questioningly at me, that made him my friend and the one I, an only child, could talk to. Where was the Thomas who crawled to the edge of his water dish, then pulled himself over the edge and into it with a tiny splash? Where was the quirky head tilt? Where was my Thomas?

"Where *is* Thomas? Tell me."

"He's up in the sky." My mother looked up through the branches of the apricot tree.

"He is not! Look!" I lifted the physical Thomas in my hands.

My mother stared at the sky as though searching for something. "He's in the clouds—with God. God needed Thomas."

I remembered hearing about God in Sunday school but nothing about his needing turtles.

It was unfathomable to me. "God?" I paused. "Like Santa Claus?"

"Not quite, hon."

"The tooth fairy? Did the tooth fairy take Thomas?"

"No." My mother rubbed her forehead. "Well, maybe."

"Is God a girl or a boy?"

My mother sighed. "I don't know."

Tears ran down my cheeks. "What would God want with my Thomas? Why would she take him from me? What could she possibly want with my turtle? I've only had him for a few days!"

My mother stood up and straightened her apron.

"Thomas is dead, Gay. I know it's hard for you to understand, but he simply *is* no more."

There was nothing *simple* about my turtle not existing. This was serious stuff.

My mother gently drew Thomas from my hands and placed him in the grass between us.

"He's gone, Gay. Every living thing must die sometime. None of us lives forever."

I looked up. "Huh?" Believing the tooth fairy had taken Thomas to her fantasy den was far less scary than hearing this. But my mother didn't lie. I looked down at Thomas. "What do we feel when we die?" I whispered.

"I'm not sure."" My mother looked tired. "I don't know." Thank goodness she didn't hit me with the story about all good creatures and people going to heaven and the bad ones plummeting into an endless hell. I don't think I could have taken that—though, for sure, Thomas would have gone straight to heaven, for he was a good and faithful turtle.

I glanced around trying to get a bead on what she was telling me. "Where do we go when we die?"

"Some people think we go to a really nice place in the sky."

I looked straight up through the apricot boughs but only saw endless blue punctuated by white marshmallow-fluff clouds. I didn't see any people or animals up there.

"Are you and Daddy going to die?" I looked at Thomas.

"Yes, dear, but not for a very long time."

"Am I going to die?"

"Not for a very, very long time. We'll all be together for years and years. And you shouldn't be concerned about dying because it's all so far off for all of us."

"Is Thomas a ghost?" I thought of Halloween, of white, flitty, flying things.

"Some people think the dead come back as ghosts, but that's not really true. Ghosts are imaginary, made up." My mother put her arms around me. "I don't want you to worry about dead things right now, because you and Daddy and I aren't going to die for a long time. Now, say goodbye to Thomas and come inside." With that she walked back to the porch, turned once more toward me, opened the screen door, and disappeared inside.

I was left alone with my dead turtle. I picked him up, turned him over on his back, and rubbed his belly with my index finger. More tears dribbled down my cheek, and then I couldn't see Thomas very well. He was a blur in my hands. I sniffed, wiped my eyes, and Thomas came into focus again.

"Give back my Thomas, you bad tooth fairy." But I had already been sitting most of the afternoon with the immobile creature, and something told me he wouldn't suddenly come back to life. And something also told me a generous fairy who only wanted children's teeth wouldn't really be interested in absconding with my turtle.

I was frustrated, robbed by something I couldn't fight or talk to, and scared of this thing called death. For minutes I sat with Thomas in my lap and stroked his little thin legs. Then I patted down a section of grass about the size of my softball and laid him in it. I arranged his legs neatly underneath his shell and tried to put his tiny head back inside where it would be more comfortable, but it wouldn't budge, frozen on the outside. Next I found a good-sized stick.

I had no idea what I was doing but felt compelled to keep doing it. I laid Thomas aside and tore out the grass I had patted down moments before. Then I began poking at the roots with the stick. It was tough going, and all I knew was that I needed to make a safer spot for Thomas. I dug and dug, but the grass roots were strong.

As I hacked furiously at the ground, I suddenly noticed my mother's shoes beside me. I looked up, and she was smiling. She bent down, wiped my face, and showed me something. A spoon. She demonstrated how to dig, then put the handle in my hand. When she saw a little pile of dirt next to a hole, she knew I had the situation under control and left.

In minutes I had dug a little grave about four inches wide and long by two inches deep, hardly deep enough to protect the dead turtle from weather or predators but deep enough to cover him with a snug blanket of earth. Gently I placed Thomas inside the hole, rearranged his legs and neck again, patted him once more, and sprinkled dirt on him. Then I patted the rounded grave with my little hands and sat back, looking.

Why did I put him under the ground? I didn't know. I only knew that the desire had come from inside my head, something insistent, a feeling so intense I couldn't refuse it. I was compelled by a force as mysterious as death itself.

I stood up and went into the house, to the kitchen, where my mother was finishing a batch of tapioca pudding, and went to the cabinet beside the oven. From it I took out a clean plastic margarine tub.

"Can I have this?"

"Sure, sweetheart."

"Would you fill it with water for me?" My mother held the plastic tub under the faucet, then placed it in my hands. "Be careful so you don't spill it."

Carefully I walked outside and over to Thomas's little hill of dirt. I set the margarine tub half-filled with water next to the grave. "There, Thomas. Now, wherever you are, your pool is close by."

I wiped away the last tear and headed for the house, spoon in hand.

****

Many years have passed since Thomas died. Unfortunately the "tooth fairy" didn't stop her carnage of my beloved animal friends. She stole Grace the kitten, whom I desperately tried to keep alive after her lower jaw was shot off by a hunter. She stole my family's dogs—Pal the collie and two German shepherds, Greta and Heidi. And she wasn't content pillaging my parade of animals as I grew up and went to college. In that time death came to my grandmother's dog and her bird and then Gramma herself. Death robbed me of my Gramma Eckensberger, who taught me to love and respect nature and animals as much as I loved her and myself. And even though death intruded more often as time went by, I found it as incomprehensible at the age of forty as it had been when I was five.

Yet for all its callousness, death has taught me things—not the least of which is to live life with the enthusiasm of a child.

****

A recent death jogged my sensibilities about people and their relationships to their animals. This happened when I had buried our old barn cat Elaine, accidentally rolled on and suffocated by a sleeping pot-bellied pig. Elaine had been my friend and companion through all my horse-showing days, always accompanying me around the farm and helping me with my stall-cleaning chores. She had the simplest of motives, content to merely attend, and the huge emptiness her death left in my heart made me realize that the loss of an animal friend could have just as much impact as losing a human family member or best friend.

In fact, for me, losing a pot-bellied pig, a horse, or one of my house or barn cats was far more heart-wrenching than hearing about a distant relative's passing. Was there something wrong with me for feeling this way? To be truthful, the death of a human acquaintance affected me far less than the deaths of my horses Merry, Fancy, Fax, and Nicholas and my house cats Robert, Milton, Wendy, and Ricky. I wondered if other people questioned their grief when their animal friends died. In fact, I have decided after much deliberation that a life, even if it be a species different from human, is richly deserving of human grief and the ceremonies and tributes that accompany it. And I don't apologize for that sentiment.

The pet impacts a human's life in ways that other humans cannot. I have found that the human-animal bond is incredibly strong, strong enough to compel us to honor the animal's memory. Why are they thus deserving?

Honesty. That is part of the answer. I believe the human-animal bond is at all times honest, for an animal cannot be otherwise, and in the presence of a guileless creature, most humans behave honestly because they gain nothing by being false. And, with their authentic personalities, the animals let us recall the capacity for these qualities in ourselves. They are like mirrors to us. If we look inside them we will see, reflected there, the capacity for honesty within ourselves. Our pets challenge us to rise above common humanity.

Honesty is but one of the incalculable gifts we receive from our animal friends. Add to that loyalty, trust, unconditional love, and the many other qualities common to pets, and it's no wonder humans suffer profoundly when their animal friends die. When a pet dies, we don't just lose the animal, we lose our own essence and the self-acceptance we felt in the company of that animal.

So it is understandable and logical that the bond with our pets is incredibly strong and that we feel compelled to offer our furry or scaly friend a deserving burial. Burial or cremation is a way to give back, to seek balance, to do a favor in return.

And not only does the dead pet need burial, as people need burial, for the respectful and sanitary disposing of a body, but the dead animal friend also deserves a memorial. The human's gift is all bound up in a need—instinctual, perhaps, to memorialize the pet in a personal way, with ceremony, with praise, and above all with gratitude for her companion who loved and played and taught invaluable lessons.

The day I buried my faithful barn cat in one of my T-shirts, I began to wonder about the practice of pet burial and how other people make tributes for their animals, just as I had for Elaine. That questioning led me to write this book. The true stories here affirm the importance of the bond between animals and people and showcase the many gifts pets offer their humans. Every animal's life story reaps a gift in return—a memorial: simple or extravagant, conventional or eccentric, an instinctive and significant act of honor, tribute, and need.

****

So sits my cat cemetery—single smooth rocks marking each grave—not nearly as grand or elegant as some depicted in the pages that follow. All my "good teachers" are buried together, each lovingly wrapped in one of my T-shirts beneath the old oak trees under which, as kittens, they loved to run, hide, and torment the shrews and ground beetles. When they were grown, we shared our love of the stillness in those trees, the earthy smell of the matted leaves, the faint odor of honeysuckle. And now they lie, buried with love, beneath their moss-covered bower.

Table of Contents

Chapter One
A Spirit in the Clouds

Species: Canine—German Rottweiler
Name: Wools, Ms. Tee, Tee-Tee
Born: July 23, 1997
Died: Feb 12, 2007
Human companions: Diane & Rob Mayer

Diane held her dying mother's frail hand. "Mom, what should I do about this litter of puppies?" A curtain flickered in the breeze and drew fleeting shadows over the bed.

Her mother lifted her head, her lips strained. "You need a puppy of your own—to help you."

"But, Mom, I don't think I can handle all this—my divorce, moving my business, moving my home, and caring for you. I'm stressed, scared. What will happen without you? How am I going to take care of a puppy, too?"

A crow cawed beyond the sickroom window. The bird called loudly—feathered energy. The mother forced a whisper. "Choose a female from your litter. The one who will take charge. She'll…" She struggled to catch her breath. "…help you."

That evening Diane drove the three-hour ride from her childhood home where she first raised her own puppy. She had always felt protected there; no matter the problem, she could always run home, lock the door behind her, and feel safe, nestled within the soft, dark walls of the house. But her visits home these days felt different—home didn't feel as safe with death lurking around the corners.

Listening to the murmur of the tires, she thought maybe her mother was right—she needed a dog to help her through life.

The next day Diane awoke to the puppies' mewling and yipping. They were hungry for breakfast. She loaded the puppy chow into five ceramic bowls and placed each neatly in the twelve-foot square pen built for ten energetic Rottweiler pups. The pups, twirl-barking and dance-hopping, mobbed the dishes as she set them on the mat. "Okay, okay already. You guys aren't really starving, are you? You *did* have something to eat last night." Nine puppies crowded the bowls, slurping and gulping, their heads deep inside the dishes. But one puppy stood alone, watching, patiently waiting for her turn.

Diane smiled down at the pup. "Well, look at you, you beautiful thing. Why aren't you eating with the others?"

The puppy looked up, regarded the others devouring their food, then promptly picked out a dish. Having worked dogs in agility, utility, and obedience classes, and having bred these puppies' parents, Diane knew most everything there was to know about canines. She'd be the first to admit she understood dog behavior far better than she understood what motivated people. For sure that pup had been waiting for the others to eat first.

Diane reached over the dog pen and scooped the pup into her arms. "What a good pup you are, waiting for your brothers and sisters to eat first." She spun the animal around. "Huh, you're a little girl." The pup peered into her eyes, and immediately Diane recognized something special. The puppy's gaze was intense, as though she knew, even at so young an age, exactly what her human was thinking. "I get it. You're the one." She held the animal high, but the pup never took her eyes away from Diane's—their gazes locked.

Diane held the little female to her chest. "I don't know what kind of spell you just put over me, but it worked. What you just did for the other pups—letting them eat first—was very special. Do you like me well enough to be my lifetime companion?" The puppy lay limp in her hands, neither wriggling nor whimpering to be put down—just watching, scrutinizing Diane. Then the pup opened her mouth, yawned, and her lips drew back in a big Rottweiler grin. Diane laughed. "Great. We're gonna be pals, you wooly thing. Now, get something to eat before there's nothing left."

Diane's hunch about the female pup was right. Every day she observed Wools, named for her thick hair coat, doing something fairly uncommon for a young dog. When the other puppies were called inside, she stood back while the others, anxious for treats, rushed through the kitchen door. Only after walking the perimeter of the yard and accounting for everyone did the puppy follow the others inside where she allowed herself a treat.

Wools seemed born with a worldliness, a knowledge usually credited to humans, certainly not to animals. But Wools' wisdom was of a different kind—

sophisticated yet innocent. In those eyes that had hard-gazed Diane into accepting her as her own, lived a being who valued unselfishness, caring, and compassion for others over herself. Hers were simple needs: if all was right with her human and dog family, only then did she do for herself. She was otherworldly. Selflessness was her *modus operandi.*

Just a few weeks later, Wools' selflessness eased Diane through the hard times, including the death of her mother. At night when Diane startled awake from a dark dream, Wools rose to her bedside, laying her head next to Diane's trembling hand. Wools' presence soothed, nurtured, protected—through divorce, through moving a business and a house. And years later Wools—Diane's "home base" as she called her—stood by her side through her father's death.

Though Wools commiserated with Diane much as a human friend would, she delighted in living life as a dog, as well—especially when it came to the outdoors. Wools' initiation into the Mayers' love of hiking and nature began when the pup was only fourteen weeks old. Five members of the family—Diane; friend, Rob; Ian, Wools' pup brother; and Bodhi, their three-year-old Golden Retriever—regularly explored Chadds Ford, a wooded area in Pennsylvania near the Delaware border. Here Wools honed her hunting skills, creep-crawling among the vines and rhododendrons in search of a chipmunk or a butterfly. She played and rolled with her brother Ian in the leaves, loving the roughness of the fight and the feel of the rich, dark ground on her back. When Ian and Wools tired themselves on the trail, Diane and Rob put them into their knapsacks for the trek back.

Stalking critters in the woods was strenuous work for a puppy, but by the time Wools reached adolescence, she was an expert, hunting down larger prey such as groundhogs and foxes, and, on one occasion, with the help of her brother, a deer. When she saw something move in the distance, she came to a point, analyzing the creature's smell, waiting and waiting and waiting...sometimes for half an hour, and, then, with one huge *Pounce!* she had it.

Diane and Rob hiked most of Delaware's state parks, Wools happy beside them. She romped the beach at Henlopen State Park, through the stands of oak at Brandywine State Park, and along the water's edge at Bellevue State Park. As gentle as she was at home in the living room, when hiking in the woods and on the beach, she morphed into a powerhouse, barreling after a crab or other creature or tearing off the beaten woodland trail to forge a path of her own.

Her performance on the hiking trails and her reputation as Super Dog amongst the Mayers' neighbors led them to ponder Wools' abilities in dog competitions. So Diane signed her up for her first obedience class.

Wools succeeded at both obedience training and utility training. She followed Diane's directions as though she anticipated her human's thoughts. While she accomplished the utility and obedience courses with ease, Diane knew she was bored, so she signed her up for an agility course.

Rottweilers were bred as herders and guardians, so it was no wonder, considering Wools' intelligence blended with her natural-born penchant for ruggedness and speed, that she excelled in all her classes—

particularly the agility classes. Agility allowed Wools, built more like a male dog and weighing a fit one hundred ten pounds, and Diane, her diminutive coach, the perfect balance—speed and athleticism finessed with fine communication skills.

In one competition Diane ran alongside Wools. "Slow down, hunch down, and dip into the tunnel, Wools." And Wools did exactly as Diane said, slowing up to the entrance, crunching her body, then speeding through the plastic cave and rushing out the other end like water from a sewer pipe. She was hell on paws when she heard the starter whistle and attacked the maze unlike any dog the trainers had ever seen. Running the agility course fulfilled Wools. She loved extreme sports.

"Wow! Look at that Rotty! She's terrific!" An agility instructor remained awe-stricken as Wools flashed past and over the third fence.

Another stood up clapping. "Tremendous job!"

A spectator yelled from the stands. "Too much!"

The crowd yelled and applauded the speeding bullet-dog as the announcer went berserk. "Top notch!" From then on Wools' nickname became Ms. Tee, Ms. Tiptop, Ms. Tremendous, Ms. Terrific. Tee-Tee wooed all the dog trainers with her keen intelligence and her willingness to exceed even herself. Darting through the hoops, down the teeter-totter, through the tunnel, over the fences, she and coach Diane showed everyone how Ms. Tee and Diane worked together, how in sync they were, not only during the competition but also when relaxing together between rounds. She and Diane became known in the competitive circuit gossip as "the team to beat." Rob affectionately called them the

"Extreme Tee-am."

Diane whispered as Wools watched television with them one Sunday evening. "Look at her now. She's so laid back with us." She smiled. "You'd never think that this afternoon she was racing like a maniac, hurdling fences and barrel-assing through a plastic tunnel." Wools looked up, smiled widely, and placed her head back on her crossed front legs.

As serious as Wools was about her competitions was how silly she could be at play, as when she acted out "Killer Snowman," her favorite winter sport. After Rob and Diane spent an afternoon constructing a human-sized snowman, Rob gave Wools the go-ahead. "Okay, Wools, get 'im." Wools revved up, biting the snow between her legs, scrunching down, then leaping up and racing toward the snowman. *Blam*! She dove into the snowman's stomach and burst out the other side.

The snowman teetered for a moment while the snow-laced Wools turned and prepared for another attack. With another blast to his hind end, the snowman blew apart into a snow-feathered flurry. Then, cheered on by Rob and Diane, Wools dismembered, decapitated, and battered his remains. Every winter hike ended with the Killer Snowman game, and Wools had killed upwards of seventy of them by the end.

One evening in their living room, Diane watched Wools, a finger pressed to her lip. "She's all about balance, isn't she? As extreme a competitor as she is, that's also how quiet and relaxed she can be. As serious as she is hunting is as goofy as she is playing Killer Snowman. This dog does a perfect job balancing her life."

Rob looked up at the ceiling. "Yeah, that's something we could all use a little of."

****

Wools really enjoyed a unique communication with Diane. Her ability to understand both what Diane was saying and what she was thinking happened consistently during Diane's own dog training classes. During Diane's course for dog owners, Doggie Massage 101, Wools agreed to be Diane's demo dog. The evening began with a friendly introduction. Eight people sat gathered in a semicircle around Diane and Wools, who sat quietly beside her.

Diane began to explain the first step in relaxing a tense dog. Without a word Ms. Tee lay down, though clearly not tense. Diane, thinking nothing of it, began to run her open hand along Wools' back. When she had demonstrated the preliminary massage techniques, Diane offered to repeat the same demonstration on Wools for the people on their off-side. Without being told, Wools stood up, sauntered over to her left side, and lay down in the exact same position. Only vaguely did Diane realize people were talking and not listening.

"Did you see that?"

"Yeah—pretty amazing. The dog just got up and positioned herself without being told to."

"Just like she knew what her owner was saying."

Diane regarded the crowd. "All right. I would like each person to practice some massage techniques on Wools." Wools looked up and smiled, her teeth glint-gleaming. Then she laid her big head down and waited for the first person to sit down beside her. One by one each participant manipulated Wools' legs, her toes, her neck, even the base of her stubby tail. She didn't budge

20

an inch. She was soaking up the attention, enjoying the participants' massaging her muscles like well-risen lumps of dough.

****

One day a neighbor thought she heard Diane talking to someone.

Sheryl hesitated on the doorstep. "Is there someone here, Diane? I hope I'm not interrupting something."

"Oh, you aren't. It's only Wools and me. She and I were just talking." Wools sat quietly beside the kitchen table.

"You talk with your dog?" Sheryl's eyebrows knitted. Ms. Tee was smiling broadly.

"Yep, we talk all the time." Diane smiled at Wools. "And don't look at me like I'm nuts. She tells me profound things about life." Wools smiled again, tongue lolling. "To live on the edge—always push the envelope. We were just discussing Robert Frost, as a matter of fact. Wools thinks we need to go off the trails more often when we hike. She thinks Rob and I should take the path less traveled.

"She says if we look beyond what we can actually see, look past the trail, past the next person, past the idea, the dream, the goal, it'll make us face our fears. We'll be stronger for it."

Sheryl pursed her lips. "She told you this?"

"Yeah, you think I'm nuts, but I'm not. It's uncanny the way we can talk with each other. Did you know that's why Rottweilers don't make very good police dogs? It's because they think too much. They won't blindly run into the path of danger without first thinking it all out. And cops don't like a dog that hesitates and takes time to think."

Not walking on the beaten path was only one piece of advice Diane took from Wools. The angel in a dog's suit taught her, by example, to reach beyond this physical earth, to explore all possibilities. She taught Diane and Rob they should stop hustling, stop "rabbiting" and relax as she demonstrated during a massage. Her behavior exemplified living naturally and instinctively.

In her more playful moods, Wools could be as silly as a big kid—like the afternoon they hiked to the river's edge during a drought. Immediately upon seeing the muddy river's edge, Wools charged into the slop, pawed furiously, scooping mud, water, and gravel high into the air behind her, and sniffing, feeling with her paws for one of her favorite toys—a tire. She sank her teeth into the exposed edge of the tire and began to pull, yanking with all her strength, her haunches braced deep in the silt. She pulled, and soon the tire sucked loose with an explosive *Pop!* Rob and Diane roared with laughter while she dragged her prey up the hill—her souvenir.

Years of hiking, catching small creatures off the trail, running agility courses, fighting with tires, and lounging with Rob and Diane on a Sunday afternoon passed by far too quickly. The Mayers hiked their last trail with Wools at Mink Brook Trail in New Hampshire in January 2007.

In the forest where Wools and her family had romped when she was much younger, the Mayers and their dear old dog stood for the last time together in the deep snow. The trees sheltered them safely beneath their crystal-covered boughs under the spell of togetherness and love. A soft snow began falling, and the sound of quiet encompassed them. So alone, so solitary in the wild within the comforting woods, their only sense was of their strength together. Each, amongst the others, centered on their being one—as a family. The feeling of belonging to the trees, the water, the snow and ice, enveloped them as a light snow fell, on their parkas, on Wools' thick coat. A critter's lone tracks disappeared down the ridge to a safe place beneath a mountain laurel. The three, each aware of the others alongside, looked out over the creek, breathing the crisp moist air of the woods while the falling snow enfolded them in a soft blanket.

Wools died a month later, on February 12, 2007.

****

Wools' Memorials

Rob Mayer had been in the restaurant business for seventeen years, the past twelve as the general manager of a popular Irish pub, the Logan House. Under his supervision twenty-four employees worked weekends and evenings in an atmosphere of revelry and camaraderie, and they, along with Rob, delighted in the pub's social scene of live local bands and Irish fiddlers. Rob found his social life full and his patrons' friendships fulfilling, but in time, he realized he wasn't truly happy—something was missing.

One evening after the last server had said good-bye, Bill Bewley, Rob's close elderly friend and the restaurant's accountant, saw Rob hunched over the bar, his head in his hands.

Bill sat on a stool next to him. "Something wrong, Rob?" The bar area smelled of beer and cigarettes, and usually Rob didn't mind the odor, but that night it hung acrid, nauseating.

Rob looked up, his face pale. "I don't know, Bill. Ya know, we've discussed this issue before. Is this really what I want to do for the rest of my life? Look, it's 1:30 in the morning." He paused. "I really don't have much of a life here." He glanced around the bar and the seating area where most of the chairs sat askew. A few napkins lay, discarded, on the floor, and crumbs littered the tabletops.

Always a fatalist, Bill looked down into his clenched fists. "You'll know when the time is right, Rob. Something will give you a clue. Right now, this place allows you a pretty secure life. Maybe the time will come when you can make that lifestyle change. Until then, just keep plugging."

"Guess so." Rob sighed as he closed the door behind him.

For another half a year Rob and Bill worked the pub, each the other's friend and support. The restaurant business was all Rob knew, so he continued to serve up good food, drink, and relative happiness at Logan's.

But Wools' passing set the wheels of change in motion.

****

On February 13th, 2007 when Diane and Rob went to the Delaware Pet Crematorium to pick up Wools' ashes, they arrived devastated. Diane felt her guardian angel had been stolen, and Rob felt angry he'd never again share lengthy conversations with his canine buddy. With her death had been stolen their energy and lust for life—Rob and Diane were sucked dry with grief.

Yet, for all the emptiness, being able to hold her ashes provided some comfort. Rob held Wools' cremation urn, turning it round and round in his hands, feeling its cool weight. As the crematory owner stood by, Rob turned the urn in his hands. "She was everything to us. She taught us so much. I can't take it. I can't believe she's dead—in this bottle."

Ron Fox, the man who had handed Rob the container, looked down. "Her job was done, Rob. She was put on this earth to give you unconditional love, honesty, and positive energy. Her mission was accomplished.

"I want you to know that's not a bunch of bunk. I really believe what I just said. Our pets are sometimes our only solace. Each one, as I did with Wools, I handle with the greatest respect because I know that dog or cat has given so much of themselves to their human family. And cremating them is the cleanest, most pure way of disposing of their bodies."

He paused. "But I won't be doing this much longer. I'm getting ready to retire. So I'm spreading the word, waiting for the right person to come along. That person's gotta love animals, first and foremost."

Rob held Wools' cremation urn in his hands and turned it around, feeling the smooth metal. "Really? You're thinking of retiring?"

"It's time for a younger person to take over, but I don't want just anyone. Every day I live other people's sadness. Whoever takes over this job has to be a very caring and understanding person. And he can't want to do this for the money. He must want to provide a very necessary service for people during some of the worst times of their lives."

Diane and Rob looked at each other. Rob petted Wools' urn. "I think I might be interested in that job.

How about if I think it over and call you in a couple of months? Maybe you'd show me the ropes here? Right now, I'd like to take Wools home and just be with her."

"I understand perfectly."

A winter storm began as Rob and Diane drove away from the crematorium. They drove for quite a while before pulling into the gravel parking lot of Bellevue State Park, Wools' favorite hiking spot. Rob, with Diane shielding Wools' urn, forged through the driving snow, already five inches deep. They braced against the wind as they battled their way up the mountain so familiar to them and Wools. Finally, Rob and Diane arrived at Wools' favorite spot where pine trees growing close together had made a low-hanging archway. Wools had always enjoyed sitting in its center, watching the chipmunks and squirrels. It was her outpost where she had played sentry.

Rob and Diane stood beneath the branches with their backs against the wind. Diane took the urn from beneath her jacket and unscrewed the lid. She reached inside with her thumb and index finger and took a pinch of ashes, letting them be taken by the wind and snow. Then Rob reached inside, tears streaming down his face. He, too, let nature take Wools with her into the woods.

"Our good, good Wools." Diane waved good-bye. "My angel, my protector. Rest here, Wools, in your favorite spot." She paused. "Next year I'll come back here and bring you a fairy house where your freed spirit can play. I'll build it out of all the things you loved in the woods—all the things you carried in your mouth when we hiked here. I promise, Wools."

Since Wools had hiked and loved all the state parks

in Delaware, Rob lovingly carried Wools' ashes to each one. He put her ashes into the sand on the beach at Cape Henlopen State Park and even blew some into the ocean itself. The next week Rob sprinkled ashes into the stream at Brandywine Creek State Park. When he released the ashes into a breeze at Chadds Ford, he smiled a smile as grand as Wools' and took the half-filled urn back to the car.

In the weeks following Wools' death, Ron Fox, Rob, Diane, and Bill Bewley had many discussions about Rob's possible career change. In addition to the talks, Ron and Rob met several times at the crematorium where Ron showed him how to run the business.

Rob and Diane mulled the possibilities. Yet Rob still couldn't make such a huge decision. The more he thought about his popular Irish pub and the security it provided, the more he doubted whether he could make the crematory a go. In order to think, he often set out alone, backpack in place, into the woods around Chadds Ford. He climbed to the special boulder where he and Wools had often rested, and then he thought and talked things over with Wools' spirit.

Then, only days after that, his dear friend and mentor, Bill, died. With both Wools and Bill gone, Rob contemplated his way. What should he do?

Days later, a telephone call rousted Rob from his chair. A professor who was a regular at his pub was heading a three-week hiking and study trip to Tibet, and one spot was available if he wanted it. The hikers would visit all eleven major monasteries, including Jokang, where the original Buddha, of 600 A.D., had once sat. Having studied Buddhism when he was younger, Rob thought seriously about taking the trip. If he went, he could take his mind off Wools' and Bill's deaths for a while.

Diane nodded. "Go. You need to get away for a while. Take the opportunity, and go, Rob."

****

Rob and his fellow travelers arrived in Tibet on July 2, 2007. At Jokang, the oldest Buddhist monastery in Lhasa, the capital of Tibet and most revered Buddhist holy site, Rob opened his knapsack, took out Diane's face mask jar, which at one time had held exfoliation cream, and unscrewed the lid. He shook some dust into the palm of his hand, then flicked it into the air, where a light breeze carried it away. "Be free, here, Wools. Let your spirit be free. You're in a good place here."

The culmination of the trip was climbing to Mount Everest's base camp. There Rob said a prayer for his friend Bill and laid the old man's photo in the snow. Then, while the others were photographing Her Snowy Highness, Rob walked back to his sack and took out Diane's jar. Holding an eight-by-ten photo of Wools, Rob walked over to a rocky outcropping punctuated by scores of pink and yellow wildflowers. He gathered snow from the mountain into a pile. Then he opened the jar. Sifting Wools' ashes between his fingers, and looking up at Everest, he spread them over the pile of snow. "We made it, Wools—you and me—together. This is the highest hike we've ever done, ya know? Seventeen thousand feet we climbed." Rob placed the rest of Wools' ashes atop a pile of snow with her picture next to them.

Rob's trip to Tibet with Wools riding in his knapsack sealed his decision to quit his Irish pub and begin life anew at Ron's pet crematory. He had witnessed a simpler, purer, and more honest life in Tibet—one reflective of Wools herself. Wools had found fulfillment simply by sharing life with her human companions. She hadn't needed material things to be happy; she simply had been content to *be*. Rob, too, would be content with the simpler life the crematory could provide.

****

Diane's Memorial for Wools

As Diane promised Wools when she died, she built a fairy house to commemorate Wools' one-year passing anniversary. With two rocks Rob had taken from Everest's base camp, Diane constructed a twelve-inch-tall by eight-inch-wide fairy house of moss, Bodhi leaves, oak leaves, flower petal, pines, feathers, and a giant dandelion "wish"—mostly items Wools had retrieved on their many hikes. When it was finished, Rob and Diane hiked to Bellevue State Park and set it where Wools used to sit under the "cathedral" created by the three pines. To this day the fairy house lies sheltered beneath the pines, another memorial for Wools, one dog who touched so many people—a spirit at play in the Everest clouds.

****

Rob Mayer continues to operate Delaware Pet Crematorium at Robinson Lane, Wilmington, DE 19805. More information about this business can be found at www.theanimalsoul.com and by calling 302-656-5737.

In conjunction with his business, Diane Mayer operates a farm in Avondale, PA, dedicated to the human-animal bond. The website for her farm is www.thewhitefeatherfarm.com. Here Diane specializes in canine holistic medicine, canine massage, pool therapy, and pet grief counseling. Diane's training in animals' life-after-death experiences culminated after fifteen years of study in Nepal and with Native Americans. With this background Diane currently works, with Wools' spirit working alongside her, with people after their pet family member has died, counseling them about the technology of what happens after animals die.

Chapter Two
Chloe's Garden

Species: Pot-bellied pigs
Names: Chloe & Zack
Born: Chloe 1994; Zack 1993
Died: July 2002; Sept. 6, 2007
Human Companions: Donna and Eric Prust

Donna cooed as she held the black and white nine-week-old pot-bellied piglet in her arms. "Look at her. Isn't she precious?" Donna and her husband, Eric, had just left the 4-H farm and were taking the two-hour drive home to Livermore in northern California. "You're beautiful, aren't you?" Donna whisper-looked into Chloe's eyes. Wrapped in a soft pink cotton blanket, the piglet, no bigger than a chunky soup can, stared wide-eyed into her new owner's eyes. "Aren't you *beautiful*?" Donna repeated and snuggled her face against Chloe's soft, quarter-sized nozzle.

Chloe answered in swine-guage. *"Fru-u-u-up, fru-u-u-up, fru-u-u-up."*

Eric understood the tone of her voice and for a second looked away from the road. "I'm jealous. I don't think I like this."

Chloe sounded worried. *"Mre-e-e, mre-e-e-e, mre-e-e!"*

"It's okay, Chloe," Donna said in a soft, lilting

voice, a voice made for soothing baby pigs. "Don't be afraid of him, he's just teasing us. You can hang out all the time with me—you'll be my cuddle piggy, won't you?"

Chloe chirped, content.

****

Pot-bellied pigs have become the pet *de rigueur*. Clean, tidy, and highly intelligent, pigs' behavior and human-like traits belie the myths that give them an unearned negative image. Much research and experience with pigs as pets have proven them friendly, forgiving, protective, loyal, affectionate, and fastidious animal friends. Their intelligence rivals a three-year-old child's, they have a comedian's sense of timing, and they exhibit emotions and sensitivities mostly attributed to humans. Pigs make wonderful house pets, and a properly cared for pig hasn't so much as a whiff of unpleasant odor.

As demonstrated by Donna's cuddling little Chloe, baby pigs are delightful animals to hold and talk with. Totally focused on the person in whose arms they lie, these little creatures seem to realize just how adorable they are. They use their beautiful eyes and long eyelashes to enamor their human friends. It isn't hard to do, for pigs' eyes are like humans' in shape and size, and the pupils, so unlike those of cats and horses, are round like people's. The chocolate eyes follow their owners' movements and react like human eyes, darting at strange noises and quick movements. The pig's eye is an intelligent eye, a knowing, perceptive eye that reflects awareness when an enamored person looks into it.

Chloe fit right into the Prust household the minute

she set hoof there. She had no other animals to compete with for her humans' attention. She had it all. When Donna was cooking, Chloe sat waiting on the kitchen mat for the carrot ends, the pieces of celery, the morsels of chicken skin. She licked the brownie bowl and cleaned up any scraps of just about anything that fell by the wayside.

An hour before dinner, Donna gave her a dish of grayish-brown pig chow, accented with bits of fresh broccoli, lettuce stumps, and baby carrots. Like most pigs, Chloe had a hearty appetite even for bland manufactured food, and in two minutes her dish was licked slick-clean.

As soon as Donna and Eric sat down at the dining table, Chloe rushed in, frantic, like a little kid zeroing in on birthday cake. Just as they began to pass the fragrant roast beef, buttered mashed potatoes, and the most pig-tempting vegetable, sweet corn, Chloe leapt, her front hooves striking the edge of a dining room chair, huffing and complaining in pig language, demanding her share.

The family's quiet dinners quickly became memories of the past. During each meal Chloe begged for one more bit of hot dog or sweet potato, her voice so plaintive, so pitiful that she charmed dinner delicacies out of Donna and Eric again and again.

****

In a matter of days Chloe had become the queen of the condominium, bossing everyone in sight: she wanted a walk, she wanted a grape, she wanted a belly-rub, she wanted, she wanted, she wanted. One morning Donna heard yelling and cussing downstairs. It was her adult son, Matt. Chloe, sashaying her way through the living room to the kitchen, had bitten his big toe while he slept on a lounge chair. Similarly, her Pig-Highness asserted herself via temper tantrums, nips to the shins, or simple takeovers of territory, like usurping Eric's lounge chair.

Despite her tyrannical hold over everyone she met, Chloe's family—especially Donna—adored her. Just as Donna predicted the first day, Chloe became her cuddle-pig, burrowing under the blanket with Donna while everyone watched Alfred Hitchcock reruns in the late evening. Donna always had her heating-pad pig next to her, warming her thigh.

Then came a night when Chloe couldn't get comfortable, thanks to Eric's hoggish spread-eagle position in what she felt was *her* bed. She wriggled against his sleep-dead legs, but they wouldn't budge. She pushed with her nose, putting her weight behind the push, and when the legs refused to give way, she sank her teeth into an ankle.

"Yeo-o-o-oow!" Eric bolted upright. "What the hell was that?" Chloe leapt to Donna's side of the bed. Donna sat up, dazed, and curled an arm around the pig.

Eric rubbed the bite. "That's it! She's dethroned! We have no rights in this household, and I say we stage a coup against this tyrant-swine. She needs some other vassal to dominate."

"Well, who?" Donna's voice was thick with sleep. "I take her for walks, let her meet the neighbors. What more can I do?"

"We need to get her a friend—a pig friend. Maybe that'll take her mind off us. Call someone about adopting another pig. Tomorrow morning."

****

The next day Donna, with a pig crate in the back of

her SUV, drove to a nearby pig-rescue and sanctuary. After meeting the director and accompanying her to a large, clean dirt yard where perhaps thirty pigs were busy sniffing and snorting dirt clouds into the air, Donna noticed one totally black pig all by himself, squeezed into a corner of the yard.

Donna pointed to the lone animal. "I'd like to meet that one over there. He looks about my Chloe's age."

The director scowled. "I don't think you want him. He's not at all friendly. Doesn't have much use for people."

Donna stared. "I want to see him anyway. Can I go inside?"

"Sure. But I'm telling you, he's not very nice. His name's Zack."

The director opened the gate to the yard, and the other pigs scattered as Donna approached the pig standing by himself in the darkest corner.

She called to him from several feet away. "Hey, Zack. Are you having a good day today? Do you want to come over here?" With that, the black pig faced Donna and charged across the pen to her. He came to a sliding halt as she bent down, her hand outstretched. He looked at her for a second, then presented his head for petting. With her hand on his coal-black head, he let out a deep sigh.

The director looked amazed. "I can't believe it!"

"He's the one. I'll take him with me right now."

While Donna was filling out the paperwork, she asked about Zack's history. The director told her Zack was about a year old and had arrived there four months ago from someone who'd kept him confined to a closet.

Donna's shoulders slumped. "A *closet*?"

"When our people went to rescue him, he was in a clothes closet, standing up to his belly in shoes, belts, jeans, and junk. All the guy's other clothes were hanging over his head—he barely had enough room to turn around. When we forced him out, he could hardly see, he'd been in the dark for so long. Almost completely blind. Absolutely pitiful." The director shook his head.

"Cooped up in a clothes closet for a year! Well, we'll make up for that—starting now."

****

Back home, Queen Chloe didn't appreciate an interloper invading her territory. As is common with rival pigs, there was the usual pig-posturing and threatening stares, the occasional charges and teeth chomping that signify impending battle. In Chloe's case none of this was necessary—Zack graciously submitted to Chloe the minute he laid eyes on her. Though Chloe felt her supremacy threatened, Zack was just glad to have a caring, clean, well-lit place to spend the night.

Acclimating Zack to his new family was trying at first, especially with Chloe defending her territory, but Zack made himself at home. During the first days, Zack enjoyed the good homemade lunches and paraded, clearly delighted, through the kitchen, past the softly talking television and Eric snore-purring in his chair, through each of the bedrooms, checking to make sure his own pig bed was safe beside his humans' bed. The Prusts' living room was spacious, and he luxuriated in the time it took to go from one corner of it to another. Indeed, this was no closet house. He enjoyed his moments outside even more, quickly learning to use the large dog door to go outside to relieve himself.

Once Chloe laid down the rules of the household and was sure Zack posed no threat to her queendom, they became best friends. Though they ate and slept separately, they were always glad to see each other after breakfast, and then the planning began. Chloe, of course, decided the day's agenda, which might begin with lying out in the morning sun until snack time or excavating a patch of backyard in search of grubs and spring shoots.

Their greatest thrill was sharing outdoor time with the Prusts as they tended the gardens. Chloe and Zack helped with the gardening, careful to pull out and eat only the weeds. The garden was lovely, packed with purple grasses, dainty yellow daisies, coral bells, nasturtiums, a variety of snapdragons, cool blue lobelia, kalanchoe, and begonias

Zack loved the kiddy pool where he and Chloe splashed and rolled on scorching days. He found calm in the bird songs, sniffed the air, and dreamed of delicacies cooking on the neighbors' grills. When he pushed back inside through the dog door after an afternoon outdoors, he looked around tentatively, as though, Donna decided, he feared this life was too good to last.

Now that Chloe had a pig mate, he became her primary audience, and what an admiring audience Zack was. Chloe loved being in the spotlight, so when Eric picked up his fiddle to play some old country tunes, she began to dance.

And oh, how she could dance! Clearly enthralled, Zack watched the splendid Chloe zigging and zagging to the strains of the country fiddle. She spun around in the center of the living room as the violin reached high notes, and her rump swayed and switched left, then right. She was a beautiful sight, her body lilting and spinning and twisting. Zack was so impressed with Chloe's show he was speechless—for the first time since the Prusts had known him.

Zack's special talent, no less impressive than Chloe's dancing, was his gift for gab. He was a porcine conversationalist, murmuring pig-thoughts out loud as he enjoyed his fifteenth trip through the living room. When he wasn't talking to himself, commenting on the new rug that squished so differently beneath his hooves or muttering under his breath about the incorrigible Chloe, who poked him awake and stole his bed, he talked with Donna and Eric.

Donna watched one Sunday afternoon as Zack marched through the pig door into the kitchen. "What's up, Zack?" She was deep-frying doughnuts, Eric's, Zack's, and Chloe's favorite treat.

Zack looked up and smiled. *"Vrup, ...vrup, ...vrup."* Then with hooves clattering on the hard kitchen floor, he sashayed into the living room.

"How's it goin', Zacky-Boy?" Eric sat in his lounge chair while peering over his reading glasses. "Busy day? Things to do, places to go, huh?"

Zack stopped at Eric's chair. *"Mree, ...mreee, ...mr-r-r-r-e-e-e-e."* He was complaining.

"So you're bored. Want me to go outside with you? I'll watch you while you cool off in the kiddy pool."

"Whre-e-e-e! Whre-e-e-e-e!" Then Zack turned around and looked over his shoulder at Eric.

"Okay. I'm coming, I'm coming." Eric got out of his chair and walked to the kitchen, but Zack stopped dead, blocking the door.

"Bra-a-a-ah, bra-a-a-ah, bra-a-a-ah."

"Raisins? You want a couple of raisins? Okay." And with that Eric grabbed a box of raisins and Zack trotted after him.

"Ra," Zack said. *Thank you.*

****

Most people don't realize that pigs have thirty-two different vocalizations and only by living with a swiner can they appreciate their ability to speak piglish with their porcine friends. Even if they're meeting a pig for the first time, most people listen and will understand if the pig is happy, frightened, angry, disgruntled, frustrated, or asking for a snack or a place to relax. Their ability to communicate with humans and other animals is uncanny, and that is only one reason they make exceptional pets.

****

On a day in which the temperature had reached one hundred eight degrees, Zack was busy eating the heads off dandelions. Eric decided to shower him with the garden hose. The second water landed on Zack's back, the pig whipped around and barked. *"Ru-u-u-uck! Ru-u-u-uck! Ru-u-u-uck!"* Then he went flying through the dog door, spraying water throughout the kitchen.

Donna came outside, hands on hips.

Eric frowned. "He's a snitch!"

"Well, you startled him."

"But it's over a hundred degrees out here. I thought he'd like it! Besides, he didn't have to go running to you and rat me out." He looked at Zack. "You're a big sissy. And a snitch."

Zack barked back. *"Fru-u-up!"*

Donna scratched Zack behind an ear, and he leaned

all hundred and fifty pounds into her. "Zacky-Boy knows I'll protect him."

Zack stood before Eric. *"Wreee, wreee, wreee."* Eric stroked his belly until the pig wriggled in ecstasy—all was forgiven.

****

Months passed. Zack loved his new home and the Prusts and Chloe. He surely had almost forgotten the cruelty of his piglethood. But one day when Eric came home early from work with the flu, hardly strong enough to take off his shoes and slump into his lounger, Zack fell back into the past like a sailboat sucked into a maelstrom.

He was making his umpteenth stroll through the living room that afternoon, sashaying along, looking left, then right, when he stopped dead in his hoof prints. *"Re-e-e-e-e!"* He stared at the horrific things before him and screamed louder. *"Re-e-e-e! Re-e-e-e-e! Re-e-e-e-e-e-!"* His mouth was strained, his eyes wide. He let out one more horrified shriek and then spun around, knocking over a side table as he barreled down the hall. Crashing against the door jamb, he flew into the bedroom and dived under his pig bed.

Eric called to Donna. "What's wrong with Zack?"

Donna came running. "What's going on? Why all the screaming?"

"I was just sitting here, and he was coming through the living room when he stopped dead in front of my shoes. That's when he started yelling."

Back in the bedroom Zack thought he was safe and out of sight beneath his pig bed, but only his head was covered. The rest of his body was hanging out in plain sight. "Zacky, come here, honey. What's the matter?"

Donna knelt beside him and lifted the comforter from his face.

He looked at her but didn't say anything.

"Come on out, Zack. Let's go to the living room."

Gentle Zack followed, unsure but willing, as was his nature. Donna led him into the living room and stopped him in front of Eric's black dress shoes. She stroked his back, but the bristles along his mane were standing up. *"Whree, whree, whree, whree."* Zack was panting, staring hard at the shoes as though they were about to attack. *"Wrah, wrah, wrah ...wree, wree, wrah?"* He stared anxiously from Donna to Eric and then to the shoes.

"We'll get rid of those nasty shoes, Zacky." Donna whisked them out of sight. Instantly Zack stopped whining, and his bristles slowly lowered.

Eric looked sad. "Wow."

Donnas stood shocked, too. "Yeah, wow. What does that tell us?"

"It was a man who abused him—probably a businessman who came home from work, took off his shoes, and hurled them into—"

Donna finished in a sad voice. "Zack's closet. I wonder how many times Zack was hit with a shoe when that guy came home."

"By the sound of Zack's voice, probably more times than we want to know. Poor Zack."

****

After that, Eric was careful never to leave his dress shoes lying around the house. He forgot once, accidentally leaving them in the bedroom. Zack discovered them and began shrieking.

While Zack had those bouts of Post Traumatic

Stress Disorder to deal with, Chloe skipped happily through life, ordering Donna and Eric to accompany her to the gardens, demanding walks to the neighbors, and generally managing the entire household. Her one other special friend besides Zack was her rag doll, a gift from Donna, which she loved more than grapes.

Donna waved Chloe's toy in the air. "Come on, Chloe! Let's play with Dolly!" With that, Chloe charged from her house, the doll firmly clasped between her front teeth, and began to dance and spin, throwing Dolly into the air, then picking her up and sending her airborne again. Dolly survived numerous maulings by the exuberant Chloe, who was a rough and raucous mother but not an unloving one.

For many years Chloe and Zack enjoyed lazy days with their humans in California. Gentle Zack, chatting endlessly to anybody who'd listen, acquiesced to the always energetic, bossy, but loving, Chloe, and together they played and napped in the gardens behind the Prust house. They watched butterflies together and snipped the heads off tasty dandelions.

One day in July of 2002 Chloe fell asleep and never woke up.

****

Chloe's Memorial

Chloe's death left an unrelenting emptiness in Donna's heart that needed to find expression. So Donna began to work out her misery in a special memorial garden dedicated to Chloe. The physical work—designing the garden plan, buying the sculptures, planting, and potting the lavender, daisies, palms, and roses in a corner of the back yard—eased her heartache about her "cuddle pig" whom she would never hold again.

When the seven-by-five-foot garden was finished, Donna and Eric stood back from it and took in its majesty and delicacy. Every corner of the garden had something in it—the eye didn't know where to look first to capture its lusciousness and energy. Pig planters, pig sculptures, flowers of every size and color—purple violas, pansies, lavender petunias, fuchsia, geraniums, lilies, and orchids—so crowded was the space that not a single weed would find room to grow.

Donna named it Chloe's Garden because she felt it suited Chloe, a creature of nature with a personality so complex and intelligent that she enthralled every stranger she met. Queen Chloe had lived life in a grand manner, and so the garden was grand—a true reflection of the pig it memorialized.

Chloe's Garden existed for several years as a real, physical garden that grew more lush and luxurious with every growing season, yet Donna felt driven to memorialize Chloe via another avenue. She decided to open up her garden to other people who had lost their pigs. She cleared more ground and offered other pig friends "memory spots" in the garden. Each pig had a fitting sculpture or potted plant that honored his or her memory. One pig was remembered by a poem engraved on a rock; another was memorialized with a pig planter of petunias. Soon Chloe's garden was filled with twenty-something memorials. It wasn't long before Donna realized the garden simply would not hold another pig memorial. Then one day, while stroking the back of old Zack's head, she had an idea that would benefit pigs and pig owners everywhere.

"That's it, Zacky-Boy! We can make such a huge

garden we'll be able to include any pig in the world. We can share the memories of thousands and thousands of pigs in it. That's it, Zack! We'll build a *virtual* garden."

Donna set up a site in cyberspace for tributes to passed pot-bellied pigs. Each pig registered could have as many photos as the owner wished to share, as well as a written message about the pet. Donna did not limit the number of pictures nor did she edit the written words, thus allowing the owner the free expression of feelings in whatever way best described the closeness, the friendship, the special relationship formed with his or her porcine friend.

Chloe's virtual website had a wealth of pigs memorialized within it. Some of the stories were heart-wrenching accounts of abuse the pigs suffered from previous owners. Others spoke to the pig's character, his or her quirkiness or special talents or adventures. In Zack's case, because of Donna's and Eric's kindness, he managed to conquer his past and find a way to trust the species that had haunted his night dreams.

****

In September of 2007 Zack died. But his sensitive spirit lives on where he enjoyed life the most: amongst the lilies and orchids in the physical Chloe's Garden, as well as in the virtual one.

Chapter Three
Because of You, I Loved Them All

Species: Feline—domestic shorthair
Name: Spider Borbacs
Born: June 10, 1969
Died: October 9, 1986
Human Companion: Kathryn Borbacs

The young woman stormed out the back door. "I'm not staying on this farm and throwing away my life just like Aunt Doris did! I want to *be* somebody and live in an *exciting* place."

Her mother called from the clapboard farmhouse. "Please don't go, Kathryn. You'll regret it." She paused, thinking. "And don't expect your father and me to pick up the pieces if you make a mess of your life."

The lanky nineteen-year-old stood her ground. "I've always fended for myself!" Even in anger Kathryn turned heads, her oval green eyes like those of a feline, her high cheekbones and light skin framed by long, dark hair. Yet, for all her attractiveness and worldly spirit, Kathryn had never lived more than fifty miles away from home. For years every afternoon she had sat transfixed before the television in the living room she had grown up in, glued to another episode of *I Love Lucy.*

In 1966 she had graduated from the local high

school, and her ultimate dream was to live and work in New York City where Lucy and Ricky Ricardo lived next door to her friendly landlords, Fred and Ethel. She read avidly about the world's premiere city, its huge buildings, the masses of people surging along the sidewalks like the tides, the clippity-clop of carriage horses, the delicious smells rolling from the bagel shops and delis. She longed to live and feel the throbbing excitement of the big town.

Kathryn turned toward her mother. "I'm telling you for the last time: I want to live in New York City where the buildings reach the sky and never stop. I want to live in a skyrise and walk the streets elbow-to-elbow with rich and famous people."

At the end of the summer Kathryn traveled to Kansas City, Missouri, to train as a flight attendant with Pan Am Airlines, with the promise she'd be based in New York City. But when the cabbie dropped her off at a not-so-skyrise apartment building in Queens, she dropped her bags, phoned Pan Am's headquarters, and told them she was quitting. She told them, "I asked to be in the New York City of *I Love Lucy*—where all the high buildings, the museums, the busy streets, and Wall Street are—not in some place called Queens."

From there she gathered her suitcases and hailed a cab. The cabbie leaned out the window for directions. "Did you ever read *Valley of the Dolls?* Take me to the Martha Washington Hotel for Women."

The cabbie looked incredulous and shook his head. "Lady, are you sure you want to go to the Martha Washington Hotel for Women?"

Her answer was evident in her stare. The cabbie took off in the direction of Manhattan.

The cab pulled up to a narrow brick building—a single dim light bulb hanging from a broken fixture. The sidewalks were deserted, save only for a critter scurrying around the side of the building. Kathryn stood looking at the sad hotel, and then she walked up to the door and knocked. An old woman with frizzled gray hair and baked-bean teeth motioned her inside.

She looked around her fifth-floor room—no window, one dusty, old, stuffed chair, a sagging twin bed, and a dresser that had seen much better times. For fifty dollars a month she could use the bathroom down the hall. Everything smelled of Cologne du Old Folks— similar to the dank odor of dried grain. It wasn't much, but if it was good enough for the women in the *Valley of the Dolls,* it was good enough for her.

The next morning she rose early, washed her face, dabbed on some makeup, put on her best dress, and set out to find a job. When she came back in the evening with a small bag of groceries, a message was already waiting for her at the front desk: John Wiley and Sons Publishing Company had called. She was to begin work the next day.

The next day she showed up for work at John Wiley and Sons, and when her boss, Barbara, found out the naïve nineteen-year-old was living in the Martha Washington Hotel for Women, she was shocked. "No employee of mine is going to live in a dump like that. I'll find you another apartment this afternoon."

The following weekend Kathryn moved her things into an apartment for singles under the age of forty. She found it amazing that a person could actually store all her personal stuff within a space sixteen feet wide by twenty-four feet long. What a change, to go from having so much space on a farm to living one's life—from eating to sleeping to going to the bathroom—all within a single room. A Lilliputian must have designed the apartment and the claustrophobic five-by-five-foot bathroom. When she sat on the toilet, she could rest her arm on the sink and gaze into the miniature tub.

The kitchen was nearly as microscopic. When she opened the refrigerator door, it hit the wall. Next to it stood the sink and then a tiny stove. She was thrilled, however, to have four cabinets above the appliances. Still, even though it was a living space proportioned for an ant, it was a place to live, and she was at 85th and Central Park West—the heart and soul of Manhattan.

In a few months, Kathryn met a young aspiring actor. She and John soon became friends with the other tenants in the building, along with the garden lady, Miss Sally Whitehart, three floors below on the ground level. Besides cultivating a profusion of daisies, Echinacea, and lilies, she trained animals for movie producers and used her dog, Felix, and her cat, Fido, as pet actors. Next door to Kathryn lived three friendly NYU students from New Jersey, and across the hall lived Jane, a philanthropist, whose deceased parents had left her a sizeable inheritance.

One afternoon Jane invited Kathryn over for a tuna fish sandwich. Kathryn was struck by the expanse of her living quarters. "Yes, Kathryn—my apartment is huge—runs from the front of the building to the back. The rent is expensive, but…"

Kathryn caught movement out of the corner of her eye. The shadow disappeared into Jane's living room.

Kathryn sprang from her chair. "What was that?"

"Oh, that's Muggy, my cat. Every once in a while

he goes schizoid and runs back and forth through the apartment. He makes this place his own race course."

"You have a cat? Inside? In an apartment?" Kathryn's eyes were wide.

"Yes, why?"

"I used to have kittens when I was a young girl. In fact, my kittens were my only friends."

Kathryn's eyes glazed over remembering back to when she was a little girl.

****

"Mommy, Mommy! Look what I found!" The gray tiger kittens, barely two months old, squirmed, ragged and flea-bitten, in the youngster's hands.

Her mother scowled. "Just get them out of here. You know your father and I hate cats."

The year was 1958, and for probably the fourth time in her ten-year-old life, the youngster, her long brown hair pulled back into a ponytail, had taken her kittens into the barn for warmth. She had made a pile of straw for them in a corner and emptied onto the floor half a milk carton filled with leftovers from supper, half of which she had saved from her own plate. The little girl was apologetic. "I'm sorry. That's all I have. But I'll go back for more tonight."

That summer Kathryn had brought the kittens table scraps every day. "This fall is going to be different." The two kitties romped around the barn floor and darted in and out of her lap. She laughed. "You two are good and healthy, and I'm sure nothing's going to happen to you like it did my other kittens. Just stay inside the barn here, and you'll be safe."

But one fall day Kathryn ran, screaming, into the farmhouse, the screen door slamming behind her. She stopped before her mother. "Where are they?"

Her mother brushed crumbs from her apron. "Where's what?"

"My kittens! You know I was raising them in the barn all spring and summer. They're gone again! Just like last year and the year before that. Something happens to my kittens every year! One day they're here; the next day they're gone!"

"Listen, Kathryn. Cats are no good. I don't want them here, and your father doesn't want them. Stop bringing these animals home."

Kathryn sobbed. Summer took a toll on country kids living so far away from any school friends. Kathryn's only playmates had been her dear kittens she raised every summer.

The little girl gasped for breath. "What happened to them?"

Her mother was matter-of-fact. "All right, I'll tell you. Your uncle shot them."

"Uncle Tony's been shooting my cats!" Kathryn's hands flew to her mouth; she felt nauseated. Her expression was accusatory. "You told him to, didn't you?"

"Yes. We told Tony to kill them. We hate cats. They're varmints."

****

Her mother's words, as clear in Kathryn's memory as if they had been spoken yesterday, shocked her back to consciousness and Jane's apartment.

Kathryn shook off the horrible memories as Muggy raced up the backstretch, banking off Jane's living room wall and did a "wheely" toward the kitchen—a hellion on four paws. As he flew past, a large smile pasted on his face, Jane reached out and yanked him off the track.

Jane whipped the cat into her arm-cradle. "Hey, Muggins, what's the big hurry?" The cat relaxed, looking into Jane's eyes. He adored his human companion.

Kathryn reached out. "Could I hold him a little?" Jane passed the cat to Kathryn, and Muggy relaxed in Kathryn's arms, becoming as limp as an old pair of jeans. Kathryn brought the medium-sized red tabby cat up to her face and planted a kiss on his nose—he shrank away. "It's okay, Muggy. I just love cats." She stroked his fur as he lay in her lap. "Oh, Jane, he's so handsome."

****

A week later, Kathryn's buzzer went. She pressed the intercom button and asked who was there. It was a guy's voice. "John. I'm here to escort Madame Borbacs to the Museum of Natural History. Would you tell the princess her escort is here?"

Kathryn pressed another button to let John into the building. "The princess awaits her carriage, sir."

When John opened her apartment door, Kathryn saw he was carrying a shoebox. "Whatcha got in the box, John?" He untied the string and placed the gift in her hands.

A kitten popped out. It was a tabby with a white locket—a tiny brown-and-black kitten with white ticking and a white expanse of fur from the chin down to the chest. She cupped the animal in her hands. "He's gorgeous, John. Where did you get him? What are you going to do with him?"

"He's a *she*, Kath. When I found out how you

51

loved cats and that your uncle killed them all every fall, I asked Ron from next door to bring me a kitten from his parents' farm in Jersey. All week I've had her stashed in my apartment until today. She's only six weeks old. How do you like her?"

"You mean *she's mine*?" Kathryn blushed. She put the kitten on the floor, and the scared animal froze in place.

John grinned. "Yes, she's yours."

Kathryn gaped at the animal. "I can't have her! Are you nuts?" She turned around to face John, her fists clenched. "Are you out of your mind? I don't know the first thing about taking care of a cat *inside* a house! I only ever had barn cats. Where will it go to the bathroom, for heaven's sake?" Kathryn was nearly frantic.

Then she looked down at the shivering kitten at her feet. She picked her up and held her next to her face. She felt the purring vibrato on her skin that she remembered so well from the kittens she had had at home on the farm, the ones her uncle had executed every fall. A tear fell from her eyes. "I absolutely love her, John, but I don't know the first thing about keeping her. All they ever got was table scraps and food I saved from my own plate." The kitten looked up at Kathryn, her eyes wide and questioning, and her purr grew louder. Kathryn had a determined look. "Jane, next door, has a cat, Muggy. She'll tell me what to do."

****

Jane told Kathryn it was very simple taking care of a cat, and that's why they made the perfect apartment pet.

Kathryn had no knowledge of keeping a cat

indoors. "But where does Muggy go to the bathroom?"

Jane was incredulous. "Where all inside cats go—in a box."

So Jane took the shoebox the kitten came in and poured in some clay litter from the five-and-dime. The kitten's first day was going well until she had to use her box. Scratching furiously in the shoebox, she finally perched over the hole and peed for probably two minutes. Suddenly Kathryn noticed a wet trail oozing from under the box.

The kitten jumped out just as Kathryn leaped for the box, the bottom bulging and dripping. She threw the box in the bathroom sink where she heard the pee trickling down the pipe. Hands on hips, she stared at the sunken box, its bottom wet and fragile. Then she went to the cupboard and tore out a large piece of aluminum foil. She got another cardboard box, lined it with foil, and set it down on the floor.

That night Kathryn crawled into bed, turned onto her side, pulling the covers up around her neck, and stared into her kitten's eyes. She reached down and hoisted the kitten into her bed where she curled round and round, finally settling on the pillow Kathryn's Aunt Doris had made for Kathryn's christening. The only cherished item she had brought to New York City from the farm, the small, pink, goose-filled pillow had been Kathryn's from her birth, and it accompanied her everywhere.

The next morning the kitten had to use her litter box. Afterwards Kathryn was horrified to see slivers of aluminum and litter clay all over the floor.

In the morning Kathryn confided her concerns to Jane. "I just don't know what I'm going to do with this kitten. I got a box, just like you said, but it leaked the first time, so I lined another one with aluminum foil. Then, when she went to the bathroom this morning, she tore up the foil and…"

Jane was confused. "The box leaked?"

"Yeah, the shoebox leaked."

Jane laughed. "Ya don't use a regular box, silly! You buy a litter box specially made for cats. Boy, you weren't kidding when you said you knew nothing about keeping a cat."

Kathryn went right out and purchased a litter box. Of course, "only in New York," as the phrase goes, could a person find a toilet box for cats and gourmet food for them, as well.

****

The new kitten lifted Kathryn's spirits as nothing else could. Every evening after work, her kitty waited atop the kitchen table for her human companion. The first thing she did after she got home was give her kitten a walking tour of the apartment. She showed her the garden below, naming each flower; then she carried her to the refrigerator and explained the goodies inside. The kitten lolled in Kathryn's arms, her eyes wide and curious.

During the daily tour Kathryn kept a running conversation with her cat. "Yep, my walk to work seemed a lot longer today, kitty. It's not easy walking forty blocks, from Eighty-Fifth Street to Fortieth and Third, especially in the rain, but Mommy can't afford to take a bus. And everyone wonders why I'm so skinny. But every step is worth it, Sweetie, knowing you're waiting for me."

After the tour, Kathryn sat on the trundle bed and

cheered her kitten's antics as she began to play—probably in celebration of Kathryn's homecoming. She raced around the tiny one-room apartment, jumping from the bed to a chair to the kitchen table to the kitchen counter, over the stove, through the sink, and back to the bed again.

When John visited the next weekend, Kathryn gushed about the kitten. "I love my kitten. She's gentle; she's playful; but, most of all, she's my best friend. I never realized, even though I had cats as friends when I was little, that anyone could get so close to an animal. She's like having another person in this apartment. She paused. "Still, I just can't think of a good name for her. It's got to be something special because she's so special."

Just then the kitten galloped past. John gaped in awe. "Wow, look at 'er go!"

"Yeah, she does that a lot. I think she's exercising. There's not a whole lot of room in here, ya know. Just when she gets going, she's at the other end of the room. Sometimes she flies around here so fast, she's like a toboggan on an ice run—ya know the way the sleds climb the walls of the run. She banks up the wall."

As if for a demonstration, the kitten raced past them again, sliding across the kitchen table between the two and dropping with a thud to the floor. John and Kathryn watched as she galloped past, her tiny feet making unusually loud hollow sounds on the hardwood floor. Then suddenly she was clinging to the wall—stalking John's shadow.

Kathryn's eyes grew wide. "Look at her! She's got all four feet stuck onto the wall. Now I not only have a new cat, I've got a free wall-hanging!"

The kitten hung there, spread-eagled, all four paws nailed into the wallboard.

Kathryn thought for a moment. "Ya know, she kinda looks like a spider, doesn't she, clinging there?"

Suddenly the kitten slid down the wall and raced up and over the bathroom sink. She plopped to the floor and then took off running again, swerving up the wall and down again. Then she came to a screeching halt at Kathryn's feet. Kathryn picked her up. "You're just like a little spider. So that will be your name—Spider." Then Kathryn held her close to her face, and Spider began to purr. Kathryn felt the vibrations through her neck and cheeks, and she closed her eyes.

****

One morning Kathryn, who acquired her apartment's furniture from the castoffs lining the streets on garbage day, set her alarm for six a.m. in order to get first dibs on a particular dinette table discarded on the curb at 87th Street. Once Kathryn hauled it up the stairs and into her apartment, Spider found the perfect scratching post on one of the table's wooden legs. After a few months of her sharpening her claws there, the leg looked as though it had gone through a schizophrenic milling machine. Spider's "scratching post" had become thinner and took on an irregular fuzzy look with its hair-like splinters.

Another brilliant summer day Kathryn threw open the double-hung window and carried Spider to where she could smell the fresh air. Spider looked down from Kathryn's arms at Sally Whitehart's garden where the impatiens were in full bloom. "Just look, Spider. Aren't her flowers beautiful? I wish we could both go down there to play."

Kathryn put Spider down on her pink baby pillow, but Spider didn't want to sleep. Instead, she wanted to help Kathryn clean by curling around her legs and running after the dust towel. Finally, Spider settled down on the bed, so Kathryn tiptoed into the kitchen. A few minutes later she looked back to check on Spider.

She gasped.

Framed in the open window was Spider's butt, her feet teetering on the window ledge.

"Spider!"

With that Kathryn heard Spider's front legs scrabbling for purchase against the outside bricks. Then the cat disappeared over the edge.

Kathryn ran to her window, three stories high. "Oh, my God, Spider!"

Kathryn heard a thud. The cat had fallen onto Sally Whitehart's awning. Spider looked up, unsure what to do.

"I'll be right down. Stay there!"

Minutes later she was banging on Sally Whitehart's apartment door. "I'm sorry, Miss Whitehart, but, uh, my cat, Spider, just fell out the window. I have to get her, and, well, she's on your awning."

Miss Whitehart ushered her through her lavish apartment with its French Provincial furniture, a baby grand piano, and what looked to be a valuable, antique sideboard. "You should be very careful of any animal in the city." The woman fetched a stepstool, and Kathryn scruffed Spider from the awning.

****

Later that day Kathryn knocked on Janie's apartment. "Janie, I don't know what to do with Spider. I think she's bored in my tiny room. Today she was looking out the window and fell out. Luckily Sally Whitehart's awning caught her; otherwise, she could've been really hurt, falling three stories."

"Why don't you bring Spider over here and let her play with Muggy? I bet since he's a boy—he's fixed, of course—they'd get along well. They could chase each other all over the place."

Muggy and Spider loved each other from the beginning. The one chased the other to the front of Jane's apartment, through the kitchen and Oriental dining room, into the sitting room, around the entertainment area, and, finally, back to the front formal living room. For hours they played, slept together, ate together. Jane even cooked them little hamburgers for snacks. Jane enjoyed all the activity as much as Muggy did.

Two days later Kathryn knocked on Jane's door. "Jane—Spider would like to come over and play with Muggy."

Jane opened the door and smiled. "Of course. Anytime Spider wants to play with Muggy, she is welcome." Kathryn put Spider on the floor, and she flew to the living room in search of Muggy. Again the racing started, the *"thrump, thrump, thrumping"* over the hardwood floors. Kathryn and Jane watched as their cats flew through the air, over the furniture, and around the tables and chairs.

Jane laughed. "What a couple of maniacs."

On another day, Kathryn almost forgot her keys as she opened her apartment door to leave. On her way out, she noticed the door chain still hooked but gaping enough to let a cat through. Through the opening Kathryn spied Spider sitting at Jane's door, scratching to go inside.

Spider sat, staring at the door. Suddenly, one paw came up and touched the door, *"Skrch, Skrch, Skrch, Skrch."*

A moment later, Jane's door opened. "Good afternoon, Spider. Want to come in and see Muggy? Come on inside." Spider disappeared inside.

Several months later a frantic knocking sounded on Jane's door. It was Kathryn: something was wrong with Spider. "Look at Spider. She's been crouching so funny, and she's yelling like she's in terrible pain. She must have a bellyache or something."

Jane's brow wrinkled, and she bent down to Spider, who, instead of running to play with Muggy, lay immobile on the floor. Jane stroked Spider's back. "What's the matter, Spider?"

Spider sang, and she stood up on her back toes, her rump pointed to the ceiling.

"Br-r-r-r-rp, br-r-r-r-rp, br-r-r-r-rp."

Kathryn's hands flew to her mouth. "Oh, no—something's really wrong. Look at her!"

Jane laughed, shaking her head. "Kathryn, haven't you ever seen a cat in heat?"

"She has a fever? Can you tell she has a fever just by looking at her?" Kathryn was wringing her hands.

Kathryn's naiveté was almost too much to believe. Jane giggled. "No, 'heat' means she wants to attract a mate."

"That's what she's doing? Is that all it is? Oh, thank God! I thought there was something really wrong with her. I was so worried she'd have to have an operation. I don't have money for an operation."

"Well, you'll probably have to spay Spider." Jane

snickered at Kathryn's clueless look. "That means she has to have her reproductive organs removed so that she doesn't have lots of babies. Besides, you don't want to have a cat in heat all the time—all that yelling and pedaling behind. I'll pay for her spay when it comes time, so don't worry. She'll stop doing this in a couple of days, and then she'll do it again in about a month, you know, just like us girls."

Kathryn just stared in amazement.

****

Once Kathryn got into the swing of things at work and felt totally settled into her apartment, she began inviting friends and neighbors over. One Saturday night Kathryn decided to show John Spider's latest accomplishment. As a security device most New York apartment houses have a buzzer system that allows a guest to buzz up to an apartment. When the person upstairs hears who's downstairs, he or she returns a message via the intercom and presses a button to allow them into their apartment.

"Watch this, John." The buzzer sounded in the apartment.

Spider flew off her lap, jumped onto the dinette table, and pressed the call button. A voice began to speak. "Kathryn, it's Barbara." Spider cocked her head at the sound coming from the little speaker. She batted at it and said in a questioning voice, *"Re-ow?"*

"Kathryn? Are you there? Tell me that wasn't Spider on the intercom, was it?"

John was wide-eyed. Kathryn gave him a look of "Isn't my cat ingenious?" and ran to the speaker button. "Actually, Barbara, it *was* Spider. She's my door lady now. Come on up."

Kathryn even tried the speaker trick herself when she came home from work. From the foyer, she buzzed up to her apartment, knowing well that the only one home was Spider. Seconds later through the speaker in the entryway, she heard a tinny, *"Re-ow, re-ow?"*

Kathryn whispered into the intercom. "Hey, Spider. Mommy's home. I'll be right up."

Life in New York City was grand for Kathryn and Spider. Kathryn loved the city; she loved her editing job; she loved her neighbors and friends; she loved it all. It was the Age of Aquarius, and though she didn't particularly consider herself a hippie, she, John, Jane, and the three college guys often hung out together, dancing in Kathryn's apartment, playing Led Zeppelin so loud that Spider ran to Jane's apartment to escape the noise, and dancing across bed sheets with Day-Glo fluorescent paint on their feet. The psychedelic sheets made cheap wall art.

As usual, Spider continued to scratch at Jane's door so that she could romp with Muggy and share Jane's good home cooking, particularly her beef cubes with potatoes, though Jane's shrimp and green beans were Spider's favorite meal. By ten o'clock when Spider tired of Muggy, Jane let her back into the hallway, where she scratched at Kathryn's door to be let in.

****

Those two years in the City were idyllic, but after much careful consideration, in 1971 Kathryn decided to move back to Allentown and get an apartment of her own.

Not too long after she and Spider settled into their new place, the doorman told her about a feral mother cat and two kittens living near the drain pipe behind the apartment house. Kathryn, who because of Spider had come to love cats as much as her parents had always hated them, caught the mother and took the two kittens into her apartment. Though she couldn't touch the mother, whom she named Mother, the kittens learned to trust her, and she named them Tuxedo and Shorty. They and Spider became good friends and accompanied Kathryn through a few more moves until she settled into her home in Lehighton.

****

In the time Spider lived with Kathryn, she taught her human companion so much: for one, how comforting a pet could be during sadness and depression. Living alone and trying to get along in a large city and scrimping on food and clothes was easier when a person had a best friend to come home to. Spider also had been Kathryn's liaison, as well, connecting Kathryn to the other people in the apartment. Running down the hall to greet the college guys and darting into Jane's apartment after Muggy, Spider attracted other people to her, and, therefore, to her human companion as well. Spider became the connection, as well, during Kathryn's psychedelic parties, where she acted the hostess. In all, Spider had been Kathryn's faithful moral support, her buddy, and confidante—her dear friend. Spider was Kathryn's comic relief, her little clown—her living wall art.

Spider died on October 9, 1986.

****

Spider's Memorial

Kathryn sent out obituary cards to her friends and co-workers—those who had known Spider well, as well as those who only knew Kathryn but understood that

Spider had been an integral part of her life. The text was a simple memorial. "Our dear Spider was born on a farm in New Jersey. She resided in New York City for two years before moving back to the Lehigh Valley in 1971. She died peacefully at home in Lehighton."

Spider was the first official pet Kathryn ever lost, and she had never experienced an emptiness as full as this. During the viewing held at Cloud Nine Pet Cemetery in Breinigsville, PA, Spider rested on Kathryn's treasured goose down pink pillow her grandmother made for her when she was born in 1948. Kathryn had taken that sixteen-inch square baby's pillow with her through all her moves, and from the moment she got Spider, the kitten had made that pillow her bed. It was only fitting that Spider should have her pillow in death as she had in life.

For Spider's funeral, Kathryn composed the passages that the funeral director of Cloud Nine Pet Cemetery read. "Because of you, I loved them all." Lynn described the unique relationship that had developed between Spider and Kathryn. Because of Spider and the unconditional love she gave her human companion, Kathryn grew to love all cats and joined the humane society auxiliary in Allentown in order to rescue and foster other abandoned and neglected cats. Because of Spider's love, when Kathryn visited her mother back at the farm, she rescued two other kittens, Peaches and Toader. The neighbor had locked them in a corncrib to die. Later, she took in a neglected mother cat with four kittens. Unfortunately the mother died, but Fred, Bernice, Rusty, and Pepper, whom Kathryn nicknamed "The Babes," survived and became part of Kathryn's feline family.

During the ceremony, Kathryn carried Spider in her satin-lined casket in her arms as she had carried her on her many walking tours. She walked her for the last time to her burial place amid the pine trees and other headstones overlooking the green valley. The breeze wafted around the tombstones, brushing them gently with caressing fingers, for nature herself adored her treasures—her children—lying there beneath the ground.

At Cloud Nine Pet Cemetery, Spider's tombstone became the first of twelve to honor Kathryn's entire feline family—each one of which had some measure of Spider's spunk, her affection, and clownish personality. Kathryn's friends gathered round her while they laid daisies, tulips, and catnip toys at Spider's grave.

Spider's granite tombstone, as enduring a rock as Spider's memory will always be, bears Spider's photograph and reads affectionately, "My Old Lady."

Chapter Four
Captivating Canines

Species: canine—Belgian Tervuren
Name: Micah
Born: August 5, 1993
Died: March 12, 2008
Human companions: Lori & Stan Schoch

One puppy stood out from the rest of his littermates—the fuzz ball with the yellow collar. In fact, the breeder, Jenny, decided Mr. Yellow was the perfect dog for her longtime friend and fellow dog trainer Lori Schoch. Out of all eight puppies, Mr. Yellow proved himself the feistiest, the most playful, and the most energetic of the group. Because her friend Lori had similar traits, always running to stay fit, working out at the gym, playing ball with her German Rottweilers, Molly and Samson, or playing with her two naughty cats, Casey and Sylvester, Jenny knew Lori would find her high-energy dog and animal partner in Mr. Yellow.

Back at his new home in El Paso, Texas, Mr. Yellow's new human companion renamed him Micah. From the start the seven-week-old pup relished his short, daily morning runs with his equally tiny human companion, Lori, a five-foot-two-inch, ebony-haired young lady who ran tiny steps beside her pup of infinite energy. Later in the day, when the sun rained down, cooking everything and everyone to a crisp, Lori took Micah, Molly, and Samson to a shaded park for a walk.

From the very first Micah loved being the center of attention. His need for Lori's adoration bordered on selfishness, for when the cats, Casey or Sylvester, curled around Lori's legs, Micah got up and ran them off, standing at attention at his mistress' feet. Even as a very young pup, he seemed to consider the other pets' presence an invasion of his space, and his lips emitted a high-toned, gurgling puppy growl.

A more gregarious canine was hard to find. When guests came through the door, he ran around the living room like a whirling dervish, first grabbing one of his plush balls, then sailing it through the air in a celebration of company. Smiling, his lips drawn back to his ears in an extreme doggy grin, he greeted the guests with his soft presents, either a blanket from the couch or a pillow or something else cuddly that could endear him to them.

Micah was renowned for his smile, his endless energy, and his warm receptions, but as he grew older, his one weakness continued to haunt him: his fear of thunderstorms. Micah was friendly and brave in so many respects, but from a puppy, he was deathly afraid of thunder and howling wind. At just a year old, he experienced his first thunderstorm. With the crack of close thunder, he jerked upright on the couch, eyes glued to the high windows flashing with searing light. Micah sat rigid, his eyes wide, unblinking.

Lori walked over to him and stared at her dog. "What's wrong, Micah?" He said nothing, catatonic on the couch, and then she noticed his huge belly. She went over and felt his stomach; it was bloated skin-tight. In the driving rain and wind, Lori whisked him off to the vet, who took an X-ray and preliminary blood work totaling a whopping two hundred dollars. Finally, stymied by the absence of any definitive diagnosis from the X-ray or blood work, the vet diagnosed Micah with severe gastric distention provoked by thunderstorm anxiety.

As Micah grew into adulthood, his fear of storms only increased despite Lori's treating his anxiety with homeopathic herbs, flower essences, and holistic remedies. She refused to give him regular anti-anxiety drugs, and, despite intense conditioning and behavior modification, he continued to become unglued when a storm hit, like the time he was in Lori's bedroom by himself. With each clash of thunder, he went bezoomny, tearing the walls with his claws and biting at the bedroom door. In a matter of minutes, Micah had shredded the door to bits—another two-hundred-dollar thunder-bill.

Though fear of lightning storms was Micah's weakness, he was an ideal dog in every other sense, particularly when it came to learning things. His breeder and dog trainer, Jenny, met with Lori to teach Micah tracking and sheep-herding skills, but Lori couldn't stomach the possibility of meeting snakes out in the countryside, so she declined honing those skills. Instead, Lori tried agility training with Micah. Because he was so athletic and intelligent, he excelled at the sport. Throughout the years he never competed as an agility dog, but he loved running the agility courses: jumping through hoops, boring through the tunnels and chutes, scrambling over the teeter-totter, leaping over the jumps, weaving through the poles, and climbing the

A-frame. He loved the speed and the excitement of running an agility course.

At the age of two years, Micah began his career in obedience training. Lori, in no hurry to win Micah's Companion Dog title, in which a dog had to collect one hundred seventy points out of two hundred from each of three different judges, finally took him to his title in 1998. Micah demonstrated with expertise his ability to heel on lead and off lead; perform re-call (a sitting dog across the ring must come and sit before its owner in the heeling position); execute long sits (a dog must sit without moving in a row of dogs for one minute); master long downs (a dog must lie down in a row of dogs for three minutes); and stand for an exam and allow a judge to touch him. Micah loved obedience because of its built-in desire to please a human companion. More than anything, Micah wanted to please Lori.

Excelling in obedience classes helped satisfy Micah's longing for exercise, but he was happiest when he could mix his high energy with Lori's high energy. Galloping beside Lori during her morning two-mile run, Micah stopped, disappointed, at the trail's end. *"Okay, that was fun,"* he seemed to say, his big face grinning at her. *"Now what are we gonna do?"* Sometimes Micah's energy flabbergasted Lori, as it seemed all she did all day was "feed" his boundless enthusiasm. Lori could easily interpret what Micah, her hyper dog-child, was mumbling at any time. *"Oh, boy, we're goin' someplace different. Here we go. Oh, boy. Oh, boy."*

When Micah wasn't thinking in his big, energetic, *"Here we go again"* hurry, he was speaking it in dog language. Even as a puppy he growled when Casey or

Sylvester came too close. But as he grew older, he talked in many different tones and with different intonations. Often he'd plead for more even after the morning's run had ended. *"Yeow-ow-owl, yeow-ow-ow-owl."* At times he mumbled under his breath. *"Ra-owl, ra-raowl, ra-raowl."* Lori translated his "doglish" as his asking where his ball or blanket was. At other times his message and tone of bark came through crystal clear. A solid *"Wo-o-of! Wo-o-of!"* signaled he was ready for dinner or a ride in the car.

Micah's gift for gab was remarkable, as the time he tried to get Stan to notice him. The Schochs had just moved and settled into their house in Austin. One evening after work, as Stan walked through the door, he spied Micah lying on the floor next to the couch. Instead of going right over to Micah and greeting him as he usually did, Stan pretended he couldn't find him. Stan called into the kitchen, "Hey, Lori? Where's Micah?"

Over the years this game of tease had become routine, the likes of Abbott and Costello. Lori played along. "Why, I don't know where Micah is, Stan."

Stan shielded his hand over his eyes, like a sailor searching for land, and he looked around the living room—under the chair where not even a cat could hide, let alone a large dog—behind the couch, at the side of the hassock, behind the curtains. He looked everywhere, but he deliberately wouldn't look at Micah, who sat at his feet. "Where's Micah? Where do you suppose Micah is?" His voice was megaphone loud.

Micah stood directly in front of Stan and "woofed" twice. *"Look! Here I am! Look here! I'm right in front of you!"*

But Stan didn't respond.

After another five minutes of Stan's turning and calling for Micah, the dog began barking furiously. He ran circles around Stan, yet Stan kept calling, blind to Micah's antics. Micah barked. Stan turned to search under a chair, around the side of the piano, on the staircase. And each time Micah flew around to face Stan, barking in his face as though to say, *"For the love of God. Look here—I'm right in front of you!"*

Finally, Micah had had enough. He decided that if Stan couldn't see or hear him, then he'd surely be able to feel him. So he bit him in the ass.

Micah's bite was more a wake-up call than a real bite. Stan started laughing, and Lori, privy to the joke, came out of the kitchen howling, too. And as his two human companions laughed, stroking his long hair, so, too, did Micah join them in the amusement, his lips drawn back in a huge smile.

Micah, indeed, had a sense of humor. Each day before Lori left to teach junior high school, she penned Micah in the kitchen behind a baby gate. Each day when she came home he was in the kitchen where she had left him. One day, however, she was late getting home. After she pulled into the garage and charged through the back kitchen door to let Micah outside to go potty, she was shocked to witness Micah crash-jumping back into the kitchen over the baby gate. His expression gloomed guilty. Then, at once, his face morphed into a smile. Lori laughed, wondering how many weeks he had been spending the day couching it up in the living room and then leaping back into the kitchen right before she came home.

Another time, while Stan was sleeping in his Lazy Boy, Micah, looking for something to do, sauntered over to Stan's chair. Micah thought that breathing on Stan's arm would be enough to awaken him to play ball, but when Micah discovered his breath not hot enough to rouse him, he devised another method of getting his attention. Very quietly, Micah tiptoed around the back of the chair to where Stan's baseball cap sat precariously on his head. Micah eyed it, thought for half a second, and then snatched it. Stan woke up, his arms flying to his head. Micah was gone. He had disappeared behind the side of the couch. Stan pretended not to notice, and a minute later Micah slinked from behind the sofa, the hat in his mouth, his lips strained back in a huge, mischievous grin.

Wherever Micah went, even to the mall, he captivated people with his animal magnetism. Though Micah never approached people, always respectful of their space, he lured them toward him in his own otherworldly way. Outside a store he sat quietly on a loose leash and tried to make eye contact with each passerby. He stared and stared at the person until the stranger felt the weight of his gaze—like some kind of magnetic thing. Then, unable to endure the feeling any longer, the person turned toward Micah. Once they caught his eye, he opened his mouth, his tongue lolling out, and his lips strained up and back to his ears in the widest of grins. His body started shaking, excitement building, and, invariably, the person came over, stroked his long, silky fur, and talked with him.

As much as he loved people, Micah was ferociously protective of his home. A stranger inside the home, one that Lori or Stan had invited in, was his friend, but someone outside the home was an intruder. Micah felt it his job to protect his family's home. So one day when the gardener came too close to the living room window, somehow turning the leaf blower onto the picture window, Micah became enraged. The eighty-pound Micah flew at the window. The window broke, the man ran, and Micah was taken to the vet for stitches.

With other people formally, or not so formally, introduced to him, he was friendly and all about fun and games. For instance, when Stan and Lori walked through the door, their luggage in hand, back from a trip to Hawaii, they found the animal sitter, Nicky, standing, flabbergasted, in the kitchen. As it happened, Micah had stolen Nicky's towel as she was coming out of the shower. So she quickly dressed and went after the towel, which Micah had dragged through his doggy door and into the back yard. Nicky told Lori and Stan that she had, for probably the fifth time, gone into the yard after Micah to get the towel, but each time she came close to him, he darted back, with the towel, through his doggy door and into the house.

Nicky was frustrated. "I don't know how to get the towel from him. He just keeps playing games with me."

Stan looked at Nicky and laughed. "This is what you do. Watch." Stan turned to Micah, standing in the middle of the yard, the towel dangling from his mouth. "Micah, bring me the towel." With that Micah marched right up to Stan and dropped the towel at his feet. "He's a champion obedience dog. He'll do whatever you tell him to do." Stan laughed.

Micah loved games and running. He loved blowing off steam in Austin's Zilker Park. Of course, Lori was his number one running partner. The two ran together every morning. He was an extreme dog with extreme energy. Besides running, he loved swimming in Austin's Barton Creek. On particularly hot summer days, he jumped into the creek and leaped, bunny-hopping, in the water. Then he came roaring from the stream, shaking his soaked coat over Lori and Stan. He loved watching his humans run from his dog-shower. And while they were running he was right behind, threatening to douse them again.

Micah was a nature lover as much as a lover of people. Active until his final days, Micah enjoyed playing ball in the Schochs' back yard in Lakeway, a suburban community outside Austin. As a respite from activity, he especially loved hunkering down in one of the webbed lawn chairs behind the house where he could watch the squirrels scamper beneath the brush and the birds skim water off the swimming pool. Huge crows swooped from the Bradford pear to the ligustrum and viburnum bushes, and he watched them collect grasses, nibble on wild berries, and squabble with each other. Micah gazed over the hills beyond the limestone wall that edged the Schochs' back yard, relaxing to the sounds of the swimming pool's waterfall, and from his lawn chair he could see beyond the fence to the cedar woods beyond. And he contemplated the golf course a half mile away, where Lori took him, now that he was older, for his daily walk. His vista from the back of the porch was a view wherein he could breathe in the entire countryside.

The property beyond the Schochs' home held other fascinations for Micah. At least once a week, when Lori reached for the bag of apple slices and another bag of tortilla chips, Micah grinned. He knew what was coming. "Let's go see Mommy and Gertie, Micah." Then Lori shook the bags of food. With Micah on his leash, Lori took him to visit the deer family he watched almost daily from his lawn chair. The elegant mother deer, at sight of Lori and Micah, ran from the brushy undergrowth beneath the cedar trees, her daughters and cousins right behind. Focused on the bags of food, the deer trotted right up to Lori and Micah and begged for their favorite treats.

While a dog behaviorist would suspect a dog would naturally want to chase down a deer, in Micah's case they would be wrong. To the contrary, Micah touched the doe's nose, smelling her essence, sensing her wildness, and her calm. He must have recognized some kinship with the deer, as equally unafraid of Micah as they were of Lori, handing out the treats as fast as she could. Such a sight between different animal species is rare, a gem of nature, humbling men and women who doubt nature's unfathomable curiosity.

Micah died March 12, 2008.

****

Micah's Memorial

Micah, Lori Schoch's Belgian Tervuren, lives on in a shadowbox created especially for him by Westlake Animal Hospital's client service manager, Erin Wright. Micah's shadowbox contains several locks of hair from his lush tail, his name tag, a few small, ceramic doves and rosebuds, and his paw print fired into clay. A part of Micah graces the shadowbox and is a constant reminder of the love between a woman and her dog.

The idea of creating shadowboxes for long-time clients whose pets had died and whom the Westlake

Veterinary Clinic had treated and cared for all their lives came to Erin Wright one day. She was saddened that many grief-stricken clients opted to abandon their best friend's cremains—the transformation of their pet into a cache of charcoal fragments.

In order to preserve the pet's memory in a more forgiving way, Erin began to construct simple but meaningful boxes that could be hung on a wall or set in a corner. First, she bought a five-by-seven-inch box from a craft store, then stained and lacquered the wood to a fine sheen. Before the pet was sent for cremation, she made an imprint of the paw in a lump of clay, along with the pet's name. Then, she had it kiln-dried. Sometimes with a small photo included, Erin hot-glued a sample of the pet's hair, the miniature doves, a few flowers, and the paw print into the box.

"It's my way of giving back to our faithful clients, who, after hundreds of visits to our vet clinic, have to face one of the worst events in their lives—losing a dear family member. Their furry children were the biggest, most fundamental parts of their lives, and I want our clients, our friends, to know that their pets and they, too, were and are very special to us. Having a part of their animal preserved in this way makes losing them just a tiny bit easier." Erin loves her shadowbox tributes. "People who don't live with animals may not have any concept of the loss one feels when their pet dies. I've been told some pretty fantastic stories by owners about their animals. Their pets are truly family members."

Chapter Five
A Heaven for All Animals

Species: Canine
Names: Rusty & Rusty Joe
Breed: Rusty, mixed breed; Rusty Joe, Australian shepherd mix
Born: both unknown (adopted from shelters)
Died: Rusty, November 11, 1996; Rusty Joe, May 18, 2000
Human companion: Father Salvatore Livolsi

Rusty

Ordained in 1948, Fr. Livolsi served churches for twenty-five years in Jersey City, Bayonne, Union City, and Newark. In 1972, Father Salvatore Livolsi and church volunteers built a mountain retreat, Blessed Sanctuary of Mary, Our Lady of the Holy Spirit, atop a hill in Frankford County in Branchville, New Jersey. The refuge, nestled among the mountains of Stokes State Forest, offered the Father a quiet place to live and his followers a tranquil place to worship God within His natural creation.

The Father lived in the retreat by himself, amid the large oak trees and the creatures of the woods. The handsome, dark-haired priest puttered around his sanctuary, clearing land to build shrines to various saints and set crosses along a wooded path. When he wasn't ministering to pilgrim or retreat groups seeking peace and personal resolve at his refuge, he was involved with local town festivals and community groups, and served as the chaplain for the Frankford Fire Department. His life was perfectly balanced between community and activities of his faith, yet he felt as though something was lacking in his life.

****

Father Livolsi had often seen his neighbor Jan walking her dog, Xena, past his retreat. Each time the two passed, Father yelled, "Good morning!" in his deep, thunderous voice, and several times he invited her and Xena inside. Over many cups of coffee, Jan and the Father became good friends, and because he was so intrigued by Xena's personality, he asked Jan to help him find a dog of his own.

At the local animal shelter, Father's heart softened toward a yellow lab-mix dog. The mutt with rather large, pointed ears was a medium-sized, rather nondescript animal, but his personality was as large as a shepherd's. An hour later Father and his new companion, Rusty, were at home in the Father's forest retreat. There, amongst the critters scurrying in the woods, Rusty gazed in awe at his natural surroundings. With miles of running room and the scent of pine in the air, he thought he had reached heaven.

Rusty soon became the Father's sidekick in his ministry. Since everyone in Branchville knew of or had experienced the inspiration the bold, deep-throated Father Livolsi worked among his parishioners, businessmen and homeowners throughout the town often welcomed the Father and his dog into their places. When Salvatore needed a couple of bolts to fix a table, he and Rusty headed to the hardware store, where Rusty accompanied him inside, at the invitation of the store's owner, Mr. Chadwick. Though Rusty could smell the aroma of dog bones at the front of the store, Rusty never left Fr. Livolsi's side, content to help him search bins for bolts and nuts.

After the hardware store, Rusty and Salvatore stopped for lunch at Loni's diner, where Patsy and Fred Cannelloni served the Father his favorite lunch: a BLT with a side of fries. Patsy and Fred sat in the booth opposite the Father and his dog, who sneaked a few fries from the priest's plate. The four sat around talking about the Father's renovations to his retreat and the deer that snatched birdseed from the Father's birdfeeders. Fr. Livolsi told them he had made a special feeder for the squirrels, creatures he found comical and intelligent and needing food, too, in the harsh winter. Through the conversation, Rusty sat straight and attentive on the bench next to his human companion.

Rusty didn't lack for lunch at Loni's, either. Patsy brought him a piece of cooked cow's liver, cut into small slices, and Rusty ate neatly from his plate. Rusty sensed the convivial mood of people eating, and he soaked up their conversation and joy. As they talked, especially when Salvatore laughed and his loud, husky voice boomed through the diner, he sat upright in the booth, his lips drawn back into a huge smile.

Wherever Father Livolsi went in town, people invited him and Rusty into their homes, for the Father entertained everyone with his interesting and funny conversation. Hunkered around a friend's kitchen table, light discussions ensued which sometimes grew into serious, philosophical discussions about death and birth and the possibilities of reincarnation, heaven, and hell. During the discussions, the women passed around cookies or blueberry pie, which Salvatore always shared with Rusty.

Rusty also accompanied Father Livolsi to the many hospitals where the Father administered to the sick and the dying. In those instances Rusty waited out in the car. When the Father came back, Rusty wagged his tail so hard he almost propelled himself onto the floor. But sometimes when his dad came back from the hospital, Rusty sensed something was wrong. Rusty noticed the Father's contemplative look, the crossed brows, the corners of his mouth turned down. When his dad wore that look, Rusty crawled over and snuggled next to him, and Father Livolsi's limp hand dropped onto his dog's back. Sometimes Rusty couldn't love the Father away from his sadness, and it would take an overnight's sleep to bring back his human companion as he knew him.

Most of all, Rusty enjoyed Father Livolsi's trips to the nursing homes where Rusty immersed himself in the throng of oldsters. Along the endless hallways Rusty trotted up and down the rows of wheelchairs and nuzzled each wrinkled hand. Rusty proved himself worthy of his own kind of counseling. When the elderly, bed-bound folks lay curled up in despair, Rusty approached them with an attitude of calm and caring. The dog moved slowly, looking into their strained eyes, and Rusty's eyes drooped, too. Then he sat at their bedsides and looked up, his mouth partially open as if to say, *"It's okay. I'm here. You can pet me and talk to me if you like."*

To the more lively guests of the home, Rusty laughed and did a few tricks for them—twirling in place, standing up on his hind legs, taking a treat from their hands. Rusty was the hit at the nursing homes, even more so than the Father himself.

Over the years Rusty's love for humans earned him the townspeople's respect that comes with being the Father's healing partner in the religious and non-religious community. Early on, Salvatore noticed how when Rusty accompanied him to friends' or acquaintances' homes, Rusty sensed the moods of the people. When people were loud, laughing, and celebratory, Rusty was up, active, happy, and his tail wagged him. When others were down, he became calm and reticent, and his eyes grew soft and understanding.

Rusty and Father Livolsi had developed a partnership of common love for all people. Rusty, in his own way, supported the Father's efforts with his parishioners, and he supported the Father himself when the priest's job became too much to bear.

Rusty died November 11, 1996.

****

Rusty Joe

Rusty's death led to several conversations between Jan and Father Livolsi about the possibility of animals having souls. Though his formal religious training determined that an animal's having a soul was doubtful, the Father discovered quite the opposite. What he had witnessed with Rusty's uncanny ability to sense and react appropriately to people's moods, his patience while the Father tended to his parishioners, his congenial personality and willingness to just be the Father's companion, made the Father question his Roman Catholic teachings.

Father Livolsi knew his God well. The Father's

God wouldn't have created such an animal capable of uplifting people in dour moods, joyful with those who were happy, and loving everyone without offering that same animal its own salvation. The Father's God was a kind and all-encompassing God, who, the priest felt, would not create such a creature and then abandon it at its time of death.

Jan agreed the problematic issue of animals having souls should be resolved by religious authorities. Guaranteeing animals their God-given souls would certainly impact animal welfare laws, animal rights issues, factory farm production methods, and, in general, would encourage humane treatment of all animals, including farm animals, in a modern society.

****

Jan, seeing how devastated and lonely Salvatore was after Rusty's death, took the Father back to the shelter to pick out another dog. This one he named Rusty Joe, in tribute to the original Rusty. But Rusty Joe wasn't as amiable right from the start as Rusty had been. He was a more reticent, shy dog—not as naturally friendly and outgoing as Rusty had been. When Salvatore went to see someone sick in the hospital or bed-bound in his home, Rusty Joe waited in the car but lost patience, often escaping to the outside if the Father left the window open.

Over the next year, however, Rusty Joe learned to love people the way the Father did, and he became less shy and more outgoing the more places they visited. Rusty Joe followed the Father wherever he went—on short walks around their retreat and sitting on his dad's homemade bench that looked out to Sunrise Mountain. Rusty Joe, like Rusty, just loved being in the moment with his human companion. He didn't expect much, only Salvatore's company, with which he was happiest. Each evening the Father and Rusty Joe enjoyed a couple of TV shows together, and they often fell asleep, Rusty Joe in his Father's lap.

Unfortunately, Rusty Joe became sick and died within a few years of the priest's adopting him. Again Salvatore was heartbroken.

Rusty Joe died May 18, 2000.

****

Rusty and Rusty Joe's Memorial

At seventy-eight years of age, the Father was alone, and though he chose not to take in another dog for fear of having his heart broken for a third time, he confided in Jan he had decided to memorialize both Rusty and Rusty Joe in a special way. His Rustys, he told her, had been his strength, his family, his partners in his ministry. Each had been such a unique, loving, selfless animal, not demanding nor critical. He proposed to memorialize them by building a wooden monument and placing it outside his Christian retreat chapel.

Father Livolsi's tribute is a four-foot-high wooden pedestal topped with a wicker basket holding a dog statue. On the front of the pedestal is a bronze plaque with both dogs' names and the dates of Rusty's and Rusty Joe's deaths. A written tribute, "Rainbow Bridge," author unknown, sits nearby:

Rainbow Bridge

Just this side of heaven is a place called Rainbow Bridge.

When an animal dies that has been especially close
To someone here, that pet goes to Rainbow Bridge.

Where are meadows and hills for all of our special
Friends so they can run and play together. There is
Plenty of food, water and sunshine, and our friends
Are warm and comfortable.

~

All the animals who had been ill and old are restored
To health and vigor. Those who were hurt or maimed
Are made whole and strong again, just as we
Remember them in our dreams of days and times
Gone by. The animals are happy and content, except
For one small thing; they each miss someone very
Special to them, who had to be left behind.

~

They all run and play together, but the day comes
When one suddenly stops and looks into the distance.
His bright eyes are intent. His eager body quivers.
Suddenly he begins to run from the group, flying
Over the green grass, his legs carrying him faster
And faster.

~

You have been spotted, and when you and your
Special friend finally meet, you cling together in
Joyous reunion, never to be parted again. The happy
Kisses rain upon your face; your hands again caress
The beloved head, and you look once more into the
Trusting eyes of your pet, so long gone from your life
But never absent from your heart.

~

Then you cross Rainbow Bridge together....
****

In mid-February of 2008, as Father Livolsi lay sick
in a hospital, the eighty-five-year-old priest shared with
his long-time friend Jan some thoughts about the life he

had enjoyed with his two dogs. "I lived many years with those dogs, and they taught me and all my friends and parishioners how to accept life's unfairness. They taught me how to feel joy and how to appreciate the simple things in life. If anyone deserves a place in heaven, they do." He swallowed hard. "I've thought about it and thought about it, trying to reconcile my findings with my theological background which, as we talked about before, is doubtful on animals' having souls." His voice began to quiver. "Surely the church must be mistaken. I believe Rusty and Rusty Joe not only had souls but very special souls. And I believe, as I lie here dying, my spirit will be fortunate enough to run in the heavenly fields alongside them. It will only be heaven for me if my dogs are there to greet me."

Father Livolsi died at the age of 85 on February 16, 2008.

****

Much information herein was gathered by Jan, one of the founders of the Sussex County Friends of Animals Shelter in Sparta, New Jersey, days before Father Livolsi greeted his best dog-friends in heaven.

Chapter Six
To See With One's Heart

Breed: canine—dachshund
Name: Heinrich
Born: September 12, 1992
Died: November 2005
Human companions: Phoebe & Jerry Mossey

What dog could want for a kinder, more selfless owner than one working for the International Fund for Animal Welfare, an agency that improves the welfare of wild and domestic animals by reducing their exploitation, protecting wildlife habitats, and helping animals in distress? The day the worker from IFAW's World Headquarters in Yarmouth, Massachusetts, arrived at the dachshund breeder's home would be the luckiest day in the life of one pup.

Only days ago Phoebe had lost her dachshund of twelve years. She was heartbroken and saw an ad for puppies in the classifieds. She felt it was too early to get another pup, but her husband insisted they visit the puppies anyway.

At the local breeder's home Phoebe leaned over the playpen at the one lonely ten-inch puppy. As Phoebe held the shivering pup in her lap, the breeder explained that his two brothers were like a couple of gang members, always beating up on the weakest one of the three. The last pup wore his scars as bravely as Henry Fleming had his badges of courage.

Phoebe's husband Jerry found the little pup with the beat-up head so vulnerable and pathetic that he wanted to take him right home. Phoebe, however, despite the pup's kind personality and ability to withstand brutality, wasn't sure because the emotional wound from having lost her first dachshund was still sore. So the couple left without the little dachshund. That evening Phoebe glanced into the corner where her old dachshund had had his feed and water bowls. She burst into tears.

The next day Jerry returned to the breeders and bought the runt, who literally jumped into Jerry's arms. Jerry marveled at how little the eight-week-old pup weighed—less than a five-pound bag of sugar—and he wasn't as long as he should have been. He took the pup with him in the car, wedging him inside his coat, and he drove to Phoebe's office in Yarmouth Port.

Quietly Jerry walked into her office where Phoebe was busy at the computer. "Hey." She turned from her desk and saw the pup's head sticking out from inside Jerry's coat. She slowly stood up, her eyes bright, and she held out her hands.

Jerry put the puppy in her arms, and she held him to her chest. "Oh, thank goodness. I couldn't sleep all night just thinking about him all alone in that playpen, probably thinking he'd never get adopted. Now he's ours." She sighed, and the long, skinny body relaxed against her chest. "His name will be Heinrich."

From the beginning Heinrich slept in the big, queen-sized people bed. But Heinrich's first night with Phoebe, alone since Jerry worked the night shift, was scary for the little pup. He was in a strange place with a strange woman, on top of a huge plain resembling the Sahara—a great, flat expanse of cotton and heavy blankets. In fact he could hardly walk in the desert of blankets, getting stuck in the dunes and hills. He felt completely overwhelmed by all the material and began to whimper.

Phoebe switched on the light and held Heinrich close, fully aware he was missing his mom. He must have felt much better in her arms instead of floundering amidst the huge hills and vales of the comforter. Phoebe decided to turn on the TV so that its thrumming noise might ease Heinrich to sleep. An old Japanese monster movie was playing, and Heinrich's eyes lit up once he heard the dinosaur roaring and stomping over the prehistoric earth. Phoebe and Heinrich watched the monster movie until he fell asleep in her arms and she in his.

As a pup, Heinrich loved to hunt and fight his toys. Once Heinrich adjusted to his new home, he grabbed his stuffed dinosaur by the neck, shaking him, growling, and biting him until his prehistoric "guts" were running out his nose. Then Heinrich, making sure the monster was dead, stood over him, watching for movement. Growling, his hair standing up like a punk-rocker along his back, Heinrich always "killed" his toys and checked them later, muttering at them to dare come back to life.

Similarly he was very aggressive with his orange ball. With it he honed his skills as a hockey player, earning him the nickname Goalie Dog. Whenever Phoebe rolled his orange ball on the kitchen floor, Heinrich ran to the side and ahead of it, watching, laughing at it, and then, finally, jumping ahead and blocking it until it stopped at his feet.

Phoebe cheered Heinrich on—as excited as though watching a real hockey game. "Yay! One block for Heinrich!"

He liked playing hide-and-seek with his orange ball. Wherever Phoebe rolled his ball—under one of several chairs, under the sofa, under the refrigerator—he sniffed it out, then stood "talking," asking his mom to come help him get it out. "Well, where is it, Heinrich? I don't see it anywhere." And Heinrich hopped in place, muttering and laughing for her to come. *"Right here. Right here."* Then Phoebe ran to Heinrich's side and, using either her arms or a yardstick, she rolled the ball out, all the while with Heinrich talking and gurgling and pawing at her arm.

From the time Heinrich was a puppy, Phoebe took him to work with her to the World Headquarters of the International Fund for Animal Welfare. While she worked, Heinrich visited Phoebe's co-workers, not being a pest but just checking out each room, sticking his nose inside the door, if it was open, to say *"Hello."* All the workers were glad to talk with Heinrich and be distracted from work for a while.

Many of the others brought their own dogs or cats to work, too. Heinrich wasn't really crazy about other dogs, probably having flashbacks to his puppyhood when he had been constantly pummeled by his brothers, so he avoided the dog offices. He could wait to talk to those people at lunchtime when his mom was around to protect him. To warn other dog owners to avoid bringing their dogs into her office, Phoebe posted a sign on her door that could be changed to read, "Monster

Dog Is In" or "Monster Dog Is Out" depending on whether Heinrich came to work that day.

On the other hand, he liked the cats. When his nose told him that one office contained a worker's cat, he went inside, marched over to the cat, who was more his own size, made nose contact, turned around, helped himself to a few pieces of his or her dry cat food, and walked back out. For Heinrich something about a cat must have seemed calm and unintimidating. One time Phoebe took in a stray cat who had babies a week after arriving at the office. He liked to sniff the babies, who mewled and slept a lot. They made funny, burpy noises, and they made him feel warm and happy.

During staff meetings Heinrich fell asleep to the murmurings and discussions filling the room. Their talking was like white noise to him, and he never realized that his snoring interrupted some of their most serious discussions. Heinrich's loud snores, however, served as comic relief for many of the workers, whose jobs were sometimes stressful, requiring them to be constantly armed against and battling the harm humans perpetrate on the animal world. Heinrich provided them all with a little stress relief.

When it was lunchtime, Heinrich grew excited when he heard Phoebe's keys taken from her purse. He hopped in place because he more than likely knew he would get a favorite treat at Wendy's. Almost every day he climbed into Phoebe's lap as she drove him to the Wendy's take-out window where he looked at the woman behind the opening and "talked" to place his order. Laughing, Phoebe ordered her own lunch and gave Heinrich a tiny piece of her burger, careful to watch his weight since fat dachshunds are prone to back problems. When the workers behind the Wendy's counter saw the cute dachshund sitting in Phoebe's lap murmuring and muttering, they all gathered around the window to talk to him.

Not only did Heinrich get a take-out "lunch" at Wendy's, but every morning before work Phoebe pulled into Dunkin' Donuts. He just loved to ride his mom's lap when she pulled up to the drive-through window. When she began to order, Heinrich stood up with his front paws on the side of the door, looking anxiously at the donut girl. He waited until she came back with his box of munchkins. While the box was meant for the workers at the office, he knew he'd get at least half of one for a snack in the morning and the other half for a snack in the afternoon. During the ride to work, Heinrich guarded that box of munchkins, sitting beside them, a most serious expression on his face.

When he wasn't busy at Phoebe's office, checking to make sure Phoebe's co-workers and their animals were busy helping other animals the world over, Heinrich was at home sharing long walks with his mom and dad. Heinrich's huge backyard bordered a pond for about a hundred feet, and he cherished his walks outdoors where he chased the ducks and geese. Just like he did with his dinosaur, Heinrich wanted to kill the geese and ducks, but they knew they could fly away and he couldn't follow. One day he even challenged a swan, which must have been a definite boost to his morale. And he barked at and ran after squirrels, chipmunks, and rabbits. Even after his progressive retinal atrophy caused him to go totally blind later in life, he continued sniffing out the wildlife's trail, and he growled at the images surely forming in his mind of ducks and geese and squirrels and such. Anyone could see he took his hunting skills very seriously.

While life was idyllic, in 1998 at the age of six years, Heinrich was diagnosed with back trouble—a spinal disk problem common to dachshunds. In weeks he became paralyzed—both back legs limp as blades of grass, and while many dachshunds with the disease end up using a set of wheels to support their back ends, Heinrich, with no surgery and after many chiropractic treatments and much physical therapy and much more courage and determination, made a complete recovery in several months.

Those months of physical therapy found Heinrich particularly happy to get away from it all. He knew when he saw Jerry hosing the camper and cleaning out the inside that they were going on vacation again. He carefully trotted in circles, wondering what he should do, and then he dashed back inside the house and began packing his toys.

Several times a year Phoebe and Jerry took their camper to the Massachusetts beaches. Heinrich loved to ride the ferry to Nantucket Island. The dachshund adored any kind of riding, be it in a boat or a car or a canoe: the swaying, the vibrations of the wheels on the road, the humming of the engines. In the car he mostly rode the whole way in Phoebe's arms, but sometimes he curled up on the back seat where the humming of the engine and Phoebe's and Jerry's quiet talking put him to sleep, though most times he surely only pretended to be asleep, so excited he was to be on vacation.

Before Heinrich knew it, they were at the beach, where Jerry popped up the camper and got the family settled in the park. Then they spent the day beachcombing, mostly on Cape Cod, but sometimes shopping on Nantucket where the ladies in the shops fussed over him. Once he even had a shop owner give him a little dish of peanut butter ice cream. He had never tasted anything so delightful in his life.

Beachcombing was thrilling, and the salty, moist air of the ocean soothed his joints and back. All kinds of treasures that enticed a dog lay buried in the sand: rotting clams, pieces of driftwood, some living creature burrowed deep into the sand and exhaling air bubbles from his below-home. Heinrich played, too, with the ocean, scooting away when the thin line of a wave tried to catch him. Then, when the wave ran from him—obviously scared of the brave dachshund—he chased after it, barking and warning it not to come back. But it did, and he refused to run from it, simply skipping nonchalantly sideways. He wouldn't give the ocean the satisfaction.

Heinrich's trips to Maine, New Hampshire, Canada, and Vermont must have made him feel worldly. What were his big brothers doing now as he was being introduced to important business people in the shops of so many villages and hotels? While Heinrich and his family always crashed, exhausted, into their camper at night, Heinrich's days were filled with walking, being held, visiting important folks, snacking on foods he had never eaten before, and smelling the fresh air, be it in the mountains or along the ocean's beaches.

The first thing Heinrich did when the car door opened at their destination was to sniff the air. Sometimes it smelled like pine, sometimes like flowers;

most of the time the atmosphere had a briny odor. Then he knew he was at the ocean where he could run and run, playing "chase and escape" with the waves.

One of his most memorable vacation experiences was visiting Ground Zero in New York City. There he felt something sad and sorrowful coming from Phoebe and Jerry when they stood looking into what he thought must be a different kind of beach-hole. Why did the hole not smell like salt? Whenever Phoebe and Jerry took him on vacation, the air was always nice, fragrant, enticing, oceanic, or he smelled things like French fries, hamburgers, or popcorn.

Heinrich didn't enjoy the black hole. He wasn't allowed to go inside and walk around. He could only stay in his mother's arms, and they were trembling. He felt drips of water on his back and looked up. Phoebe was crying. And again he must've wondered why they came on vacation to such a place. But Heinrich had no way of knowing his dad was a fireman at home and needed to be there—where it all happened. Once they took him away from the hole, he felt much better. The three of them stopped at a street vendor, and he ate part of Jerry's hot dog.

On the vacation to the black hole, Heinrich noticed their big white camper hadn't followed them there as it had to other vacations. In New York City they stayed in a hotel, and he rode something called an elevator—its lurching made his guts leap in a decidedly thrilling way. The hotel staff fussed over him, and he met several new friends there. He tried telling his mom he wouldn't mind visiting this place again, providing he didn't have to go to that nasty hole again. The hole wasn't a happy place.

As the years passed, Phoebe began to notice that Heinrich couldn't see very well in twilight. He always hesitated, even if he was following Phoebe, to enter a dark room. Phoebe didn't know that he felt he was walking into a deep, unfathomable pit, much like the one on the bad vacation. When Phoebe took him to see Dr. Venezia, the doctor told Phoebe that his gradual loss of night vision was the first stage of retinal atrophy, a disease common in dachshunds. He told her that he would gradually lose his eyesight, but that she shouldn't worry because dogs adapt very well to blindness since their main senses are smell and hearing, and his were just fine.

Heinrich went totally blind by the age of eleven, at which time he was also diagnosed with Cushing's disease, a nuisance thyroid condition the specialists decided not to treat because of Heinrich's heart murmur. Blindness did nothing to diminish Heinrich's life. He learned to sniff his way all around the house, the back yard, the vet hospital where he received occasional treatments for his heart condition, and Phoebe's office. Heinrich's nose followed his own scent trails wherever they had been before, and he was so expert at finding his way that people didn't even know he was blind until Phoebe told them.

Phoebe found it amazing that Heinrich even seemed to know where he was going in the car. Though he didn't place his front legs on the dashboard or the side of his car door anymore because he couldn't see anything, somehow he knew in what direction Phoebe was driving, whether it was south to Dunkin' Donuts or whether it was north to Wendy's. Every time they drew close to one of those places and even when they were pulling into Phoebe's driveway, he began to chatter as he always did, excited to be going for a piece of donut, a hamburger, or back home.

Having congestive heart failure, Heinrich wasn't expected to live to his twelfth birthday, but, thanks to Dr. Venezia, he was able to celebrate his thirteenth birthday.

For his special day people fussed wildly over him at Phoebe's office, and he wore a yellow lei for the occasion. Then Phoebe took him to see Dr. Venezia; she took him to Wendy's, and they had an absolutely happy and busy time.

All his life Heinrich was a happy, enthusiastic dog, even though he began it as a runt. His courage and determination to beat the odds were remarkable: he challenged hind end paralysis and won; he went blind but learned to "see" with his nose and ears, and he endured congestive heart failure and the treatments that went with it—many medications in pills and injections, monthly echocardiograms, blood pressure checks, blood work and occasional chest X-rays. He endured all the doctoring and medical procedures with courage and willingness. He was always polite, never attempting to bite or struggle, as though he knew his vet-tech girlfriends were trying to help him. Though he was in poor health the last couple of years, he never lost his enthusiasm for life.

Toward the end Heinrich didn't have the energy to chase his geese and ducks, but he still had the fighting instinct in him. So, from the comfort of his favorite chair, he chewed and shook and growled at his favorite stuffed snowman toy as his proud parents watched and smiled.

Heinrich died in November 2005.

Phoebe received a bouquet of flowers from the staff at Dunkin' Donuts when they heard of Heinrich's passing.

****

Heinrich's Memorials

Heinrich was a very lucky dachshund.

Being the subject of a human's adoration had many benefits, not only in life but also in death. Heinrich's life with his human companion, Phoebe, was as rich and colorful as a crazy quilt, decorated with so many variegations of passion, humor, affection, tranquility, and courage that Phoebe didn't know quite where to begin to pay tribute to her patchwork dog.

First, she began filling the gigantic death hole in her heart by seeking a living tribute to Heinrich. She wanted to adopt a dog who was the mirror image of Heinrich—another old, blind dachsie—Maggie Mae. Maggie's owners had dropped off the fourteen-year-old blind animal with Cushing's disease at a veterinarian's office. "She has no quality of life." Instead of putting the old dog to sleep, however, the vets turned her over to Coast to Coast Dachshund Rescue where, in February of 2007, Phoebe found her. Phoebe drove all the way from Yarmouth Port, Massachusetts to Ohio to adopt an elderly blind dachshund. From that day onward, the happy, vibrant Maggie Mae accompanied Phoebe to work every day.

Phoebe has paid tribute to her dearest dog, Heinrich, in several ways. She has made provisions in her will to create the Heinrich Mossey Scholarship at Cornell University College of Veterinary Medicine, from which Heinrich's veterinarian, Dr. Venezia, had graduated. Phoebe wanted to provide funding available to vet students to help animals as Dr. Venezia had helped Heinrich.

In addition to making a tribute to Heinrich in her will, each year Phoebe purchases a quarter-page ad in the auction booklet for the annual MSPCA "Spirit of Kindness" auction. Heinrich's picture is in the ad and includes the quote, "You were living proof that blind dogs see with their hearts."

Also in honor of Heinrich, Phoebe and her younger dachshund, Venice, walk in the Walk for Animals, which benefits the MSPCA shelter. Spectators and other walkers can see her T-shirt with its meaningful logo. "Venice and I are walking in loving memory of Heinrich."

Finally, when Heinrich was diagnosed with severe heart disease in mid-2003 and given only six months to live, Phoebe began a scrapbook honoring Heinrich. Not only did it help keep her worries in check, but it would some day become a tribute and book of memories of her beloved dog-son. She purchased the scrapbook from the Creative Memories company and began to fill it with photos of Heinrich and mementos such as several of his baby teeth, license tags, programs from fundraising walks for the local animal shelter, and the many sympathy cards and emails from people all over the world.

Heinrich's scrapbook of memories is truly memorable. Among the more impressive pages is the "Blessings" page covering the 2005 Blessing of the Animals that happens every September at the West Yarmouth Congregational Church. That page is particularly special to Phoebe because Heinrich had nearly died several nights before the blessing, from a congestive heart failure crisis. And he would die after the Blessing in November of the same year.

Within the scrapbook are two pages showcasing Heinrich as the little brat he could sometimes be. For instance, he hated being groomed, so when Phoebe got out his brush, he attacked the brush, biting it and hanging onto it so she couldn't use it. And he loved tearing up paper bags, so that if Phoebe ever left a grocery bag on the floor, the next time she came into the room, it was in pieces, Heinrich standing in the middle of the mess. And if Heinrich ever sneaked over to his wrapped birthday or Christmas gifts before the days of celebration, he opened them, too, shredding and tossing aside the paper until the bare box was showing. And, as a brat would, he bared his teeth in a naughty grin.

Heinrich, even though he couldn't see during the last few years of his life, still liked to "ham it up" in front of the camera. He knew the sound of the camera's motor when Phoebe turned it on, and from wherever she stood and called him to look, he turned in that direction and held his pose, his legs held out to each side like a boxer prepared to fight. One of those photos in the scrapbook shows Heinrich wearing a blue wig, which, in actuality, was a scarf knitted by one of Phoebe's co-workers. Heinrich had been flipping the scarf into the air and stomping on it, so Phoebe decided to make him a turban of sorts. Heinrich, wearing a very serious expression, probably thought he was playing the King of Siam in that photo.

On another page of the scrapbook sits a handmade birthday card sent to Heinrich in 2005 for his thirteenth birthday. It celebrates the Boston Red Sox, Heinrich's favorite team. The other photos on that page show Heinrich parading around in a yellow Hawaiian lei, which he wore throughout his "miracle" birthday party that celebrated his living over a year longer than expected. Pictures of his thirteenth birthday show him being fussed over by all Phoebe's co-workers, receiving lots of toys, doggie bones, and a huge piece of a birthday cake. Then Heinrich had his picture taken with Dr. Venezia and his favorite veterinary technicians during their lunch hour. After visiting the veterinary hospital, Phoebe took him to his favorite restaurant, Wendy's, where he had his picture taken eating a cheeseburger without the bun or nasty-tasting pickles.

The "Memories" pages in Heinrich's scrapbook hold sympathy cards, and one cites a quote by Rabindranath Tagore: "Death does not extinguish the light, rather it puts out the lamp because the dawn has come." Since Phoebe worked for an international organization, she received sympathy cards from all Heinrich's friends living in the United Kingdom, Canada, South Africa, France, and Australia. She was amazed at how many lives Heinrich had touched. Phoebe has placed these cards in the "Memories" section of Heinrich's scrapbook along with a card bearing the poem, "The Rainbow Bridge."

How such a comparatively small animal impacted people around the world, his technicians and his veterinarian, Phoebe herself, as well as her co-workers, is proof that animals, in the very simplest of ways, touch people deeply. Heinrich showed during his illness, in no deliberate effort and in no way to impress, uncommon courage, stamina, and a sense of humor—

traits truly admirable and distinguishing for any animal. For such a small animal, his depth of courage was immeasurable.

Chapter Seven
A Badge of Courage

Species: African elephant
Name: Sonny
Born: January 1982
Died: February 2001
Zookeeper and human companion: John Bergmann

John Bergmann laughed and grabbed for the elephant's trunk, but Sonny was too quick. Suddenly a rush of water, fire-hose thick, burst from its end, hitting John squarely in the face. He wiped his cheek on his sleeve, blinking the muddy water from his eyes. "That wasn't nice, Sonny." He shook the water from his curly hair. "In fact, that was downright sneaky."

Sonny lifted his trunk and smiled a "gotcha" grin. Through John's muddied eyes, the gash on Sonny's trunk was barely visible. The six-inch gaping wound, his physical badge of courage, masked the emotional one buried deep within the animal's psyche much as it did in people with psychological disturbances. That part of Sonny was something he couldn't help—it had become a part of him—after the culling.

The killing of Sonny's elephant herd in Zimbabwe in 1983 resulted in the annihilation of his family as well as his sense of security. In the settling dust along the river's edge where the grand animals had been grazing one afternoon, eighty adult elephants, some shot through the head, others wounded in their legs and bellies, lay slowly dying. The African bush glowed with fire-blood, and the river frothed tomato red. Though mortally wounded, a handful of bull elephants still struggled to rise in a last attempt to defend the youngsters. Sitting on their haunches, blood streaming down their sides, they trumpeted in weak but insistent voices as other adult elephants shot in the throat and chest lay fighting for breath, barely able to answer the yearlings' calls for help. Most of those eighty adults had been luckier than those expiring by the river's edge, for the humans' aim had hit their targets well. Shot in the heart or brain, most had dropped—stone dead— Sonny's mother and many of his aunts among them.

While the year-old elephant struggled to make sense of the chaos around him, the second phase of the attack began. After the adult elephants had been eradicated, hundreds of two-legged creatures ran, yelling, jumping, and spitting like hyenas, at the forty scared young elephants. They leapt and charged Sonny and his brothers and sisters with an arsenal of hooks, spears, heavy chains, and ropes the diameter of grape vines. Sonny feared this enemy more than those of the African bush. Though he had never liked the lionesses as they eased, slinking, past his herd, their eyes scanning the sick amongst them, he knew they were seldom a threat. Circling around him and the other yearlings, the adults, especially his mom and aunts, of which he had ten, had only to stomp their feet at the lioness and trumpet a warning. Then she crawled away in search of easier prey.

The predator that had Sonny's legs tied with heavy

ropes was nothing like the lioness. Unlike the solitary, hungry feline, these things killed in packs, like the wild dogs in the bush. They maimed in large numbers—more lethal than a single large cat on the hunt. And these comparatively small but agile creatures wielded weapons he had never seen before, their tools as sharp as the tip of a split branch. And when he got in their way, his skin ripped as easily as an elephant tearing a limb from an acacia tree. When Sonny charged one of the two-legs, it flung something at him, and a shock of pain rippled along his back—a deep gash in his trunk gaped like a hippo's mouth, and it leaked blood onto his front feet.

These small nimble creatures, mostly black, some white, also knew how to use big moving steel things the size of Sonny himself. Four round black things under each box rolled, turned, and moved the steel compartments in any direction. Those boxes could move as slow as a sick, elderly antelope, or they could dart as fast as a cheetah. They were nightmarish—those walking, rolling vaults—and they slowly crowded him and his cousins, surrounding them, pressing them into a tight circle.

Sonny leaned against the other young, panic-stricken elephants. At least they had each other. Sonny longed for his mother. She had always defended him against ill-tempered bull elephants and had charged hungry lionesses. *Where was she? Why wasn't his mother helping him?*

The yearlings, pressed together, trumpeted balefully. Some fell to the ground gasping, their trunks limp with exhaustion, and tears streamed down their skin-cracks. This wily predator was tenacious. Soon the baby elephants' calls slowed, weakened. Defenseless without their elders, they massed together as one—alone and without any will to fight. As the baby elephants leaned into each other, rigid with fear, the two-leg enemies disappeared inside their boxes—silent and staring with piercing white eyes.

In two hours the young elephants found themselves huddled together inside those same dark containers, four elephants to each of the caravan's ten boxes. As each dark cave began to move, Sonny and the other yearlings braced themselves against its unforgiving metal sides. For what seemed like days, the terrified animals hunched together to keep from falling, leaning against each other for balance as well as for courage. The only sound was the rattling of steel beneath them and, inside, the gentle weeping of the elephants.

The morning of that day was the last taste of freedom for Sonny. He and the other thirty-nine young elephants, from which he would soon be separated, were being moved continents away from his native Africa. They would no longer follow their mothers to the river's edge, would no longer be groomed by their aunts within the herd, would no longer sleep, surrounded by the protection of the herd's matriarchs, beneath the deep, black, star-studded African sky. That bloody evening while Sonny struggled to maintain his balance, he felt lost and thrown into the chaos of something hateful—something he could not understand.

Sonny had met humans.

****

John Bergmann grabbed the garden hose he used to water Sonny, Oliver the steer, the monkeys, and the goats, and sprayed the elephant's feet. "Ha-ha, Sonny.

You're not the only one with a hose." He laughed. The elephant tilted his head to the side. Then he dunked his whole trunk into his water trough and began sucking, hoovering as much water as he could hold, all the while eyeing John.

Bergmann gasped as he watched Sonny suck nearly an inch of the trough's water into his trunk. Sensing his disadvantage, he dropped the garden hose and took off running to the protection of his makeshift office desk, about ten feet from Sonny's pen, as the first wave of muddy water sailed through the air. John roared with laughter from behind his desk, and water rained, pattering all around him. Then, knowing he missed his target, Sonny turned around and emptied the rest onto his friend Oliver the steer, who delighted in Sonny's cool shower.

Sonny and John Bergmann had not always been on such good and playful terms. Sometimes Sonny still had his moments, those moments fueled by the past, by the haunting memories of his river-friend running crimson, of his silenced herd, of the two-leg creatures that had beaten and stabbed him, taken his freedom and his family. In those moments, he ached with emptiness and turned his back to Bergmann, who reminded him of the two-legs. In those moods he refused to accept Bergmann's treats—the overly ripe bananas, the halves of cantaloupe, the tasty watermelons. Those remembrances killed his appetite, and John swore that, at those times, he could detect a tear-trail on Sonny's face.

****

When Sonny first walked into the zoo, he was a weary and distrustful world traveler. In 1989 he didn't know he had come to the Popcorn Park Zoo in Forked River, New Jersey, all the way from Zimbabwe via Texas and New Mexico. The two-legs had bought his travel ticket to the Popcorn Park Zoo after first tormenting him in a place they called Texas. There they chained his legs raw, whipped him, beat him, and confined him to a small pen. They cowed him into frightened submission by revving a chainsaw inches from his pen. Through it all, Sonny suffered welts and scars, of both the physical and emotional kind, because he refused to submit, refused to cower. Finally, when he had blasted for the third time through his pen at another zoo in New Mexico, the officials declared him a *rogue* elephant. And rogue elephants—good for nothing—earned another ticket—a one-way ticket to the town of Euthanasia.

The Popcorn Park Zoo, however, learned of Sonny's plight, and, true to their mission of serving abused and neglected animals, they decided to adopt Sonny, the incorrigible bull elephant. So when Sonny stepped onto the grounds that first evening, the first two-leg he saw was John Bergmann, and unlike the other two-legs, this one seemed different. This one didn't carry a spear or whip. He didn't even brandish a shovel in Sonny's direction. He just sat quietly next to Sonny's pen.

John Bergmann had a low, soothing voice that animals loved. "Hi, Sonny. Welcome to Popcorn Park. It's good to have you here." Then he got up, took half a cantaloupe, and gently rolled it through the bars. It came to a stop at Sonny's feet. Oliver, the steer in a neighboring pen, roared a greeting, but Sonny began to sway with anxiety.

"It's okay, boy. You're safe here. Taste the cantaloupe. I'm going to stay with you tonight until you feel safe. Don't worry—I won't leave you. I'll be right back." Then Bergmann opened the large garage doors at the far end of the seventy-five-foot by fifty-foot triage barn where new animals were acclimated to the staff and the new environment before being placed into their outdoor pens. Sonny stared anxiously and rocked in place as the two-leg disappeared.

In moments one of those boxes—the metal boxes of Sonny's memory—rolled through the doors. Sonny bellowed, grabbed one of the two-inch pipes that formed his cage, and pulled with all his weight. He had to get out. But the bars didn't budge. Sonny roared again, and then the moving box stood still and silent. Sonny's back softened once the noise of the box stopped, and then he saw the zookeeper step from it along with a much smaller, miniature two-leg.

John led his seven-year-old son by the hand. "Sonny—I want you to meet Jonathan."

Sonny had retreated to the far end of his pipe-cage at sight of the mechanical box, but he approached with caution once he saw the smaller two-leg. Another cantaloupe rolled into his pen, but he didn't trust it—a trick. Then the little two-leg called to him in a high voice, "Sonny, don't be afraid. You're going to like it here. Daddy and I are going to stay right here with you all night so you're not afraid, aren't we, Dad?" Such a tiny voice Sonny had never heard from a two-leg before. He just remembered their shouting, yelling, and hooting. None had sounded like this.

That evening Sonny paced his pen, eyeing the steel box like those of which he had horrific recollections.

While Sonny paced, trunk-touching all the bars for an exit, John slept fitfully in the truck cab with Jonathan curled in a blanket beside him. Jonathan woke up. "What's that noise, Dad?"

A low rumble sounded from Sonny's pen.

"It's Sonny, son. He's still worried about us and his new home. I think he may be talking to Oliver and the goats, too. I don't really know."

"Is he talking to us, do you think?"

"No, he's not talking to us. Someday—maybe—but not now. Go back to sleep."

Sonny didn't sleep until the third night. Had Bergmann known that his "box" was the demon of Sonny's dreams, he would have driven it away, but he didn't realize it was the immediate source of Sonny's discomfort. The third night, however, Sonny was too exhausted not to sleep. And he slept in as grand a manner as any of his species, snoring loudly and rhythmically, his belly full of this different two-leg's cantaloupes, watermelons, and good grass hay.

For all the suffering Sonny bore at the hands of people, he adjusted well to his new surroundings and zookeeper Bergmann and his staff. In a few months everyone liked Sonny, though he still had moments when he retreated to a corner to brood. Then the staff were notified to be extra quiet and careful around Sonny because he was in one of his despondent moods.

Sonny, by the age of eight or nine years, learned to accept his confinement in his large outdoor pen. At least he could talk with Oliver and the tapir and hippo across the way. His pen was clean, facing south so that he could warm his back in the sun, and it even had a large pool area for him to enjoy a mudpack against flies.

While Sonny wasn't as free as he had been in the African bush, and while he didn't have his loving herd to protect him, this place seemed like a decent compromise—far better than the other two places he had lived. Order and organization ruled here, and the two-legs spoke softly and massaged his trunk with light fingers. The two-legs always delivered his breakfast of oranges, grapefruit, cantaloupe, watermelons and hay early in the morning. Then they sprayed fresh water into his trough from a very long, thin trunk.

On days when Bergmann was on feed duty, Sonny listened for the low rumbling of his zookeeper's truck, which he could hear from a quarter mile away. At the sound he lifted his trunk and awakened the entire zoo with his trumpeting. When John finally arrived at Sonny's pen with the food barrow, John couldn't roll the pumpkins and lettuce heads fast enough into Sonny's cage. And when John pushed another vegetable into Sonny's kiddy-pool food dish, Sonny tapped the top of John's head for him to hurry—he was starving. "Yeah, you're starving, just as much as I am, Sonny. Both of us could stand to lose a couple of pounds." He laughed as he sailed a flake of hay at Sonny's feet.

After only a few months at the zoo, Sonny began to warm up to the other staffers. He coaxed them near by hanging his trunk between the pipes and waving it. Melanie, one of the animal crew, found Sonny's beckoning trunk irresistible, and though she wasn't allowed to get into the pen with him, she let him touch her face and hands with his trunk. Giggling, she submitted to his exploration of her face, much as a blind person feels the contours of people's faces in order to "see" their friends. Sonny's trunk felt ticklish to her, the tip of the trunk so delicate and soft.

Melanie and Sonny quickly became buddies. While on her daily rounds, Melanie always stopped for a few minutes to scratch Sonny behind the ears. She went up to the bars, and whatever Sonny was doing—pulling on a tree stump or searching his dry moat with his trunk— he stopped, knowing it was time for his massage. Then, he sidled slowly up to his friend and waited. As Melanie raised her arm—the signal for a scratch— Sonny slid his thin, skin-cracked ear through the pipes.

One who cares for large animals doesn't scratch an elephant's ear the way she would tackle an itch of her own. On the contrary, scratching an elephant's ear was done with as much vigor and strength as scraping away paint peeling from the side of a barn. With his ear curling and waving between the bars and her body bending and reaching toward him, Melanie rubbed the soft, silky area behind the ear. With that Sonny smiled, his trunk raised, his mouth open, and a slow rumbling, a giant "purring," erupted inside the elephant.

Soon Sonny wasn't content with having only his ears scratched. Between feedings, if any of the animal crew happened past, he sidled up to the pipes and put his weight into them so that the skin on his flank protruded between the pipes. The animal crew used kiddy rakes then and simply raked his cracked, dry skin, and Sonny helped them by moving his sides up and down in rhythm to their strokes. When summer came, another element was added to the body massage—as three members of the animal crew stroked Sonny with rakes, John sprayed him with the hose. To complete the massage, John used an orchard sprayer to spray mineral oil over the elephant's body and legs. Sonny smiled widely. He thought living at the Popcorn Park Zoo was not so bad a life after all, not with daily massages, exfoliation treatments, and cool, moisturizing showers.

Sonny grew to love John and Melanie and the rest of the animal crew—something he never would have dreamed of since they were two-legs. Now he relished each morning when they all came whistling and chatting toward his enclosure with fruit barrows and offers of back scratches. Before they were even out the door with the goodies, Sonny's trunk was flailing through the pipes, urging them to hurry.

Still, though it was certain Sonny was happy at Popcorn Park Zoo, he had his moments of depression. Then everyone respected his need to be alone, to remember his mother, his aunts, African rainstorms, but, most of all, his freedom in the African bush. During those moments of sadness and irritability, enduring the barrier of pipes that kept him a prisoner, he took his dejection out on the noisy, ill-mannered monkeys in a nearby pen.

The monkeys were as intelligent as Sonny, and they knew perfectly well that their loud chattering annoyed him, so they tantalized him, screeching, running, attacking each other, and just acting very "two-leg." The final straw was their throwing scraps of food at him. Seeing him hit broadside, the monkeys wailed with ape-laughter. *"Kree…kree…kree-e-e-e-!"* So when Sonny had finally had enough, he hurled the first of many dung-pancakes at them. Shocked, the monkeys darted inside their enclosure, silent for the first time. Sonny felt triumphant. Each time he flung his turds into the monkey cage, he trumpeted an expletive, no doubt, in elephant language.

Sonny's intelligence, much like that of the monkeys, was clearly keen. One morning when Sonny walked into his outdoor area, as was usual, John was removing the soiled sawdust from the pen. Like a playful child, Sonny, trunk tucked under his chin so as not to expose himself, peeked out from behind his enclosure. John shrieked with feigned surprise, and Sonny wore a mischievous grin. Sonny loved playing hide-and-seek. Another time, Sonny had been sniffing rocks at the edge of his moat, a six-foot-wide, ten-foot-deep trench. The moat, though not filled with water, could still discourage an angry elephant from charging a crowd and breaking out of his enclosure.

That day, while Sonny explored the edge of the moat, he suddenly lost his balance and slipped into the trench. Sonny lay thrashing at the bottom of the pit, and his trunk flailed, frantic for something to grab. Sonny trumpeted his predicament in ear-shattering hysteria. John, Melanie, and other crew members ran to his camp and found Sonny in the dry moat up to his shoulders. Sonny was stuck. Surrounded on all sides by dirt walls, he was panic-stricken.

When John knelt at the edge of the moat, the marooned elephant laid his trunk at the side, and John stroked it quietly, speaking in soothing tones. Soon Sonny calmed enough to think. First, with much difficulty, he rolled, stood up, and turned himself around. Then he braced his trunk against the dirt wall in front of him. Pushing against the opposite wall with his trunk, he was able to back himself up the emergency staircase that led out of the trench. But soon he ran out of trunk with which to push. So he stepped back down and turned around to face John.

"Here, Sonny." John showed the elephant a ridge behind the last step at the top of the moat. "Grab here and hoist yourself up the steps. Right here." John tapped the concrete. "Right here."

Sonny gave John the tip of his trunk, and John placed it on the ridge. The tip of the trunk scaled the edge, exploring, contemplating. Then it grabbed the concrete, and with it Sonny hoisted himself up the steps and out of the trap. John and a crowd of zoo-goers and staff clapped and cheered.

Sonny was admired not only for his intelligence, his affectionate and playful personality, but also for his size. The massive animal had experienced, in his travels and through his suffering at the hands of man, a depth of knowledge at once innocent yet sophisticated beyond that of much human experience. Sonny, despite it all, reserved inside himself a capacity, as large as his physical self, for noble-mindedness. His was a good and heroic heart.

After enjoying life for twelve years with John Bergmann at the Popcorn Park Zoo in Forked River, New Jersey, Sonny died at the age of twenty-one in February of 2001.

****

Sonny's Memorial

Mourners from the New Jersey Humane Society as well as staff from The Popcorn Park Zoo and Sonny's human friends and admirers from several different states gathered on March 10, 2001, to attend Sonny's memorial services given by Rev. William Donahue at

Layton's Home for Funerals. Complete with flowers, bows, and catered refreshments, along with a kite a little three-year-old made so that Sonny could fly to heaven, Sonny's friends lined up at Sonny's compound back at the zoo while a bagpiper played a funeral dirge.

In a funeral service in which the room was decorated with a bouquet of flowers shaped like an elephant, a broken heart flower arrangement, and two elephant footprints signifying Sonny's journey, Rev. Donahue said, in part, during his sermon:

"I began in my own life to realize that my closest contact with God was looking into the eyes of a dog or a cat. I began to realize that the life they fulfilled was not so I could train them, but so they could teach me.... [Sonny's] mission has been accomplished. He has assisted the earthlings in demonstrating love and kindness and compassion so we have all grown as a result of an elephant named Sonny."

As the Reverend's funeral service came to a quiet end, John Bergmann, tears welling his eyes, remembered his animal friend and the touching moments they shared.

****

A week after Sonny's funeral, John appeared, Sonny's photo in hand, at the tombstone engraver's shop. John placed the photo of an elephant on the man's desk. "I need a tombstone for Sonny."

The man glanced at the photo. "So you want an elephant etched onto a piece of granite?"

John contemplated the moment. "No. I don't just want a photo of an elephant. I want the etching to be of Sonny, not just any elephant."

"Okay, sir. I'll try my best."

It sometimes takes months to etch granite, and Sonny's gravestone took no less time to create. The placing of Sonny's stone happened months after his funeral service. When the truck finally pulled up to the Popcorn Park Zoo that summer day in 2001 and backed into place before Sonny's burial site, John and his staff stood transfixed before the masterpiece that was Sonny's headstone.

Melanie dabbed her eyes. "It looks just like Sonny."

John's lips were trembling. "It *is* Sonny." Then he smiled. He looked at the stone engraver. "Thank you. It's Sonny."

Atop the mound of earth that is Sonny's grave, his headstone reflects Sonny's grandeur. If any animal ever deserved such a memorial, it was certainly Sonny, who lived to forgive the two-legs who had tortured him and grew to love those that helped heal him.

When the headstone had been placed on its concrete pad, John commented how it sparkled in the sunlight. "It's exquisite granite. Where is it from?"

The man wiped his eyes, clearly touched by his own creation. "You're not gonna believe this..."

"Where did it come from?"

"This granite came from Zimbabwe."

****

Donations to the Popcorn Park Zoo are needed and greatly appreciated. Anyone wishing to contribute to Sonny's memorial fund may mail a donation to Sonny Memorial Fund, Popcorn Park Zoo, Humane Way, Box 43, Forked River, NJ 08731-0043.

Chapter Eight
Our Royal Swineherd

Species: pot-bellied pig
Name: Duchess; Duke
Born: May 5, 1997; May 5, 1997
Died: May 28, 1999; September 26, 2005
Human companions: Barbara and Bob Baker

On May 5, 1997, Lulabelle, Ross Mill Farm's pregnant breeding sow, furiously began tearing up newspapers, readying a cozy nest for her piglets. Finally, after scratching the shredded papers into a heap, she lay down with her full, pendulous belly and gave birth to three little pigs hardly bigger than hamsters. Susan Magidson, Lulabelle's owner, knelt beside them, proud as though she were the mother herself.

Susan fussed over her pig. "Oh, Lulabelle. Look what you made. You made another you." Susan picked up one of the piglets. Indeed, Lulabelle had replicated herself in one of the piglets. The tiny black-and-white female was truly fancy, sporting a lot of "chrome"—a full white collar, four white legs and white tail. The second piglet had only a bit of white on him, and he already had a human family waiting for him in Virginia. Then Susan scooped up a smaller, all-black male piglet. He chirped as she held him against her chest. "And you, too, are just as handsome. Wait until I call your new parents in Florida and tell them how handsome you are."

For the next four months the babies romped the woods around the farm with their mother—their common interest hunting wild mushrooms and berries beneath the oaks and dogwood trees. Though they loved the outdoors, what Duke and Duchess, names their Florida parents had already given them through an email, loved more than anything was their human companion, Susan. She cooed and tweaked them whenever they passed. She carried them around in her arms and stroked their backs until they fell asleep in her arms and talked to them and whispered soft words in their tiny, sensitive ears. When Susan called the piglets to "Come along!" for dinner, Duke outran Duchess and his brother to the house.

Loving humans was a trait that made the piggies comfortable with their new parents, the Bakers, in their home in Florida. Barbara Baker fussed over the newly weaned babies, setting up fluffy beds for them to sleep in, teaching them tricks with Cheerios for rewards and taking them on their leashes for walks in the neighborhood. At night the Bakers took Duchess and Duke and planted them between their legs as they watched TV before going to bed. Duke and Duchess loved their new humans.

Pot-bellies love warmth and being toasty, so Duke and Duchess luxuriated in the Florida weather. Bob even bought them a kiddy pool in which to cool off when the heat and humidity became overwhelming. When Duchess overheated from playing with her brother in the back yard, she jumped into the pool, spinning around on her haunches and splashing everyone in sight. And Duke, too, seeing his sister having so much fun, flopped down in the water, squidging the water all over his back and sides.

Though the Bakers and the tropical-like weather were ideal, the piglets hadn't anticipated one problem— two other pigs lived in the Baker household, two massive, imposing step-pigs who had had an established reign over their territory and did not appreciate the tiny invaders from rural Pennsylvania. Her Royal Highness Lady Lee and His Excellency Lord Chapman ruled the patch with Napoleonic fervor. In particular, Lord ruled the home with an iron hoof.

Compared with Duchess and Duke, as small as soft drink cans, Lord Chapman was loveseat size, and the combination of his incredibly hulkish body with his aggressive temperament put the two newcomers at a disadvantage that Lord, himself, realized and relished. Duchess, being of a more assertive temperament than Duke, however, rose to the occasion whenever Lord regarded her as a toy to be chased or pummeled. Instead of running from Lord, Duchess stood her ground, posturing threats, raising her hackles and chomping her teeth. Then she turned her tiny body sideways, bristles sticking out much like the spines on an inflated blowfish, to make herself look larger and more threatening than she really was. Somehow Duchess' ruse worked, and Lord, presented with the horrific visage of Duchess doing her intimidation dance, slinked away. Then, as magically as Duchess had blown herself up, she deflated and ran off to find Duke.

Meanwhile, Duke, witnessing the confrontation, escaped to one of his many secret hiding places, for, from the beginning, Lord disliked Duke. Lord probably thought of Duke as a rival male and a threat to his kingdom. As on so many occasions, when Duke felt threatened by Lord Almighty, he hid. For the first few weeks the Bakers remarked that perhaps they had really only brought home one pig because Duke was always hiding behind the sofa, a chair, behind the water heater, behind a planter, all to be out of range of Lord the Terrible. Eventually, however, Duke realized that his best defense was his sister, Duchess the Brave.

Duchess understood that Duke was afraid of Lord, and so every morning she scouted outside and inside the house for signs of Lord's presence. She became Duke's protector. With Duke following closely behind, Duchess walked outside, checked out the porch area, then the garage, then the flower beds. If the outside was clear, Duke knew he could go his own way for a while, but he never let Duchess out of his sight for very long. Duke and Duchess had a symbiotic relationship. It wasn't long before Duke realized that Duchess couldn't hear anything. Duke must have wondered why his sister always ignored their parents, especially not racing to the house when called for dinner. When Duke tried to converse with Duchess himself, he knew she couldn't hear him because she didn't answer back. So in order to help his sister, Duke became her ears.

Barbara nodded to Bob as they watched Duke and Duchess playing outside. "I told you—it happens all the time. It's uncanny the way he gets her attention when I call them. Watch!" Barbara cupped her hands around her mouth. "Duke! Duchess!" Suddenly Duke's head popped up—listening. Barbara yelled again for the pigs. With his snout Duke poked Duchess in the side, and then they both came running.

Bob slurped his coffee. "Hm-mmm. Duke alerts her to noises. Very cool."

Duchess was such an affectionate pig it didn't matter to the Bakers she was deaf. Duchess' deafness caused few problems because Duke heard *for* her. In this way Duchess was able to live a normal life, despite her disability.

Part of the reason, unknown to the Bakers, that Duke insisted Duchess come along when their people called was because he didn't want to go anywhere alone—in case he should meet up with the biggest and scariest pig of the household. More than simply being helpful to the deaf Duchess, Duke needed Duchess's twenty-four-hour protection from Lord.

Whenever Duke unexpectedly became separated from Duchess, he lost all sense of courage. If he became caught in the same room with Lord, he ran as though the hounds of Hades were on his heels. Duke didn't share Duchess' assertive personality, but he became a master at evasive strategies. When Lord rounded a corner, sashaying into the living room where Duke lay curled on a blanket, Lord grunted a warning. Lord knew that one grunt was enough to send Duke running. Off Duke went, bolting for the kitchen, where either his parents or his sister would protect him.

Lord did nothing to boost Duke's sense of self-esteem. Every day he crept through the house—searching every crack and cranny for the grouchy Lord. And, like clockwork, whenever he was just drifting off to sleep, Lord charged him to steal his blanket.

Though Lord was a constant threat to Duke, Duke found some respite with Bob. While Duchess grew closer to Barbara, accompanying her on her cleaning chores, falling asleep in the wash basket filled with clean mountain-rain-scented clothes, helping to straighten the shower mats in the bathroom, and watching Barbara's fingers dancing across the computer keyboard, Duke became Bob's second-best buddy. When he wasn't hiding from Lord, if Duke saw Bob stretched out in the recliner, he leaped up between Bob's legs, where Bob stroked his head until they both fell asleep.

Duchess and Barbara, on the other hand, were always busy together. When Barbara was on the move, she, with Duchess in her arms, tiptoed past Bob and Duke asleep in the lounger. Barbara carried Duchess everywhere—to the basement, to the garage, upstairs to the bedroom, and out into the back yard. Duchess loved being cradled and fussed over, and Barbara loved feeling her pig-baby in her arms. Except when Duchess was guarding Duke, she and Barbara were inseparable.

****

For two years Duke and Duchess thrived under the Bakers' care. In January of 1997, however, Duchess wasn't feeling quite right. Her appetite was fussy, and even after a visit to the Florida Veterinary Specialists, she still picked at her food. The veterinarians did all the high-tech diagnostic tests and discussed Duchess' poor appetite, but they were at a loss as to what was wrong.

One morning Duchess had licked only a few crumbs from her breakfast bowl, so Barbara crouched down to urge Duchess to eat more. Barbara glanced at Duke, who hadn't even touched his food. That's when she noticed the tears. She took Duke's face in her hands and raised it to hers. Water streamed from the corners of his eyes and down the cracks around his mouth.

"Oh, my God, Bob! Duke's crying. Why's he crying?"

"Crying? Can pigs actually cry?"

"Well, how else do you explain what's coming from his eyes? And something's wrong, because he's not eating his breakfast."

For the next week, as the Bakers coaxed Duchess to eat and took her back and forth to the vets, they were not unaware that Duke was depressed, tears periodically dripping off his chin. They knew he was crying, but they didn't know why.

****

Animals feel loss and loneliness when either human or animal friends die. Before anyone really knew for sure that Duchess was just so sick, Duke knew she was dying. Could he smell it? Was her touch cooler than before? Had she told him she knew she was dying? One will never know how Duke knew Duchess, at only two years of age, was dying, but no one can deny the tears Duke shed for his best friend and sister.

Duchess died of liver failure two weeks later on May 28, 1999.

****

Duke's fearfulness haunted him daily but became worse when, at two years old, his only protector and pig friend left him forever. Duke could only lie around, despondent and crying.

It had been three weeks since Duchess died. Bob patted Duke's back. "He's crying 'cause he lost his best buddy. They took care of each other. They depended on each other—Duchess needed his ears, and Duke needed her courage. I feel so bad for him."

"I know. I feel as bad as he does." Barbara stared down at Duke. "He and I both lost our soul mates. But I can cope. Poor Duke is in rough shape. It's bad enough that Duchess has died, but now Duke is so depressed—that's upsetting me, too. I think he needs extra care from one of us."

Bob brightened. "Hey, why don't I become his Duchess, at least for a while? I'll take him with me wherever I go—in the house and outside. I'll keep Lord away from him. I'll play with him and shower him with treats."

So the shy, withdrawn Duke began to follow Bob Baker much as he had Duchess. Bob picked him up, whether Bob was eating breakfast or dinner, to sit in his lap. He took him into the bathroom for his morning constitution and for brushing his teeth. He took him outside with him to lie under the palm tree. He even took him to the grocery store.

In a few months Duke was feeling more like himself. The tears had stopped. Though he wasn't nearly as outgoing or entertaining as Duchess had been, Duke was a loving animal. He luxuriated in Bob's warm, manly smell after his shower, and every evening when Bob sat in his lounge chair, Duke stood up on his hind legs, his front hooves on the edge of Bob's chair, the pig begging to lie between Bob's outstretched legs. Lying with Bob in his recliner became a habit Duke cherished for the rest of his life. Life, as far as Duke could tell, could hardly have been better, and Bob felt much the same way.

Duke died September 2, 2005.

****

Duke's and Duchess's Memorials

Duke's cremation urn sits on a table next to Duchess's urn, beneath a painting of Duchess. Side by side lie the ashes of both pigs, brother Duke and sister Duchess, who had played together, slept with and loved each other for two years. The Bakers' comfort lay in the knowledge that they are companions in death.

****

Soon after her cremation, some of Duchess's ashes were spread at her place of birth on September 9, 1999 at Ross Mill Farm in Rushland, Pennsylvania in a memorial service attended by dozens of people. Her mother, Lulabelle, walked, a bouquet of flowers attached to her harness, with Susan, Duchess' first human friend, to the edge of the woods where Duchess and Duke had played as piglets. There, with "Trumpets Voluntary" playing from the wooden gazebo, Susan spread a few of Duchess's ashes.

During the memorial ceremony Susan spoke about Duchess and her life at the farm and with the Bakers. The ceremony was solemn and all who attended were wiping their eyes, for Duchess was a *pig-person*. Then, walking over to a sheeted object, Susan unveiled a painting of Duchess done by fellow pig friend and enthusiast, Becky DiNolfi.

When she was alone, Barbara took the painting into Susan's house and picked up one of the cards for Duchess' memorial service. She re-read the prophetic words that would eventually be a godsend for pot-bellied pigs all over the world:

In loving memory of Duchess of Pork
May 5, 1997- May 28, 1999

~

Memorial Service, Ross Mill Farm

September 9, 2000 for the scattering of some ashes.

~

The Duchess experience—
a segment—her work is not done
neither "here" nor "there."
Her work will be continued "here" by those
who perceive to have been entrusted with it.
Only Duchess knows who will be helping her
to continue her work "there."

****

In Duchess's honor Barbara and Bob Baker established a necropsy fund for pigs having died of mysterious causes as Duchess had. The necropsy fund soon grew into The Duchess Fund, an organization for funding medical expenditures and lab work and other costs for serving the medical needs of pot-bellied pigs. It was a long-awaited idea come to fruition, and the organization took off at its inception. The Duchess Fund committed itself to the following goal: "…to furnish attending veterinarians with more information and data to better equip him or her in the treatment of pot-bellied pigs."

The Duchess Fund began in the year 2000 as a medical database for pot-bellied pig medical case histories compiled with the cooperation of universities nationwide. The Duchess Fund, its first pot-bellied case being the Baker's pig, Duchess, who only lived two years, has since become assimilated into the much larger Swine Medical Database or SMD, Inc—www.swinemedicaldatabase.org. Case medical histories from the Duchess Fund can still be accessed at this web site, though The Duchess Fund site has been officially retired. Many of those cases involved reproductive, birthing, neurological, digestive and urinary problems of pot-bellies. The Swine Medical Database at www.swinemedicaldatabase.org. now serves a larger role, supervised by veterinarians, and allowing for searching and input of swine illnesses by the entire swine community, not just pot-bellied pigs. The website is supervised by veterinarians and serves lay people, owners of pigs, as well as other veterinarians lacking the training or the information to diagnose and treat all swine.

****

The Duchess Fund, and, by its extension, www.swinemedicaldatabase.org, has been a literal lifesaver for both pet pigs and other swine whose lives and those of their owners have been impacted by a mini pig they never met. Duchess continues to live on through www.swinemedicaldatabase.org.

****

Any reader interested in donating to this worthy nonprofit organization can access information at its website: www.swinemedicaldatabase.org. All donations fund swine necropsies, diagnostic tests, and other medical procedures.

Anyone interested in adopting a pet pig can go to www.rossmillfarm.com for more information.

Chapter Nine
"Puppy Up"

Species: canine—Great Pyrenees
Name: Malcolm
Born: October 31, 1997
Died: January 11, 2006
Human companion: Luke Robinson

"First and foremost, we go over the rules."

Luke plopped the roly-poly, snow-white puppy on the sofa. The Great Pyrenees sat upright on the cushions, his big paws balancing his body. He grinned, his long tongue hanging from the corner of his mouth, and sat at attention.

"I'm a man." Luke Robinson bent over, hands on hips, and stared into the puppy's round eyes. "I do things a man's way." Immediately the pup lay down, his chin on his paws.

The white pup looked the man in the eye, and his stare said it all. *Okay, I've got the point. You've got a macho issue going on here, but, hey, whatever. This looks like a pretty nice joint, and I'd like to stay.*

The six-foot, chisel-faced management consultant for hi-tech and bio-tech firms lived and worked by codes of organization and self-discipline, though his personality could be as laid back as a tugboat pilot's. The businesses for which he consulted depended on his attention to detail—the scientists demanded precision and meticulous analysis of research and data. So, too, the pup would have to learn to live by house rules, and that meant men's rules.

Luke hitched up his jeans and pulled up a chair. The pup sat up, his huge paws balancing his chubby body, and he opened his mouth in a wide yawn.

"So that's what you think, huh? Not taking this lecture too seriously? Anyway, as I told you, I'm a man." The dog grinned, his long tongue falling from his mouth and then rolling up and around his pink, leathery lips. "Don't expect me to fuss over you as a girl would." He put his finger in the dog's face. "I repeat: this is man's territory, and I'm not going to talk to you in baby talk, fuss over you, or treat you like a sissy."

The pup smiled.

"As long as we understand each other, we'll get along fine. I'll show you the routine around here, and then we'll go for a walk." Luke showed him the shiny red halter and lead. "Then we'll come back and have some dinner. But don't expect food from the table, and there will be no begging.

"You'll only get dog food. I won't give you a whole lot of special treats or anything—they're not good for you. I buy organic dog food, and you're going to eat that, even if you don't like it at first.

"As for my bachelor pad, here—well, I like organization, and I expect you to be a good dog. If you're a good dog and listen, we'll be buddies, and you'll have a nice home here."

He took the puppy off the sofa, patted him on the head, kicked off his boat shoes, and went into the kitchen. Minutes later he walked back into the living room. He stopped dead. Shards of leather lay scattered around the living room. In the middle of the mess lay the puppy, bits of leather shoe lace protruding from his mouth.

"What are you doing?" He ran for the toe section of one of the shoes and held the shoe remnant to his chest. "These cost me a hundred bucks!" The pup grinned, the heel of the shoe cupped between his front legs. "A hundred frickin' dollars!" Luke snatched the other shoe remnant from the pup, flopped onto the couch, and stared at the mangled shoe parts dangling from his hands.

****

Luke's job consulting with scientists and hi-tech businesses occupied most of his time, including weekends, but it allowed him a fairly affluent lifestyle, the kind most bachelors could appreciate—a fancy car, a house filled with modern leather furniture, plasma TVs, and a surround-sound home theatre. Though he could only spend evenings with his new pup, he hired a pet sitter to care for him during the day so that he wouldn't be lonely, so that he had his meals on time, and so that he had regular exercise and some human companionship. And he advised the sitter to keep the pup from devouring his leather lounge chair.

Luke lived with his brother in Castorville, Texas, in the Alsace-Lorraine district of San Antonio. He and Mark shared a ranchito of three acres complete with ducks, chickens, a couple of horses, and some sheep. Though the back yard was fenced in so that during the day the pup couldn't wander into dangerous territory where ranchers and farmers guarded their livestock with guns, the land beyond stretched into long horse pastures, fields of soybeans, and flat prairie. Luke made it a habit to walk his pup every evening as the sun began to set, without fear of traffic and without dread of running out of space. In Texas a person and his dog could walk forever.

Every afternoon the pup took up his post by the front gate and waited for Luke. For hours the little fellow sat, passersby stopping to pat his head and talk. He watched as all the day's workers scuttled home, hurrying along the sidewalk, speeding past in cars and trucks. With every hour the number of pedestrians dwindled until, finally, no more passed. Dusk fell, but the pup kept his vigil behind the front gate, never tiring, but only becoming more excited, knowing his reward was imminent—his dad would be taking him for a walk.

As dusk bathed the puppy in shadow, the pet sitter set his dinner in the grass, and he ate ravenously, as most puppies do. Then he sat back down, his face and ears turned toward the direction from which he knew Luke would be coming. Suddenly his ears pricked. He heard that lovely sound, the quiet purring of his dad's car.

Luke stuck his head out the car window as he pulled into the driveway. "Hey, pup! I'll be right there." He ran into the house to change into hiking boots. The pup galloped to the kitchen door. In minutes Luke flew from the house and attached the lead to the pup's harness. All the while the puppy sat like a stoic. He was shivering with anticipation but contained his enthusiasm as a man's dog should.

When they arrived at the river minutes later, Luke stopped and squatted beside his puppy. "Okay, Bud. I know I've taken a long time to come up with just the right name for you, but a name is very important. I wasn't going to make that decision rashly. I had to feel you out in order to choose the one that fits you best. I've thought long and hard about this, and Mark and I have come to a conclusion. Your name is going to be Malcolm—of *Macbeth* fame. What do you think?" The pup smiled, his tongue falling from his mouth, then curling around his lips. "You're my dog. You deserve a royal name. And something manly, too. So, it's Malcolm."

Malcolm stared into Luke's eyes and smiled, his lips stretched across his face.

****

In several weeks Malcolm and Luke became inseparable, except for the long hours when Luke was working. On weekends, he took Malcolm with him to work where the pup sat on the concrete balcony of the office and contemplated the world beyond. Luke watched Malcolm from his desk and marveled at the animal's patience, his diligence, how he looked and analyzed his surroundings like some kind of wise man or sage—a philosopher king, of sorts.

Later in the day Luke called to his pup, "Let's go, Malcolm Big Baby!" It was time to go home. Malcolm bounced back into the office—the day of contemplation over and an evening of walking just beginning. Malcolm jumped into the car, and Luke put the top down on the convertible. Malcolm loved riding in his dad's sports car. He sat upright in the passenger's seat, sniffing the wind, his ears slicked back against his head. Just then the radio began playing Neil Diamond's song, "Sweet Caroline."

Luke grabbed an imaginary microphone and began singing, leaning into Malcolm, who turned toward him, grinning. "Where it began..." Luke crooned like Sinatra. He swung the wheel with his right hand and pointed his fist with the invisible microphone back to his mouth and continued to sing. They sped down the highway, minutes from home. When the chorus started, Luke smiled like a teenager in love and leaned in toward Malcolm again, one eye on the road, the other meeting Malcolm's curious stare. The wind strained Malcolm's lips into a laughing mouth. Luke bellowed above the sound of the radio. "Sweet Mal-colm. Good times never seemed so *swell*."

Luke stopped the car in front of their house and continued to sing into Malcolm's face. " ... the night don't seem so lonely—we load it up, just us two. La, la, la-la...I hardly hurt when I'm with you." He switched off the car's auxiliary, climbed out, and sang the chorus of "Sweet Caroline" *a cappella*. Then he opened the door for Malcolm, and the two ran to the house.

In a short time Malcolm had become Luke's soul-mate, his son. It wasn't long before all that "man-talk" Luke warned Malcolm about that first day turned to mush. Luke cooed in Malcolm's face at bedtime. "Sugar booger, Sweety Petey. Is my little bitty big baby sleepy? Does Malcolm Big Baby want to sleep in daddy's nice warm beddy tonight?"

And Luke's stern lecture about not giving snacks and table scraps went down the same drain as had his distaste for girlie language. Buying only the best for his Malcolm Big Baby, Luke brought home boxes of organic, pet health-food treats and the best, most appetizing dog food money could buy.

One morning Mark happened to walk into the kitchen just as Luke was feeding Malcolm. "Come here, Sugar Booger—my big lovey-dovey, scoopy-poopy, puppy-wuppy. Daddy has your tasty dinner. Oh, I know what you're thinking, son. You're thinking, 'Oh, Daddy, please hurry. It takes too long to chew it. Please, just hurry and put it right in my belly now. Oh, Daddy, please hurry and put it in my big, big belly!'"

"Like—well, that's so totally uncool, Luke." Mark crossed his arms.

Luke whipped around. "Uh-h-h…"

"Yeah, you're really pathetic, man. You sound like a total girl." He snickered. "All that lovey-dovey shit and daddy stuff. I don't know what happened to my macho brother, but he's *gone!*"

Luke smiled sheepishly and shrugged his shoulders. "I can't help it. He got into my brain like some kind of neural parasite—like a cranial worm. I'm all screwed up now, and it's all *his* fault. I'm in lo-o-o-ove with my boy." Luke paused and laughed. "I've never had a dog like him. He's a walkin' oxymoron. He's so simple—loves his walks, loves digging holes, loves treeing squirrels, yet he's adventurous and fearless, too. Last week when Cindy and I took him to the beach, he jumped into the waves and started swimming in the ocean—just like that! And he'd never *seen* the ocean before. The dog is brave—he'll try anything. He's *extreme.*"

****

When Luke wasn't working, Malcolm was his constant companion, and for the next year the two enjoyed the same routine—long walks into the prairie every evening, Malcolm luxuriating in the breeze that rippled his fur like stroking fingers. On their journeys into the brush, Luke loved watching the growing Malcolm sniff out a mole. Digging furiously, Malcolm raced to find the tiny rodent, and he didn't stop until he had uprooted it. And he was hell on squirrels and groundhogs, running after any one of them that had foolishly left too much ground between it and its escape tree or hole.

Yet as fearless and ferocious as he was when faced with a woodland creature, so he was just as fearful of the broom, from which he ran terrified, skidding away and raking claw marks into the hardwood floors. So it was, too, with the vacuum cleaner, which thanks to Luke's manliness he didn't see that often. But when the dust bunnies started hopping across the living room floor, not even Luke's machismo could resist them. Out came the long silver "bastard on wheels" as Malcolm's dad called it—the thing hell bent on sucking a big white dog into the maelstrom.

****

Months flew by, and Malcolm grew like a Texan cornstalk—lengthening, widening, and getting taller overnight. And he and Luke became closer than ever, though Luke was disappointed that his big hairy son didn't care for snuggling.

Luke coaxed him toward overt affection. "Come on, Malcolm Big Baby." He patted the bed where he lay. "Come on up here. Jump up and come to beddy with daddy." But Malcolm didn't want to share a bed with anyone, preferring to sleep downstairs, beside the sofa.

So Luke began sleeping on the sofa.

Pulling the blanket up around his neck, Luke found

a way to feel as though Malcolm was sleeping with him. He stretched the blanket over the side of the couch so a sliver of it hung on the floor. Then, Luke called Malcolm, and Malcolm lay down, one paw touching the edge of the blanket. *Voilà!* Malcolm was sleeping with Luke.

One evening Malcolm and Luke were watching a detective channel.

"Hey, my Big Baby." Luke ran his fingers through Malcolm's thick fur.

Malcolm looked up from the side of the couch. "He's just so irresistible." Luke smiled to himself. "And he's all mine." Goosebumps erupted on Luke's forearms. Then Luke slid off the sofa and lay beside Malcolm as gunshots sounded from the television. Luke squidged himself into Malcolm's space, and for perhaps five minutes Malcolm tolerated Luke's nose snuggling his ear. But when Luke started whispering sappy stuff, Malcolm got up and walked over to the lounger and lay down.

Luke frowned. "Okay, I get it, Malcolm. Just a bit much for your taste, huh?"

Malcolm had been living with Luke for over two years, yet *the man* was still enthralled by his dog's majesty—"His Great White Presence"—as he called him. Something as inconsequential as watching Malcolm observe the outside world still thrilled him. The dog, Luke told his co-workers, looked as though he was studying the outdoors—the critters, the bugs, the sagebrush, the prairie wildflowers. He reminded Luke of the great Buddha, sitting and taking everything in, sitting for hours watching and contemplating. Gary, one of the bio-tech engineers, listened to Luke muse about his dog. "I'm telling you—it's as if Malcolm's thinking to himself, 'Well, there's a tree. Yup, there goes a car. Uh-huh, a squirrel. Here comes another car. Everything's in order here.'"

Luke found Malcolm equally amazing at dinnertime as the dog slurped his food like a man—hearty and lusty—packing it into his mouth like a contestant at a food-eating competition. His unbridled enthusiasm for his dinner, his passionate appetite, his attack of the bowl awed Luke. He felt such contentment experiencing Malcolm living in the moment of food.

Malcolm's needs were manifold—intense yet simple. He lived in the moment, the present, the occurring. Though his greatest pleasure was spending time with Luke, he found joy in other activities, too—digging a hole, sneaking over the fence, taking a walk, eating dinner, riding in the car, and sleeping. All these simple, everyday acts Malcolm relished, pouring his heart and soul into the chase or the food. Even his bedtime was punctuated with long, deep-sleeping snores.

From the beginning, Luke was impressed by Malcolm's masculinity. While Luke cooed "Puppy-wuppy" and "Malcolm Big Baby" in Malcolm's face, Malcolm tried not to disappoint, retaining his cool, not slavering kisses all over Luke's face nor crawling into Luke's bed. Malcolm even peed like a man.

The macho-piss occurred every morning. After Luke awakened Malcolm from his deep sleep, the first thing on the agenda was to relieve their bladders, so out to the back yard they both went, out of sight of the neighbors. While at their urinal tree, Luke glanced down at his man-dog and marveled at Malcolm's masculine pose—not lifting a leg as other male dogs did, but standing on all fours, his legs spread widely. Then the full stream of pee came, large and full. Luke was proud, though a bit intimidated.

The morning pee soon became a family ritual.

Then there was Malcolm's Superman pose. One evening after Luke had had an unusually long day at work, he came downstairs to find Malcolm stretched out facing the wall with one front leg extended and braced against the wall. Luke laughed, but the dog didn't move. "Hey, Superman!" But only Malcolm's ears moved—nothing else. His long leg stood straight out, like the Superman of the 1950s television series, his one arm outstretched into a fist, his white fur-cape flapping in the wind.

When he wasn't playing Superman, Super Malcolm loved accompanying Luke on his golf outings. He rode alongside Luke in the cart, and then he watched and waited for Luke to swing at the ball, never barking or fussing while Luke honed his backswing. He seemed to know that hitting a ball with a stick was very serious business, almost as serious as taking a pee.

Of all their activities, Malcolm loved camping the best. Setting out into the outdoors with backpacks and a cooler of beer, water, sandwiches, and dog food was the ultimate good time. Malcolm loved getting down and dirty camp-side, rolling in the mud alongside the river, trouncing along the river's edge in search of mouth-sized rocks, sleeping in the bed of pine needles under a spruce, and drying his mud-caked fur to an odiferous ripeness. Hiking in the outdoors, treeing squirrels, and watching the chipmunks and other critters of the woods freed Luke's spirit as well as Malcolm's. Nighttime was special—in the woods beneath the stars, man and dog were one.

But they wouldn't be one for very long because one day Luke brought home a puppy who looked just like Malcolm. Luke made the formal introduction. "This is Murphy, Malcolm." Malcolm, at three years old, lay next to the couch, watching, analyzing the pup who tripped over his own feet as he galloped through the living room. The puppy's frenetic activity embarrassed Malcolm, especially when he went charging into Luke's arms, slobbering him with big kisses. Murphy would need some lessons from Malcolm as to how to foster the proper Pyrenees' sense of cool and detachment—that is, if he ever wanted to earn a man's respect.

After several months, Malcolm and Murphy became good friends. Every so often, though, Malcolm had to remind the pup with a nip to his rump that he, Malcolm, was the king of the patch. When Luke brought home dog toys, Murphy began jumping, circling, and whining until Luke gave him the present. Then, no sooner did Murphy have it in his mouth than Malcolm got up, sauntered over, and snatched the toy from him. Malcolm didn't really want the toy—he just wanted to show Murphy that if he wanted it, he could have it. It was a macho thing.

Murphy wasn't Malcolm's only animal friend. One autumn evening, a rat terrier Luke named Flea showed up on their doorstep. Luke offered the little ratty-looking dog a home, and Malcolm accepted his company with aplomb. Flea immediately became enamored with Malcolm's thick furry coat, sidling next to Malcolm and burying his bald face in Malcolm's luxurious fur. Malcolm tried to discourage the ratty mutt's snuggling, but Flea seemed not to understand canine gestures. Malcolm soon found it easier to put up with Flea than try, without success, to dismiss him.

Luke's newborn chick, Bob, was even harder for Malcolm to tolerate. Born sickly, Luke brought him into the house where the chartreuse chick decided to take up residence in Malcolm's fur. No chick in the world had as fluffy and as warm a nest as Bob did.

By the time Bob graduated to roosterhood, Murphy had grown almost as large as Malcolm. Still, Murphy, with much instruction from Malcolm, had adopted only a fraction of his brother's aloofness. He continued to drool and whine whenever Luke entered the room.

As Murphy grew, he became the perfect partner for Malcolm's rough-housing. When Malcolm and Murphy play-wrestled in the living room, the entire house shook.

Luke yelled like a young mother from the kitchen as the vibrations from the dogs' wrestling match rattled the windows. "Hey, take it easy, you guys. Somebody's gonna get hu-u-urt. Next thing ya know, someone's gonna be crying. And we all know who that will be." As if on cue, Murphy yipped.

But Murphy had the last laugh on Malcolm one Halloween. Mark had brought home a robotic candy bowl. From the back of a bilious green bowl loomed a skeletal arm that, when the bowl was touched, pounced on the person's hand. Luke thought it would be fun to see how his Big Baby would react to the candy bowl, so he filled it with Malcolm's favorite biscuits.

"Come here, Poopy Face."

Malcolm, at six years old, and being the dog-king

of Castorville, Texas, hoisted himself up to inspect the candy dish. Luke snickered. "Here you go, Baby. Daddy has some tasty treats for you. Go ahead. Help yourself."

Malcolm looked up at Luke, smiled grandly himself, and then dipped his muzzle into the dish.

"Slap."

All hundred and ten pounds of fur-covered muscle and guts known as Malcolm the Great, Malcolm the Fearless, Malcolm the Willful, leaped straight into the air. He came down on all fours, too, like a cat, then whipped around to see what had smacked him on the head.

Luke and Mark were howling, holding their bellies tight. "Oh, God! Too much!" Malcolm stared at the horrid boney arm sprung back into position above the bowl of biscuits. Then, Malcolm strode back to his corner and lay down, a look of disgust on his face.

"Oh, he's so pissed!" Luke laughed. "Look at him—if looks could kill. Trick or treat, Malcolm. Malcolm got the trick!" Then Luke took a biscuit from the bowl, the mad hand slapping Luke's wrist, and he offered one to Malcolm. "Go ahead, take it, Malcolm. It was only a trick." Refusing food, even if it came from a manic toy, was not Malcolm's style, so he gobbled it up with little fuss.

The big, manly dog's knack for finding himself in compromising situations didn't end with the Halloween horror bowl. The day before Thanksgiving, Luke and Cindy decided to visit relatives. Already late, they packed up the car, threw the luggage into the back of the SUV, called Malcolm and Murphy to jump in, and sped off. Tromping the pedal, Luke sped down the country road until, suddenly, a road crewman waving an orange flag appeared before them.

Cindy shrieked. "Stop!"

Luke slammed on the brakes, and the SUV lurched to a grinding halt. The stop wasn't bad enough to set off any airbags, but the jolt did displace the contents of the SUV, including people, dogs, and luggage. Everyone, including the dogs, flew forward. One bag from the back whipped over the last row of seats, flew past the dogs, who had sunk their nails into the leather upholstery, and hit the back of the front seats, spilling its guts around the dogs' feet.

Luke pulled over to the side of the road to see how the boys were, and he started to howl with laughter. Cindy turned around, and she, too, began to laugh.

In the near wreck, Cindy's cosmetics case had flown to the front and blown apart, hair curlers sailing everywhere. Pink and blue Velcro hair curlers clung haphazardly throughout Malcolm's fur. One was clinging to Malcolm's left ear, and others hung twisted in his hair, on his shoulders, legs, and sides. During the cyclonic disaster inside the SUV, at least twenty spoolies and other curlers had found refuge in Malcolm's long white fur.

The look on Malcolm's face was pure surprise mixed with a tad of indignity. The thick hair on his head was standing straight up, and when he bit at a Velcro curler clinging to his front leg, he winced as it pulled his fur. He bit more at the curler, his ears cocked in disbelief, his forehead wrinkled, but it refused to budge. He looked flabbergasted.

Murphy's expression was equally disarming, but he wouldn't dare laugh at Malcolm. After Luke had freed all Malcolm's curlers, he started back on the road, Malcolm unusually quiet the whole way.

****

In May of 2004, Malcolm was diagnosed with bone cancer. Luke was devastated to immobility, but Malcolm's struggle and bravery in his fight against the disease brought Luke to a new understanding of life, a kind of spirituality he would never have predicted for himself.

Luke followed the recommendations of Malcolm's veterinary oncologist. Shortly after receiving the horrible news, Malcolm had his right front leg amputated and finished a series of chemotherapy treatments. Malcolm responded well to both the surgery and the chemotherapy. In exactly two weeks Malcolm healed from the surgery and adapted well to his disability, which he didn't regard as a disability at all. And life on the ranchito continued as usual.

One morning when Luke was on the front porch reading the *Wall Street Journal,* he noticed movement out of the corner of his eye. It was Malcolm running across the street after a squirrel. To this day the image of the giant dog standing on his back legs with his one leg on the tree is burned into Luke's memory. Malcolm, as always, proved himself a giant of a dog in every way.

Luke's initial devastation and depression finally gave way to action. Luke decided to put his hi-tech and bio-tech consulting business on hold in order to spend time with Malcolm. What was important, however, was the spirit of the moment with his dog—enjoying the rest of Malcolm's time. Life itself, beating and throbbing inside his dog and inside himself, mattered most.

Luke spent the next six months hiking and camping with Malcolm and Murphy, but he also spent time researching cancer, its causes, and its characteristics. Having been a pre-med student back in college, he had the smarts and the background to find information that might save his beloved dog. He devoted himself to researching cancer.

Luke changed in other ways, too. He admits he became more dog-like. He observed his best friend fighting the cancer with bravery only animals seem to have mastered. Perhaps, knowing they are dying, they have instincts telling them death is just another stage of life. Because Malcolm still cherished his simple needs like digging holes and treeing squirrels, Luke came to value more simple pleasures as well. Being with his dog family and allowing Malcolm his pure pleasures was all that mattered to Luke.

Recognizing the courage with which Malcolm faced his disease made Luke embrace Malcolm's spirit in all aspects. He called it "puppying up"—facing a challenge head-on. To "puppy up" meant to be unafraid in adversity and, regardless of what other people think, never let anything slow you down. Embrace life with fearlessness, embrace that which is truly important, simple, and pure—as a puppy or dog does. In meeting the challenge of Malcolm's impending death, Luke knew he could be as stoic as his ailing dog. He and his dog would live Malcolm's final months as all animals always live—in the purity of the moment.

Luke made a promise to Malcolm one evening before bedtime, but first he drew the edge of the blanket around the dog beside his sofa. "I'm going to be brave through all this. Whatever time we have left, we're going to spend together, and we're going to play, and hike, and live each day at a time." And Malcolm turned toward his man and smiled his grand smile.

For the next year and a half they did just that—playing, wrestling, sleeping, each giving the other his presence and comfort.

In Malcolm's final month, when the cancer had spread to his lungs and his death was imminent, Luke made his dog-son a promise. "I'm going to live the rest of my life for you, Baby. I'm going to live it as you have—with courage and happy simplicity. And, no matter what happens, I'm making another promise to you. I'm going to tackle this cancer bastard head on." His voice shook. "I'll fight this thing inside you, Malcolm. I'm not going to let it beat us. I don't know what it is I'll do yet, but, when the time comes, I'll know. I won't let you down, My Man."

Malcolm died January 11, 2006.

****

Malcolm's Memorial

Luke's war cry against the cancer that took his beloved Malcolm, who was Luke's rock, began a ripple effect across the United States. Currently that ripple, created by one dog and his owner, has become a veritable river of determination and fight against a scourge that plagues both man and beast. Luke continues to fulfill his promise to his dog-son and, to this day, carries on Malcolm's tradition of "puppying up" against cancer through Puppy Up walks across America and reaching people through his podcast at 2deaddogs.com.

****

On March 16, 2008, Luke, wearing a few of

Malcolm's ashes in a necklace, began the fight against canine cancer by walking, with six-year-old Murphy and one and a half-year-old Hudson, his two Great Pyrenees, on a 2,400-mile journey from Austin, Texas to Boston, Massachusetts. The funds raised from sponsors of the walk, businesses, and individual donations have been apportioned accordingly: two-thirds continues to be spent on educational awareness of canine cancer and one-third on scientific research into the causes of cancer in dogs and other companion animals. An offshoot of the research explores links between canine cancer and people cancer.

Luke's first journey—from Austin, Texas to Boston, Massachusetts—began amid a throng of volunteers, supporters, well-wishers, and TV and radio coverage. Wishing the boys and Luke good luck, animal lovers lined the Austin streets, their dogs by their sides. Those along the street of embarkation celebrated with music, carnival food, and the free-spiritedness such a challenge births. The crowd knew in their collective heart that what was about to happen was one of the bravest and most worthy and unselfish gestures of all time—a man and his two dogs were heading into the wilderness to fight the devil.

Loaded with twenty-five pounds of gear and water, Murphy waited as Luke hoisted his own pack onto his back. Other necessary gear had been sent ahead along his walking route by his brothers, friends, and volunteers to insure the dogs' safety as well as Luke's. Their equipment included a tent, packs for dogs and man, sleeping bag, hiking clothes and rain gear, dog booties, reflectors and collar lights for the dogs, and much more.

Though the Big Dog, as Luke refers to himself, and his dogs Murphy and Hudson carried their own energy food, health and nutritional support, other necessities were shipped ahead to local post offices or to local volunteers who drove the supplies to Luke's locations along the walking route. Dropped off at predetermined sites, these necessaries included a camp stove with fuel, cooking utensils, water filters and purification tablets, plastic bags, matches, and more. Boxes of kitchen items for the "boys" contained collapsible bowls, dehydrated dog food, and treats. Items such as a flashlight, light sticks, sunglasses, and duct tape comprised only a few of the other general items they took, along with personal and dog hygiene products—toilet paper, toothbrush, grooming kit, basic medicines, and foot powder. Finally, for emergencies, Luke packed first-aid kits for the dogs and himself—pepper spray, animal deterrent, and contact information. Among some of the most important items, however, were the GPS, computer, weather radio, and solar battery re-charger.

Luke anticipated meeting some hazards like feral dog packs and crossing bridges without a walking ledge, but those dangers didn't detract from his journey. The road from Cameron, Texas to Tyler was paved with difficulties—no cell phone coverage and few towns or houses from which he could re-supply his water bottles.

At night when they were too tired to take another step, they either camped in a grassy patch along the road or accepted offers to sleep at supporters' homes. At times they walked alone, with only an occasional blackbird cawing from a telephone pole. At other times, especially through the towns, they had children following, anxious to pet the grand Great Pyrenees.

Complete strangers walked for miles alongside Luke and his dogs, thanking him for his efforts on behalf of their pet dog or cat who had died of cancer or of a family member whose life it claimed. Many people and businesses made donations to Luke's fight, to his journey where each day, when he wasn't accompanied by other people, he spoke in his heart to Malcolm.

No matter the time of day or night, the spirit of Malcolm accompanied the threesome, walking right alongside them, urging them to "puppy up." He reminded them they weren't alone, that millions of animals who had died from cancer were walking right behind them, in front of them, and to the side of them. This first walk spawned Luke's organization, www.2dogs2000miles.org.

After the first step, they never walked alone again.

Luke's memorial walk for Malcolm inspired a grassroots uprising to battle canine cancer and has led to much research in comparative oncology. (See note at end of this chapter.) Luke believed that if two dogs could walk two thousand miles to fight cancer, then dogs all across America and the world could walk two million miles simultaneously, thus the founding "bones" of The Puppy Up Foundation. Currently Puppy Up walks are being sponsored all across America at any one time in many towns. The Puppy Up Foundation is headed by Ginger Morgan at 1460 Madison Avenue, Memphis, TN 38104. The phone number is (901) 619-2286 for anyone needing information on how to organize a Puppy Up walk in his or her area.

And so began the ripple effect caused by the death of Malcolm. After the Austin to Boston walk, Luke and his Great Pyrenees tackled the West Coast and the

Pacific Coast Highway where many times, without a decent road shoulder on which to walk, as well as dense fog, he and his two dogs narrowly avoided being hit by vehicles. Hudson became unable to walk much farther than the California border, but between the East and West Coast walks, Luke and his dogs amassed a total of approximately four thousand miles of road through thirty-two states.

By 2020, the Puppy Up Foundation has been working against canine cancer for ten years. When asked about her service to The Puppy Up Foundation, Morgan notes, "The monies raised through our Puppy Up walks across the country will fund grants for comparative oncology research and raise awareness about canine cancer—its prevention, causes, and treatments for both man and man's best friend. Since its inception in 2010, The Puppy Up Foundation has been able to devote $2.1 million to fulfill its mission of bringing awareness to canine cancer, its similarities to human cancers, and funding research, education, and awareness that benefits both pets and people."

Interested parties are welcome to learn more at www.2dogs2000miles.blogspot.com and at Facebook's group—www.facebook.com/PuppyUpFoundation. The Twitter address is @2milliondogs and @PuppyUpOrg.

Dog lovers can read about Luke's cross-country adventures at www.2dogs2000miles.blogspot.com. Any person interested in learning more about canine cancer and comparative oncology, as well as the Foundation's mission, can check out www.puppyuporg/puppy-up-blog or www.puppyup.org.

Be sure to check out the Foundation's social media pages—

Facebook:
www.facebook.com/PuppyUpFoundation.
Twitter: @PuppyUpOrg.
Instagram: puppyupfoundation.

In addition, Luke has developed a serial novel and podcast about his and his dogs' travels. The podcast went live Oct 9, 2019 with Episode One—World's End. The launch and drop dates are posted at www.2deaddogs.org—in memory of Malcolm and Murphy, who also died of cancer.

If interested, you can also follow the misadventures of Luke's dog Hudson, in his later years, at Fuzzbutt@ihearthudsontour, a docuseries.

****

Note: Comparative Oncology is cancer research that identifies the similarities of human and canine cancers. Recently, both human medical and veterinary researchers have discovered that many human and canine cancers have a similar genetic basis. Researchers in comparative oncology are better able to detect, through clinical trials, how canine cancer treatments may, in fact, impact human cancer treatments, and vice versa, thus coming closer to cures for cancer in both dogs and people.

Chapter Ten
Divine Swine

Species: pot-bellied pig
Name: Grace Peters
Born: March 17, 1994
Died: summer of 2007
Human companions: Charles and Barbara Peters

Amazing Grace
Charles lobbed the last shovel full of dirt atop their dog's grave. "Well, good luck, Duffy. You were a good dog."

The sheep dog's absence drilled a big empty space into the Peters' hearts, so when Barbara suggested they begin looking for a puppy, their grown daughter, Mandy, suggested a different kind of pet—a pot-bellied pig.

The Peters, occupied by work, farm chores, and sending both their son and daughter to college, soon forgot about Mandy's request for a pig until the phone rang one afternoon. A young woman explained she had heard from a friend the Peters were looking to adopt a pet pig. She and her husband were pregnant, and she thought taking care of a baby as well as a pig would be too much. Would Barbara like to meet their pig, Grace?

Barbara rolled her eyes. "I don't know if my daughter is still interested anymore. I'd have to ask her, and she's at Muhlenberg College right—"

"Oh, my goodness! How coincidental! My husband graduated from Muhlenberg. This coming weekend is alumni weekend. How 'bout if we bring Grace along for you and your husband to meet. You could spend the afternoon with her and see if you like her enough to adopt."

"Well, ah...I don't know..."

"She's only a year old and very intelligent, very gentle, too. But we have too much on our plates with this baby coming."

Barb was hesitant. Were they all ready to take on the responsibility of another animal? "But I don't even know if Mandy's still interested in a pig. That was a year ago she mentioned having a pig, and—"

The woman interrupted. "Just spend an afternoon with Grace, just to see if you like her, while we go to the reunion. Afterwards we'll come pick her up and take her home. Then you and your family can discuss whether you would like to adopt her. She's a really sweet pig, really, but, well, *we're pregnant.*"

"Yes, and your hands are full." Barb wiped her brow with more than a little irritation at the woman's unabashed insistence.

****

That Saturday afternoon the Griffiths pulled into the Peters' driveway, their pot-bellied pig, Grace, in the back seat of their sports car. The husband helped his pregnant wife carefully out of the car, folded the seat forward, and tugged on a leash. Out popped a small white pig with swirly patches of gray and black.

The round woman extended her hand. "Oh, Mrs. Peters. It's so nice to meet you. Say 'Hello' to Grace, our pig."

"Nice to meet you, Grace." Barb bent down and scratched Grace's head. Charles came around the corner of the barn as the young couple began unloading things Grace would need for an afternoon visit—an old blanket, a blue chewy toy, a cookie jar shaped like a pig and loaded with Cheerios, a foot-square piece of sheepskin, a cloth dolly, a twenty-five-pound bag of pot-bellied pig chow with a feed scoop, her crate, a litter box, and wood shavings.

Barbara and Charles stood, dumbfounded, attached to Grace by her leash as the couple drove away, smiling and waving.

Charles looked at his wife, Grace between them. "The pig needs all this stuff for an afternoon visit?" They looked down at Grace, standing quietly beside them. Then they tugged on her leash, and Grace followed them into the house.

In the afternoon they walked the farm with Grace, introducing her to the twelve sheep, the four horses, and the barn cats. Sniffing and stopping to root a few nose-holes in the soft ground, Grace seemed genuinely interested in the outbuildings, the old smokehouse, and the lilac bushes. The yearling pot belly grunted softly whenever Barb or Charles spoke, as though she wanted in on the conversation, and she walked politely with them around the edge of their pond, rustling the cattails with her nose and listening to the frogs skittering in the brush. Later Barbara knelt down beside Grace, who had almost fallen asleep in the grass, and brushed her with the horses' curry comb. Back inside the house, Barb washed the dried eye matter from her face with a soft cloth and rubbed lavender oil over her dry, flakey skin.

That evening when the Peters sat down to dinner, Grace grunted for her own dinner, so Barbara poured some pig chow into her dish. She gobbled it up without hesitation. At nine p.m. Barbara urged Grace into her crate while the Peters watched TV and waited for Grace's parents to pick her up.

But they never came to take Grace home.

College student Mandy fell in love with the abandoned pig the moment she saw her. When she needed a break from her studies, Mandy drove home and brushed Grace and took her for long walks around the pond, through the sheep pastures, out to the flower gardens, and around the old smokehouse. And the young woman confided to her pet pig about college life and her date for the evening.

Grace loved being out in the yard more than she did being in the house, especially in the long days of summer. She specialized in nipping the heads off Barbara's geraniums as well as the yellow-headed dandelions. In the fall, her favorite morning pastime was galloping to the apple orchard to stuff herself so full of apples that Barbara swore she could see each individual apple protruding through Grace's skin. Though Barbara brought Grace inside to sleep at night, during the day Grace spent almost all her time outside where, if she needed a nap, she went to her shed, climbed into her insulated dog house, and squidged, cozy, into her blankets.

Though Barbara gave Grace a choice whether to stay outside or inside during the winter, Grace always preferred the outside, unless it was terribly cold. She hunkered down in her house, drawing her blankets strategically into a bunch that blocked any drafts but still allowed her to check out the action going on in the sheep pasture. During the winter nights, Grace always slept inside, but when the sun rose, Grace wanted to go outside to her shed and den brimming with blankets.

After a foot of snow had fallen one night, early the next morning the Peters had to quickly shovel a path just wide enough for Grace to fit. When Grace stepped out the door and onto the path, the sides of which rose as high as her back, the white pig literally disappeared inside the "snow chute." Barbara laughed as Grace, running down the narrow path, reminded her of an Olympian navigating the luge.

One winter morning when the Peters came downstairs, they found Grace snuffling around the bathroom. The toilet paper roll was gone, and bits of toilet paper lay strewn over the floor. When they questioned Grace about her shenanigans, Grace looked at them with a sick expression. And, when she was offered breakfast, Grace turned away in disgust. Something was definitely wrong.

That something was the metal insert for the toilet paper holder. It was gone. The tiny bathroom wasn't hard to search, being only four feet by four feet, yet Barb and Charles could not find the metal toilet roll holder anywhere. Barbara and Charles looked at Grace's sickly face and immediately drove her to the vet.

The disbelieving veterinarian stared at Grace with grave concern as Barbara told the story. "We're sure she ate the metal tube from the toilet paper holder. I don't know how she did it, but it's gone. It must be inside her."

Charles stood completely dumbfounded. "It's gone.

She must've eaten it—she wouldn't eat any of her breakfast."

Two X-rays later, the vet said, "Good news—there's definitely no metal inside Grace. She probably won't eat because she's full from all that toilet paper. But that shouldn't hurt her—it'll pass right on through."

The next day Grace had regained her appetite, but the metal insert was never found.

Life with Grace was always interesting. Some evenings after dinner, Barbara and Grace watched old Alfred Hitchcock movies in the basement living room. Together they curled up on the sofa, and Barbara stroked Grace's rough bristles as the curdling screams from the TV resounded off the basement walls. Though Barb was scared silly, Grace often fell asleep in Barb's arms. It didn't take long for the Hitchcock hour to become a ritual and for Grace to know it was her special time alone with Barb. So when the time drew near for the Hitching Hour, if Barbara was late finishing the dinner dishes, Grace began to wail.

"Re-e-e-e-e! Re-e-e-e-e!"

Barbara joked as she dried her hands. "Gracie must've checked her watch again, Charles. It's Alfred Hitchcock time. Gotta go get Grace."

****

Throughout Grace's life, she acted as a local celebrity, visiting nursing homes, attending Charles's physician office parties, enjoying the center of attention with house guests and relatives, especially ninety-five-year-old Cousin Elizabeth, who thought Grace was the cutest pet on four hooves. Cousin Elizabeth sat bent over for close to an hour rubbing Grace's belly. Grace's hackles rose up and down in rhythm to Cousin

Elizabeth's slow stroking of her back, and Grace snore-mumbled her pleasure at the woman's steady massage.

Grace adored being the center of attention, especially while she was performing her pirouettes. Gracie loved nothing if she didn't love attention. At the farm she ran races with the youngsters of Barbara's nursing friends. To the top of the orchard Grace ran, her little hooves pushing as fast as tiny pistons, then back down the hill they all flew, the kids screaming, falling, laughing, and Grace barking and grunting until she left the kids gasping in her wake.

Living with the Peters, Grace not only had companions who actually wanted her and appreciated her company, but she, in turn, offered them companionship uniquely her own. On Mandy's sun-celebrating wedding day, with the barn dressed up and the lawn manicured, guests fussed almost as much over the pig as they did the new bride. And Grace probably felt honored to have her photo taken by her bride-friend's side, too.

For every day of the thirteen years she lived, Grace had to have known she was lucky to have been abandoned at the Peters' farm where she enjoyed their tranquil, loving world.

Grace died the summer of 2007.

****

Grace's Memorial

Walking past Grace's deserted shed sent shivers up and down Barbara's skin. Even the cats, lost without their sleeping buddy, gathered in her empty dog house. Though the sheep and horses probably didn't realize Grace was gone, the farm felt vacant without the wandering happy Grace, a fixture on the Peters' farm.

Barbara wanted to honor Grace in a way that truly reflected Grace's personality. She thought about the things Grace most loved—the orchard apples, snuffling the grass, racing children over the lawn, sharing deep conversations with the philosopher sheep, touching noses with the horses, watching TV every evening between Barbara and Charles, walking with Barbara or Mandy to the pond's edge where the geese flew as one into the clouds.

Grace had simple, pure needs. While completely at home inside the farmhouse, she had been particularly happy in the outdoors and in her shed. She loved her own small field of grass where she soaked in the sun for hours and sauntered over to the sheep to discuss the clouds and impending rain. The cats curled around her legs on their way to the horse barn in search of mice, and they had lain beside her in the grass.

Grace had loved people as well as her farm companions. Visitors and friends of the Peters offered her belly rubs, and Barbara cleaned the eye dirt from her eyes. And when Mandy was home from college, she administered luxurious full body massages. Grace had amazed visitors with her intelligence, sitting when asked, and turning a circle. Little Grace, her white coat making her unique in the pot-bellied pig world of mostly black pigs, was always a friendly, agreeable pig who needed nothing other than love and clean country air. She was the simplest and kindest of creatures.

And so Barbara designed a simple gravestone for her. Using a Dremmel tool, she took a small piece of black granite with gold flecks and carved Grace's name into it, giving the letters a fancy flair because at times Grace could be fancy, too. Then, she and Charles and

Mandy laid it atop her grave, next to Duffy and the Peters' old pony, Misty, and said goodbye.

Chapter Eleven
Call Me Comfort

Species: pot-bellied pig
Name: Lulabelle
Born: September 15, 1992
Died: February 10, 2007
Human companion: Susan Armstrong-Magidson

His name was Fester, and he was slowly dying.

Fester had been abandoned in a vacant horse stall by his human family. When Susan, the owner of a home for neglected pot-bellied pigs, found him knee-deep in manure and thin as a two-by-four, she coaxed him into a crate and drove him two hours to his new adoptive home, Ross Mill Farm.

At home, Susan and a volunteer pulled Fester's crate from the van and lifted him gently to the ground. They immediately offered him water and some pig food, which he gobbled as though it were his last meal. They opened the door, then tiptoed quietly away. The black pig peered warily outside, taking in the scenery— the historic old farmhouse, the two-story stone barn that had, long ago, been a grist mill, the woods, and the vision of a hundred other creatures that looked and smelled just like him.

Susan watched Fester from her eighteenth-century stone farmhouse as her personal pig, Lulabelle, came trundling from the barn—anxious to welcome another rescue pig who needed a bolstering of spirit due to human neglect. She would calm him, walk him to the woods, to the creek's edge, to the lawn where they would both lie down. Her quiet presence would assure him he was safe. So, as was her custom, Lulabelle sauntered up to Fester's crate, stuck her nose inside, *"oofed"* a few times, turned around, and took a few steps toward him.

When Fester didn't immediately follow, Lulabelle walked back and *"oofed"* twice. After the third coaxing Fester stepped carefully out of the crate. He trotted weakly behind Lulabelle for his home tour—a visit to the creek, then hole-digging in the woods and greeting other rescue pigs in the yard.

Watching Lulabelle in action, Susan remembered how she first met her beloved pig.

Thirteen years ago Nancy Shepherd, Susan and Richard's friend who raised pot-bellied pigs on her farm in Missouri, was showing Jezebelle and Lulabelle, her prized six-month-old gilts, at the Houston Livestock Show and Rodeo. Susan volunteered to handle Lulabelle in the show ring so that Nancy could show her favorite pig, Jezebelle. If Susan and Nancy could win against the twenty-six other gilts enrolled in the conformation class, the win would prove that Nancy's and Susan's breeding programs were setting the standard for pot-bellied pig body types—straight legs, good bone, a cobby body, a straight back, and wide, big eyes.

In preparation for the competition, Nancy advised Susan to familiarize herself with her pig. "Take Lulabelle, and work with her for a while. Train her for an hour or two. She's a very intelligent, willing pig. She's a sweetheart."

Pigs, being the fifth most intelligent animal on earth—fifth only to humans, chimps, whales, and dolphins—have a capacity for communicating at an exceptionally early age. Though they are plagued by an instinctive knowledge they are prey, once they understand someone or something poses no threat to their survival, they become independent thinkers in a matter of weeks. Pigs are quick to mature, both intellectually and physically, and can learn tricks and rules of the house within a minute or two.

That day, within the confines of their pen just fifty feet from the bulls, dairy cows, and market pigs, Susan took Lulabelle into a quiet corner and began bridge and target training. Bridge and target training is a conditioning method that works with all kinds of animals, but it works exceptionally well and fast with the most intelligent ones like dolphins and pigs.

Susan extended her hand to Lulabelle in her training session. "Here."

Lulabelle looked at Susan, then approached. When Lulabelle's nose touched her finger, Susan rewarded her with a Cheerio. "Good." Susan repeated the exercise no more than ten times, rewarding Lulabelle for touching her fingers with first a "good" and then a treat. In minutes Lulabelle came to the sound of "Here"—the bridge. Then she nudged the target— Susan's fingers.

Toward the end of the half-hour training session, Susan heard someone yelling about a loose pig. Immediately she dropped Lulabelle's leash and rushed to help catch the errant swine.

Only minutes later when Susan came back to Lulabelle's pen, she found the gate open and Lulabelle gone.

Susan froze. *Where could Lulabelle have gone?* Instinctively Susan looked toward the other livestock stalls.

She couldn't believe what she saw.

Lulabelle, who was the size of a woman's cosmetic case, was standing in the bull pen, catatonic, between the legs of a huge Holstein bull. If the bull spooked, became angry, or just shifted sideways, Lulabelle would be crushed.

Almost frozen to catatonia herself, Susan called in the same way as she had while rehearsing the bridge and target training with Lulabelle minutes earlier. "Here." As though someone had flicked on a switch, Lulabelle snapped out of her frightened torpor and marched directly out from underneath the bull and toward Susan.

Susan put her arms around Lulabelle. The little pig was shivering, and her eyes were wide. "Don't ever do that again, Lulabelle." Susan looked into Lulabelle's eyes, and Lulabelle stared back—hard. In those few seconds of eye contact, the two, one human, one animal, connected in a unique way. From that moment Susan knew that Lulabelle had to be hers.

The next day in the show ring, Lulabelle and Susan placed sixth out of twenty-six gilts.

Fairgoers passing by the pot-bellied pigs' pens stopped dead at sight of Lulabelle and her sister, two slick, black pigs no bigger than medium-sized loaves of ciabatta.

"Precious!" An older woman bent down and

extended her hand. Lulabelle sniffed politely and turned toward Susan for reassurance.

Susan smiled. "Lulabelle just loves having her belly rubbed." So the woman tentatively began to stroke the pig's belly. In a few seconds Lulabelle's legs began to shake, and the toes on one foot curled. The woman frowned and stopped rubbing.

"It's okay. You've made her feel so good and relaxed that she's ready to drop over. Pigs love getting their bellies rubbed. It moves them to ecstasy." The woman continued to rub Lulabelle's belly. Lulabelle began to sway and teeter.

Bam! A second later Lulabelle was flat out on her side in the middle of the pen. She lay stiff as a stick. Susan and the visitor laughed and rubbed her belly even more vigorously.

Back at the hotel Lulabelle sat, glued, by Susan's side until they had packed up their things to leave. While Lulabelle stared at Susan, she had to admit she was falling in love with the little pig. Nancy had noticed the connection between the two, and just as she was ready to suggest Susan take Lulabelle home, Susan put her arm around the pig. "I have to have her, Nancy. She and I have made a connection I can't ignore."

¤****

As Ross Mill Farm's pig representative and hostess, Lulabelle found her niche. Lulabelle displayed an uncanny level of awareness with regard to her role at the farm. Lulabelle flourished amid the activity of new pigs coming and going every day as they were rescued and then adopted out to loving families. Never did Lulabelle complain or challenge any of them, for she was *aware*, somehow, that the rescued animals were unsure, sad, without self-esteem, and that they needed kindness. Lulabelle became their guide, their shepherd, their pilot.

One lonely pig that Lulabelle guided to happiness was Little Awesome Annie, renamed so that she needn't bear the burden of "orphan"—no pigs were orphans at the farm. Little Awesome Annie was an eight-month-old pig, despondent and scared. Her owners threw her away with no more compunction than they would have a banana peel.

At once and as was her duty and mission, Lulabelle befriended the little pig. Just as she did with Fester, she walked right up to her, *"oofed"* a greeting, and told her to come along. Little Awesome Annie got the full tour from Lulabelle, and then, when Lulabelle decided to rest, she offered Annie a bed in her own nest next to the fireplace.

A pig's nest is her home, her personal sanctuary, her territory containing worn blankets, favorite toys, and other sundries meaningful to her. Almost never will a pig share her nest because she is very protective of it. But Lulabelle, in her generous way, and seeing the heartbreak and loneliness in Annie's eyes, allowed her a spot among her own blankets and pillows.

Part of Susan's program for helping pots included giving talks and seminars about the miniature pig as a pet. She scheduled events in many towns, taking Lulabelle along as a spokespig, informing adults and their children that though a pot is as intelligent as a three-year-old, a pig, even a young pig, can be manipulative with his or her human companions.

Susan also advised people to check their town's zoning laws for ordinances against owning pigs.

Miniature pigs were considered livestock, and livestock was banned in most towns. Checking local ordinances before adopting a pet pig would prevent a lot of future heartache for a family. Susan explained a pig could learn tricks so fast it was mind-boggling. They were also affectionate and protective of their homes, but she warned that if young pigs were left home alone for a long time, they could be destructive.

Lulabelle grew so accustomed to traveling with Susan that being in a strange place like the Schaghticoke Fair in New York was little more than routine. After Susan had spent hours setting up the living room-sized tent with a carpet, a sofa, a TV, and a bed where she and Lulabelle and four nine-month-old rescue babies the size of tissue boxes would be living for the next ten days, she fell asleep in a folding chair.

Lulabelle took that opportunity to go for a walk down the midway. When Susan woke up a half hour later, Lulabelle was gone. This time Susan's instinct told her to head straight to the food stands whose smells were wafting their way.

There, before the French fry stand, sat the little black-and-white pig. When Susan spied Lulabelle transfixed before the stand, her snout sniffing the fry-fragrant air, she resisted the urge to call out. It was a sight to savor.

The owner of the stand was leaning out the little window talking to Lulabelle,

"Hey there, Missy. You want some fries?" Lulabelle sat politely. She grunted softly. "So pretty in your pink harness. I'd give you some fries, but your mommy, wherever she is, might not like it."

Susan chuckled to herself, strode over to Lulabelle,

and took her leash. "Naughty Lulabelle. I was looking all over the place for you." Then she thanked the fry guy for watching her pig.

He asked Susan whether it would be all right to give the pig a few fries. Susan looked down at Lulabelle, and Lulabelle *"oofed."* Reluctantly, Susan took Lulabelle around the back of the fry shack, and the man bent down with a small cone of fries. Lulabelle sat politely in front of him as he picked one fry out at a time and offered it. He held it by the very tip, to insure his finger's safety, but in predictable Lulabelle fashion, she took the fry so nicely, so delicately, that he marveled at her manners.

Susan laughed. "Ya know, you've spoiled her now, and I'm probably going to lose her a couple more times before this fair is over. But at least I'll know where to look next time. If you see her again, please hang onto her until I get here."

****

Not only was Lulabelle uncannily aware that, as a pig representative, she had an important role to fill alongside Susan at public functions, but she somehow knew that Susan depended on her to nanny the two-to-nine-month-old rescue pigs. Those pigs came to the farm in all manner of attitudes. Some were wild, having never been handled by a person. Some were nasty, shy, or unsure of themselves because they had been abused or neglected. But all were capable of rehabilitation and being socialized.

Susan deliberately placed all the young rescued pigs with Lulabelle, the perfect nanny for the stressed youngsters. Her charges learned to mimic her gregariousness, and shortly they were snuggling the volunteers, following them and chortling happily around the property. The rescue piglets, who had arrived scared of the human touch, afraid of the human voice, soon adopted Lulabelle's fearlessness and friendliness. They learned to accept being petted, and, in the process, they learned to forgive people.

Lulabelle not only re-socialized the youngsters, but she also taught the rescue piglets how to have fun again. One time when Lulabelle was home alone babysitting three orphaned piglets, Lulabelle assembled them all in the kitchen.

Lulabelle looked around, listening for the sound of human footsteps. *The coast was clear.* She led the piggies to a bottom cabinet. With the tip of her nose, she pried the cabinet door open, looked around the inside, and grabbed the top of a ten-pound bag of flour. Then, with her mouth she dragged the heavy bag into the middle of the floor and ripped it open.

The piggies stood by, watching the flour flowing all over the floor, not sure what they should do. Lulabelle shook the bag, flour flying everywhere. Then she stepped into the middle of the floured floor and started licking.

In minutes the three piglets were pushing each other for a taste of flour. Soon, the scuffling spread the mess even farther around the kitchen floor. Lulabelle demonstrated to the piglets how to push the snow-like substance with their tiny snouts. The piglets were gleeful in the midst of the mess, their little faces caked ghost-white as they stood, ankle-deep, licking the flour-floor. The piggies lapped the flour as fast as they could, drool mixing it to a gluey paste. Soon their lips were coated white, as were Lulabelle's.

When Susan came home that afternoon and discovered the deed, the perpetrators stood obvious. They were the ones with the flour hardened on their whiskers, in their ears, between their toes, and in their eyebrows. Lulabelle, too, looked just as silly as the little ones. That day Lulabelle learned something from the piglets, too. She learned how much fun it was to be young and careless again, how liberating to throw caution to the wind and indulge oneself in something naughty.

As childlike as Lulabelle was with the babies, she was as serious as she could be when working to promote pigs to people. The producer of *Sesame Street* recognized Lulabelle's television appeal when he happened upon her and Susan at an educational event in New York City. Minutes later he contracted for Lulabelle to star in an introductory segment for a regular Sesame Street program about animals.

So one day, into the maze of buildings and the cacophony of streets that defines New York City, Susan drove her old blue van wherein sat Susan's redheaded granddaughter, Kelsey, along with Lulabelle lying on her blanket between the front seats. Lulabelle, her bristles clean and coiffed, in her fuchsia harness and leash, stood obediently by Kelsey's side as the camera crew filmed her walking Lulabelle down the sidewalk in front of a row of brownstones. The *Sesame Street* footage came out so well the producer asked Susan to do an entire TV show about pigs at Ross Mill Farm.

Months later, two vans of TV crew, directors, and assistants arrived at Ross Mill to film the *ZOOM* show. Filming lasted all day, with several re-takes and different shots. Finally, the director asked for the little girl and pig who starred in the *Sesame Street* show. Susan directed the crew into the farmhouse where Lulabelle was asleep in her nest by the fireplace.

The director bent toward the little girl. "Okay, Kelsey. Can you somehow get in there with Lulabelle and pretend you're sleeping with her? When I say 'Roll 'em,' I want you to get your head in as close as you can to Lulabelle's, close your eyes, and pretend to be sleeping." He turned around and whispered to his crew to be quiet so as not to disturb Lulabelle.

The end of the segment turned out perfectly. The closing of the *ZOOM* segment showed Kelsey lying with her head next to Lulabelle's. Both had their eyes closed in luxurious sleep, and then the scene faded out.

One day in the second week of December, 2006, when Susan was delivering pig food to a nearby pot-bellied pig breeding farm, the owner brought out a tiny silver-haired piglet. "Why don't you take her? You told me a while ago that Lulabelle wasn't doing very well."

Susan tried to hide her sadness. "Yes, I did." Lulabelle had really begun to slow down. Her vet told Susan that her pesky sinus infection was probably getting worse.

"Take her." That night Susan drove home with another pig friend.

The next morning Karabelle, as Susan named the little pig, woke up the whole house with her shrieking. Susan rushed downstairs. "I'm coming, Karabelle. What's wrong?" When she ran into the kitchen, Karabelle was screaming in an eardrum-bursting frenzy. Susan held her ears. The piglet's skitzing out was directed at the steel radiator doing nothing but what it was designed for—radiating heat.

Talking softly to her, Susan took the piglet in her arms and rocked her back and forth, but the little pig continued to scream. Susan didn't know what to do. She could have kicked herself for adopting Karabelle just two weeks before Christmas when there was so much to do around the farm.

Susan looked at her husband. "What am I going to do with this piglet? She's so miserable here, Richard." She was almost in tears.

Just as Lulabelle was attuned to Susan, so was she also aware of things going on within herself. Lulabelle knew she didn't have long to live, and she knew that before she died, she had one more role to fill—tending to Karabelle.

Lulabelle, with little strength left, went to Karabelle's side as she had always done with depressed piglets. She *"oof-oofed"* at the frightened piglet, and Karabelle quieted. In only a few minutes, Karabelle bonded with Lulabelle, and for the remainder of the afternoon followed her to the barn, behind the house, up to the cottage in the woods, and to the willows beside the creek. Lulabelle showed her all around, and then she lay in a patch of sun in front of the house.

Lulabelle, stretching out in the sun-soaked grass, *"oofed"* to Karabelle, and the little pig went over and lay right next to Lulabelle. They slept together for the afternoon. In the days that followed, Lulabelle coached Karabelle on climbing the ramp into the van, riding quietly in the back, and walking beside her and Susan in a harness. Finally, Lulabelle ensured that Karabelle appreciated Susan in much the same way Lulabelle had all her life. Lulabelle called the little pig to accompany her and Susan everywhere, and Lulabelle encouraged

Karabelle to lie in the blankets with her and Susan.

To this day Susan firmly believes that Lulabelle, in all her wisdom, knew Karabelle was destined to be her replacement, and she was preparing the little pig for the noble and responsible job Lulabelle held throughout her life at Ross Mill Farm.

Lulabelle died February 10, 2007.

****

Lulabelle's Memorial

Lulabelle supported many roles during her life with Susan and Richard at Ross Mill Farm. She comforted the orphaned and abused rescue pigs—she acted the dignified show pig, a nanny, an actress, and a model. But the role she loved best was being Susan's friend and confidante. More than anything, Susan wanted her best friend's resting place and memorial to reflect the calm and tranquility of Lulabelle herself.

The day after Lulabelle passed away, Susan's good friend Nancy Slocumb arrived at Ross Mill with a dogwood tree as a lasting memorial for Lulabelle. Susan watered the tree and sheltered it throughout the winter, awaiting spring when she could plant the tree, along with Lulabelle's ashes, in Lulabelle's favorite place on the farm—the lawn between the farmhouse and the pig lodge.

Once spring arrived and the ground grew soft enough to work, Susan brought the potted dogwood tree outside to Lulabelle's favorite spot. There, with the help of Richard and the volunteers at Ross Mill Farm, they planted the Lulabelle tree along with a handful of Lulabelle's ashes. Then, next to the tree, Susan placed a statue of a pig angel holding a small birdbath.

Today Lulabelle rests in a place of peace, a peace

that Lulabelle herself had given Susan and so many pigs rescued into the care of Ross Mill Farm.

****

Donations to Pig Placement Network and Ross Mill Farm & Piggy Camp are always appreciated. Foster, adopt, and support needy, abused pet pigs at www.ppn.org and www.rossmillfarm.com.

Chapter Twelve
Magic Lips

Species: Arabian horse
Name: Gabriel or Gabe
Born: April 24, 1975
Died: 2004
Human companion: Chris & Don McCutchan

They named the horse Gabriel—after an angel. But an angel he was not.

Chris McCutchan saw the muscular three-year-old gray Arabian and fell immediately in love with the horse grown fat and fuzzy over the hard Pennsylvania winter. The petite, dark-haired woman patted his head as he peered from his stall. "Would you like to be my buddy, Gabe?" She looked into his questioning dark eyes.

The feisty young Arab bobbed his head. His face typified an Arabian horse's with its chiseled features—the dished face, the small, delicate muzzle, the big, deep-set eyes and small pointed ears. He was a handsome specimen.

"Then that settles it, Gabriel. We're going to be a team." So Chris bought the handsome Arab, upon which she anticipated many long, leisurely rides through the Pocono countryside, through the thick stands of oak and pine, through cranberry bogs, and across streams lined with mountain laurel and rhododendron.

Chris' first ride, however, was less pleasurable than anticipated. While she saddled and bridled the young animal, she forgot about Gabe's former owner, who couldn't sit a toilet seat, let alone a horse. She forgot about the problems the young woman had had with Gabe. But Gabe hadn't forgotten. So when Chris climbed aboard and led him down the road past the old farmer's field, the temptation to be mischievous was too much for him. Walking over the same field where he had always dumped his rider, Gabe felt that same energy building, surging, under his skin.

When a deer popped out from the edge of the field, Gabe had the perfect excuse. He spun around like a reining horse, dumped Chris in the field, and galloped back to the barn. Chris sat in the dirt for a minute, thinking. Then she walked back to the barn, dusting her pants as she went. Back home, she met Gabe standing happily next to his pasture mate. But, instead of rewarding him with a flake of hay, which he fully expected, she remounted and worked him in the ring until he was dripping with sweat. His trick had backfired.

Gabe's previous owner had done a magnificent job of training Gabe to throw his rider and bolt back to the barn. Every time he threw her and ran back to the barn, she walked back to find him standing in his stall where she then gave him a flake of hay. On Chris's next ride, Gabe tried the same stunt again, leaping to the side and galloping as though the bats of hell were at his heels. But Chris hung on, much to his disappointment, and then she turned him in a circle, making him run—faster, longer, harder—because if he wanted to run, then she would make him run and run and run. A half hour later, Gabe was puffing and huffing like the three little pigs' wolf, his nostrils flaring, his brow wet. The smell of sweaty horse enveloped Chris, but she kept him trotting until he became even more exhausted and meek. Chris was also exhausted and out of breath, trying to urge a spent horse, but it was well worth the effort. The next time Gabe had an inkling to bolt, he might reconsider.

Though Gabe's initial bolting behavior was annoying, when she wasn't on his back she found the horse charming in every respect. Every day she freshened his water bucket. Standing with the hose, Chris stood with her back to Gabe. If he was looking out his window, when he heard the water splashing, he turned around and came up behind her.

Chris talked to him as she filled his water bucket. "What are you up to, you bad boy?"

"Ah-hem, ...Ahh-hhe-em, ...Ahh-hhe-em," Gabe murmured.

"I know. Well, I don't like the rain either."

He muttered in horse language. *"Ah-ah-ah-he."* Then he nuzzled her neck and began playing with her earrings, nudging them, and nibbling them with his rubbery lips. She laughed at his "magic lips" as he tickled her earlobes.

Though Chris often had little treats for Gabe, more than anything she had a favorite snack—a peppermint patty. Whenever she unwrapped the foil from a patty, he heard the crackling a quarter mile away and came running. Skidding to a stop in front of her, he beckoned with his elastic lips while Chris fed him one tiny piece at a time.

Still, if Chris didn't have a treat, he paraded behind her, nuzzling her neck and sending shivers down her spine. Gabe, the horse-puppy, followed Chris around the barn, shadowing her as she organized her grooming tools on his shelf, arranged his winter blankets, or just helped someone saddle her horse. He followed her everywhere, tailing her scent, her voice, her jacket he knew so well. Chris only had to look behind, and Gabe stood near.

Though Chris didn't deliberately teach Gabe many tricks, she taught him to come almost by accident. Whenever she visited the barn, she had a treat in her pocket. Before he got it, she enticed Gabe by throwing his snack into the air. "Want a mint, Gabe?" Then up went her arms, and the peppermint patty flew skyward. Gabe watched. Then he saw her catch it. "Would you like this?" Up went her arms, and the treat flipped into the air before she caught it. Again and again, Chris made sure Gabe was watching, and then, when she caught it for the fifth time, she unwrapped the treat and offered it to him. After a while Gabe associated her flailing arms with a treat. It wasn't long before all she had to do was raise her arms, and he'd come running.

The arm trick came in handy one afternoon when she and several other riders were training cross country one summer on the trails of Camelback, the Pocono mountain of ski resort fame. During the winter, skiers from New York, Pennsylvania, and New Jersey and beyond make the trip to ski the hundreds of snow trails of Camelback Mountain. In the summer, horse riders take advantage of those same trails.

So Gabe and Chris were there to prepare for an endurance competition later in the summer. Chris and three other riders were trotting along the barren, rock-lined ridge, with Gabe in the lead, when suddenly he put on the brakes, spun, and flipped Chris out of the saddle like a discus from a gamer's arm. Though she still had the reins in her hands when she hit the ground, she didn't have them for very long. Eyes googled, Gabe jerked backward, tearing the reins from her hands, and then he spun again and galloped halfway down the mountain.

Sitting on the ground, Chris was furious—until she saw what had spooked Gabe. There, not five feet from her, a rattlesnake lay coiled and ready to strike. Despite warnings to stay still when confronted with a rattler, Chris yielded to her natural instinct to run like hell, just as Gabe had. Plunging down the mountainside, Chris flew past the other riders and then tore past Gabe, who had stopped a little way down the hill. When she ran, screaming, past him, Gabe spooked again, sure the rattler was galloping close behind her. So he too took off farther down the hill and passed Chris, who was still running. Finally, he stopped another hundred yards down the mountainside.

Meanwhile the other riders saw the snake and dismounted before their horses could take off with or without them. As the snake slithered into the bushes, they wondered if Gabe would return or just continue down the mountain—a long walk for Chris, and the end of the training session for them all. Chris, too, worried Gabe would run to the base of the mountain without her, so she did the only thing she knew—she threw something into the air.

As she had done many times before, she acted the peppermint patty maneuver. "Look, Gabe! Look what I have for you!" A roll of cherry Lifesavers whipped into the air. She caught it, and flipped it back up. She threw it into the air again, caught it, and then... When Gabe saw the object flicking into the air and Chris' arms going up and down, he knew all was right with his world, and a treat was imminent. He trotted back up the mountain and stopped dead at Chris, who fed him half a roll of Lifesavers, true life savers.

As chartreuse-bellied as Gabe was at sight of a rattlesnake, he could be brave faced with other threats, such as bears. Living in the Poconos, where black bears thrived, allowed for chance meetings between bear and horse. When a young bear happened into Gabe's pasture one day, Gabe took off after him at a gallop, coming to a skidding halt in front of his face. The bear stood up on his hind legs, his eyes wide, and though his first instinct was to defend himself against the horse, he decided, faced with a large animal tossing his head and stomping the ground, to run. The bear turned and dashed under the fence and into the woods, with Gabe, snorting and tossing his head, at his heels.

****

A rider never knows what he or she is going to meet when going out on horseback—motorcycles, tractor trailers, leaping deer, squirrels rustling in the brush, groundhogs scurrying into a hole. Any unexpected sight or sound spooks most horses, even things riders recognize and have no fear of. Horses, who don't know any better, can be scared witless by dark spots on the ground, a puddle, an unusually large weed, a downed tree that was upright on the last ride, and even the horse and rider's own shadows. So depending on a horse to keep his wits in the face of a

178

loud noise, a big yellow bus, or a human out for a walk in the countryside is like depending on a three-year-old to shrug off the bogeyman in her closet.

A horse reacts to frightening things by leaping sideways and bolting back to his place of safety—usually the barn. Some horses that are dead broke may just jump in place or charge straight ahead, which is a benefit for the rider, since it's the sideways leap that most often unseats a person, even a skilled rider. Not only is the horse's reaction often unexpected, so that the rider has no time to prepare, but the spook occurs in a microsecond, taking the rider completely by surprise and out of her saddle.

The best analogy of a horse spooking sideways and leaving its rider behind is like the magician's tablecloth trick, in which a tablecloth is whisked out from under dishes that remain in place on the tabletop. The horse, equivalent to the tablecloth at the moment of the spook, whips himself right out from beneath the plate/rider, and the rider, devoid of support, hits the ground.

On another day, Chris and Gabe were riding alongside Margie and her horse Billy when the neighboring farmer's bull charged down the hill toward them. The only thing separating the angry bull from the horses was a thin strand of electrical wire the two horses couldn't see but that the bull surely knew existed. Though the bull intended to stop at the wire fence, Billy was terrified by the huge animal dieseling toward them. While Gabe had endured the bull's hissy fits on numerous occasions, the fear erupting from the other horse hit him like a contagious virus.

Gabe spooked, sliding himself tablecloth-style from underneath Chris' rump. She landed in the road, and Gabe galloped for home, his steel shoes igniting sparks on the macadam. Billy, with Margie clinging helplessly to his back, ran at Gabe's heels. But the fiasco didn't end there. Little did the farmer's goose, picking at gravel along the road edge, realize that a couple of horses were loose in his neighborhood. Before he could turn to check out the sound of clattering hooves, the bolting horses were upon him. The goose gave one tremendous honk and leaped into the air, a burst of feathers falling like snow as he tried to get airborne. The flailing goose frightened the horses again, and Gabe and Billy, with the terrified Margie hanging onto the saddle horn, put the throttle down, banking around the turn and out of sight.

Chris took off on foot after Gabe and Billy and Margie, and when she finally came around the turn, there both horses and Margie were, stopped in the road, Margie looking green as a celery stalk. Gabe and Billy stood chewing grass at the road's edge, and the goose was nonchalantly pecking the gravel at Gabe's feet.

Sometimes a rider thinks his or her horse most certainly will spook at a loud motorcycle coming over the hill, a blatting tractor trailer sailing down the road. Just when the rider is poised for the tablecloth trick, bracing herself in the stirrups, crawling up on the reins, and leaning toward the ground so that the hit is less painful, the awful thing roars by, but her horse has no reaction. This kind of undependability is what most riders dread. Just when the rider is ready to take a hit, the horse stays calm, but when the rider least expects it, the horse spins, whipping himself from underneath the tailcoats of his horseman.

Just such a completely different reaction did Gabe

have upon meeting a swarm of bees. Chris was riding Gabe through the woods alongside her friends Roxanne and husband George. Roxanne was riding her young horse, and George was riding an elderly, dead-broke horse named Sarah. Suddenly, as they came from the edge of the woods into the farmer's field—the infamous bull-charging, goose-gaggling field—a loud humming filled the air.

George stopped Sarah dead. "Stop! Don't move!" Thank goodness for the steadfast and fearless Sarah, who stood still as moss as the gigantic bee swarm buzzed past, through, around, and under the three horses. The monumental black cloud engulfed all three riders and horses. The swarm sounded like the inside of a jet at cruising speed. The sizzling and purring within it was otherworldly, and Chris thought for sure the colossal swarm of bees would spur Gabe into a gallop as no metal riding spur ever had. She thought for sure he would spin, whip his tablecloth self from under her, and abandon her to the most horrific bee stinging of her life and, possibly, her death.

Instead, he stood still. Perhaps it was his instincts telling him to be quiet in the presence of a bee swarm. Perhaps he didn't run because Sarah didn't. Perhaps he didn't run because the bees just didn't scare him. Chris hoped he hadn't run in order to protect her. No one will ever know, but Chris knew that Gabe's keeping a sane head that day surely averted a disaster.

Despite so many episodes of Gabe's spooking on the trail, unseating Chris, and running off, Gabe was the friendliest of horses, running his "magic lips" up and down all the people who fussed over him and talked with him. If Chris wrapped her arms around his head, he nudged her and slid his big loopy tongue along her chin. He gave her the sloppiest horse kisses, and he licked everyone, including the barn cats and the boarders' dogs when they greeted him. He was the barn's Don Juan.

Giving mega-kisses wasn't Gabe's only talent. He loved little kids and people he sensed were helpless in the saddle. These folks he took care of when they rode. With novice riders, Gabe commanded a fearless presence that made his riders comfortable and secure. Never did he run off with an inexperienced rider. Never did he put in danger anyone who was unsteady or off-balance on his back.

In 1984, when Gabe was middle-aged, he and Chris won their first trail competition. In such competitions, the horse and rider follow a not-so-clearly marked trail over fields, up mountains, through woods, across creeks and small, manmade obstacles. While the teams complete the hours-long endurance event as quickly as possible, each horse must stop for a vet check while the veterinarian examines the horse for lameness, pulse, and respiratory rate, and general demeanor.

That day, Gabe's natural Arabian athleticism and willing heart won him and Chris the championship. When he finished and had to undergo the final vet check, he licked the attending vet's back as the doctor leaned over to examine his legs. This display of mischievousness proved that Gabe was feeling fine enough to play, even after hours of trotting cross country.

While Gabe proved himself a superb competitor and athlete, his most unique trait was his funny personality and eagerness to please. For example, a chicken often sat, guarding the barn, in the rafters above Gabe's stall. Sometimes, however, boarders saw the chicken sitting on Gabe's back. Not only did Gabe allow the chicken to ride his back in his stall, but he also let the barn cat, Cisco, sit atop him.

Gabe's "magic lips" earned him the title of Houdini. From an early age, Gabe played with the locks on his stalls. He'd reach around over his stall walls and fiddle with the latch, wiggling it this way and that until it finally slipped out of the holder and unlocked the door. Often in the morning Chris found Gabe walking around outside the barn, completely free, while all the other horses stayed locked in their stalls.

In time, however, Gabe learned to unlock not just his own stall door but every other horse's stall door. One night he opened the door to a mare's stall, walked inside, and mounted her. Eleven months later she had a Gabe "angel" by her side. Another time when Gabe was older, he pulled another stunt as the barn's babysitter. Usually a babysitter is an older horse, male or female, to which the new foals gravitate. They are usually very calm, friendly horses that tolerate a foal's naughtiness. The babysitter also teaches the foal about pasture manners and how to submit to the older horses in the herd.

As usual, one day Gabe was standing loose in the aisle of the barn; next to him was the foal he was babysitting. He had evidently unlocked the mare's stall door. The foal walked out and skipped happily next to Grandpa Gabe, who then closed the door and locked it again, separating the mare from her foal.

Though Gabe was a master escape artist, he never

left the immediate barn area, preferring his pasture mates rather than roaming the countryside by himself. But he liked company while he was free, so he let mares, and even a stallion, loose from their stalls. If he was bored and didn't want to stay in his stall, he simply jimmied the lock and walked out. One could hardly find a smarter, more "ambi-lipstrous" horse.

Always the comedian, Gabe kept the boarders, the vets at the competitive trail-riding events, and Chris laughing. One day while she was riding, she saw something interesting on the ground. She slipped off the saddle and bent over to examine it. Gabe, noticing her intent on something on the ground, lowered his head to look, too. The two of them, said Chris' friend, Roxanne, looked comical, both bent over looking at the ground.

Not only was Gabe an equine comedy act, but he was a friendly, personable character whom everyone liked. For instance, at competitions when Chris pulled him up to a checkpoint to have a physical, Gabe sang out, calling to everyone that he was there. *"I made it!"* he seemed to say. *"Here I am!"* The vets loved him, answering his whinny and his nickering with words of encouragement and a pat on the forehead. If anyone Gabe greeted ignored him, he pawed the ground and tossed his head to get the attention he deserved. And when someone talked to him as Chris always did, he bobbed his head, as though to say, *"Yep, I agree."*

Just as Gabe was a master comedian, he could be just as sympathetic when it mattered most. Gabe sensed when Chris was having a particularly bad day. When he felt her depression, he became more quiet, almost despondent, himself, and he stayed close. He offered her his presence.

When other riders at the barn saw Gabe and Chris conversing in the aisle, they discussed how remarkably the two related to each other. While Chris fussed over Gabe, currying him to a fine sheen, not a piece of dirt clinging to his white coat, Gabe fussed over Chris, tugging at her shirt, nibbling her earrings, and just generally tasting her all over. As horses scratch each other's backs with their teeth, so, too, did Gabe try to scratch Chris' shoulder when she scratched his.

The two—one human, one horse—communicated so well Chris taught him how to bow. Once he heard the crackling sound of the peppermint patty wrapper, he began to bend one front leg, tuck it under himself, and put his muzzle under his chest. Chris showed everyone at the barn how well Gabe could bow.

While the trick fascinated the boarders at the barn, Gabe's bowing occurred at unlikely times, too. For instance, while they were on a competitive trail ride and had stopped at a vet checkpoint, as the vet was checking Gabe's respiration someone nearby was unwrapping a piece of candy. Gabe homed in on the scrunching sound of the wrapper and, to everyone's amazement, began to tuck his head down and pull back one front leg. The candy went, then, to Gabe.

Another time Chris allowed a young rider to take the aged Gabe into the show ring. At the moment the announcer called the riders to line up their horses in the center of the ring, Gabe stood stock still—until he heard a wrapper crackling somewhere. And there, in the lineup, with a rider atop him, he did his famous bow. The audience went wild, and he placed in the ribbons for that class.

For most of Gabe's life, he was boarded at

different riding facilities. Chris and husband Don promised Gabe, as he got older, they would build their own barn and fence in a pasture for him. So the last six years of his life Gabe had his very own barn and pasture, along with three pasture mates, Racer, Reesa, and Devil, horses who became his best friends. Don took in Devil, a huge, half Percheron and half Morgan horse, whose owner's health was failing, and he offered a home to a thirty-year-old, shy, red thoroughbred named Racer. And he also took in an elderly boarder, Reesa, an Arab like Gabe. Reesa, Gabe's best friend, died shortly after arriving at Heart to Heart Acres, leaving Racer and Devil Gabe's only pasture mates.

Gabe lived to be an elderly gentleman, and old age just made him more dignified, personable, and willing to please. Chris still rode him from time to time, but most of his final days he spent grazing in his own lush pasture beneath the pines, hickory, and oak trees of their woods. Though Gabe still could manage a bow, he could only bend his neck a little because of arthritis. Still, the peppermints hadn't lost their appeal. The ingenious horse continued to open his stall door, and each night after Chris threw a flake of alfalfa into his hay bunk, she put her head over the stall edge, and he, with his magic lips, gave her a slurpy kiss.

Gabe died in 2004.

****

Gabriel's Memorial

Chris wanted her horse, Gabe, buried in his favorite pasture where for six years he'd grazed the summers away. He was king of his pasture, and the green grass his comfort and sustenance, along with his equine buddies Reesa, Racer, and Devil. In his own meadow he could be himself in his field of green—content, at peace, far from the show ring or competitive trail. As well in death he lies peacefully in his heavenly pasture.

Gabe's body lies beneath a rock garden of exceptional beauty. Headed with a stone engraved with a running horse and Gabe's name, larger rocks cascade like a waterfall over the burial site. During the winter the garden is green with evergreen boxwoods, dwarf cypress, rhododendron, mountain fire Andromeda, and flaming azalea bushes. Just as the snow melts, yellow and white daffodils, robin's egg blue and canary-colored crocus, and hyacinths of every color poke their heads between the rocks in celebration of a life lived large and adventurous. During the summer, Gabe's phantasmal garden explodes in color with cascading periwinkle and peach petunias, lavender, cobalt lobelia, and purple Russian sage. Peeking from the rock crevasses are lambs' ear, hen and chicks, and aromatic herbs like spearmint, peppermint, lemon sage, and others.

Gabe's burial site is fenced off so that Devil, Malaki, a white Appaloosa, and Sunrise, a chestnut thoroughbred, can't disturb his gravesite, but Chris and Don believe Gabe is soothed knowing his equine friends are grazing right above him. Hardly could a horse have asked for a more perfect burial—in his favorite pasture and sharing the sweet-smelling earth with his horse friends.

Chapter Thirteen
In the Purity of the Moment

Species: Guinea pig
Name: Gus
Born: 1995
Died: 1997
Human Companion: Beth Anne

"I'm telling you, if I come back to this pet shop one more time, and this poor, lonely guinea pig is still here, I'm taking him, no matter what my mother says." The young West Chester college student clutched the white guinea pig to her chest and stroked his head. "He's the only one left out of that big batch of pigs from last week. Nobody wants him."

Her boyfriend shook his head. "If he's still here next week, I'll buy him for you. He's only five bucks."

The guinea pig with eyes the color of the Caribbean Sea looked at the young woman. His hair was scruffy, naturally punked—a hipster. Though some guinea pigs had smooth coats, Beth Anne loved the lonely one with the perennially bad hair day.

The next week when Beth Anne and John walked into the pet store, a fresh new load of guinea pigs had been added to the guinea pig pen—white ones, redheads, smooth-haired and scruffy ones. The pet store's newest arrivals were engaged in lively conversation, chirping gregariously in their new home. Others were chewing wood, eating bits of carrots, and hopping after one another. But the white, scruffy-haired guinea pig Beth Anne held the week before stood alone in a corner.

Beth Anne reached into the pen and rubbed the white guinea pig behind the ear. He began to purr, leaning into her fingers. The more she scratched, the deeper he purred, as if he had a rattle in his throat. Then, suddenly, he took off to the other end of the pen and spun around, facing her. Did he want to play? So Beth Anne stepped over to the other side of the pen and reached in to scratch his rump. Again he bumped and swayed his rear end against her scratching fingers, then took off running, hopping like a bunny.

Beth Anne put her hands on her hips. "That's it! He likes me, and he's mine. I'm taking him home right now."

Gus, as she named him, sat in Beth Anne's lap all the way home. When she walked into the house, she let him loose on the kitchen floor. Her mother was drying dishes at the sink.

Beth Anne's mother eyed him with suspicion. "He looks like a rat."

"He does not. He's absolutely beautiful."

"Well, don't expect me to take care of him. I want nothing to do with him."

"In a week I'll be going back to college anyway. I'm taking him with me—you won't be inconvenienced."

Beth Anne's father reached in to pet the little pig. "I think he's kinda cool, actually. I like his hairdo."

Immediately, Beth Anne began assembling Gus'

new house—a large aquarium specially made for reptiles. For bedding Beth Anne used only soft, hypoallergenic paper fiber bedding, instead of cedar shavings, to prevent any respiratory irritation. Inside the aquarium she put a small wooden hideaway under which he could sleep or run if frightened, and he could chew on its wood siding to file his teeth. Last, Beth Anne hung a water bottle and put in a ceramic dish for food. Gus' house was a pig palace.

The next week Beth Anne and Gus traveled to West Chester State College where she and another young lady shared an apartment. For the trip Gus rode in his own traveling carrier, the carrier buckled up in the seat belt, in the passenger's seat. Though he couldn't look out the windows on the way to college, he loved the rock music, particularly oldies and songs by the Grateful Dead, and as the radio blared, he danced around the carrier to the rhythm of the songs.

When they pulled onto the college campus and Beth Anne opened the car door, Gus smelled a new and exciting world. He chirped and spun around, excited. Where was he? He felt his cage jerk forward, and before he knew it, was swaying above the pavement. Once inside Beth Anne's apartment, she took him from his carrier and settled him into another glass house in her bedroom. Gus the guinea pig had a luxurious townhouse in Allentown as well as an estate in West Chester.

****

Guinea pigs, as do most animals, love routine, and early on Gus set his internal watch to Beth Anne's habits. In the morning Gus awakened to Beth Anne's stirring in bed. Then he watched her shadow float across the wall. He heard the bathroom lights flick on, the brushing of teeth, the radio softly playing. As the sun came up, he sat in the sun-yellow spot in his glass house and stretched out, bathing in the heat. Most of all he loved the morning's feeling of anticipation.

"Hey, Gus Bunny." Beth Anne pulled up her jeans and buttoned her shirt. "What do you say, Gussy? Would my lover-boy like some breakfast?"

Gus inhaled deeply. *"Vree, vree, vree, vree."* He spun around in his glass house, his bright blue eyes sparkling in the sun. Just on time, according to Gus' internal clock, a handful of guinea pig food pellets began dropping into his dish with a clinking noise he came to love. It was flavor encased in a sound.

Gus rushed to the dish and took a pellet into his mouth, munching with that sideways motion characteristic of the rodent family. He closed his eyes, concentrating, inhaling the savory scent of the pellet. He swallowed. Simply heaven. He ate another pellet, then stood back and tapped into his internal clock. He hopped in place. It would be coming soon.

Glancing up over his aquarium, he saw it coming: the bowl of goodies—ambrosia to a guinea pig's taste buds. Like a butler with her arm extended, Beth Anne carried a platter of cut-up strawberries, orange pieces, kale leaves, and cherry tomatoes. Gus saw them and shrieked—*"My veggies!"* Beth Anne laughed. Cherry tomatoes were his favorites. He loved to dive into a tomato, his front teeth popping open the tight skin from which exploded the juicy seed-flesh. He chirped and hopped in place as Beth Anne put the fruit in his dish.

Beth Anne loved watching Gus eat because he ate much like a farm pig instead of a guinea pig. He dived into a cherry tomato only to come up once for a breath of air, his tiny muzzle covered in tomato jelly and seeds. His expression was incredulous, pleasure personified.

While Gus was eating, Beth Anne readied for classes, grabbing her microbiology book, a couple of snacks, and a cell phone. Then she went over to Gus's house and stuck her face over the top ledge.

Gus had been busy chowing down his bowlful of goodies, but when Beth Anne came to say goodbye, as she did every morning, he stopped and galloped to her. Beth Anne squinched her lips toward Gus. "I'm going to be back soon, Gus, and then we'll play a bit. Now, give me a kissy-kissy."

And as though the guinea pig knew exactly what she said, he jumped up, putting his front feet on the top ledge of the glass tank, and touched his nose to Beth Anne's. In the next second, his tiny tongue flicked a guinea pig kiss to her cheek. Beth Anne smiled. "What a good boy my Gus Bunny is. I'll see you in a couple of hours." Then she patted his head and left.

Gus said goodbye in his shrill voice—a couple of *vreep, vreeps*—and raced back to his fruit dish.

****

That afternoon, as with most every afternoon, and even before Gus heard the keys jiggling in the door, he was up and running, having had a good morning nap. He was ready for his playtime. According to his clock, it was imminent. Running to the side of his glass house, he put his front feet on the side and listened for the creak of the door. He heard Beth Anne come inside, then the usual thud of her book bag hitting the kitchen table. He hopped in place—it would only be seconds…seconds…before…. The television started to speak. He checked his clock again. One second, two seconds, three….

Beth Anne opened the bedroom door. "Gus Bunny!" He hopped in a circle. "Are you ready to watch *General Hospital*? Do you want to see what Luke is going to do to Laura today?"

Gus squeaked, anxious for special playtime with his mom. Suddenly Beth Anne's hand reached down, surrounded his back, and he felt his body being lifted gently into the air. *"Vreep, vreep!"* Gus shouted, the equivalent of *"Be careful! Don't drop me!"* On the way into the living room, she grabbed a towel from the bathroom and put it on the living room floor, but Gus didn't stay there for long. He raced up to the TV, put his front feet on the screen where *General Hospital* was playing, and stared into the face of an actor. Suddenly the channel switched to a commercial, which Gus clearly wasn't interested in, so he ran back to Beth Anne, sitting with her legs spread straight out in front of her. She had a bag of baby carrots, his favorite, in her lap. When Gus ran in the "V"-shaped hallway formed by her legs, she offered him a thin carrot, which he took between his tiny paws, and he began munching, his eyes closed to slits.

Beth Anne turned to watch the show. The red-haired Bobbie appeared on the TV screen. She was sobbing. Beth Anne patted Gus. "Bobbie has so many problems right now, Gus." Gus was running back and forth, waddle-galloping inside the "V" of Beth Anne's legs, stopping only for bits of strawberries and baby carrots. He loved the attention, the exercise, but, most of all, the tasty morsels.

"Yes, poor Bobbie." Beth Anne confided everything to her pig. "She's so nice—too nice—she'll never keep a man that way. She needs to play a bit harder to get, don't you think, Gus?"

Gus sat munching a strawberry, twirling it around in his paws, licking it, his eyes closed. "She needs to be more independent and show Vince he doesn't deserve her. Then maybe he'd take notice. But I don't know what she's going to do about this baby that's not his, Gus. Sheesh, I'm glad I don't have those problems."

Gus made no comment. He didn't live in that world. He lived in a simpler world of momentary needs and desires. At the moment he was eating a strawberry, being petted, taking a nap, watching TV, running between his owner's legs. Gus's life was like a Candyland game—full of happy color, light, goodies, and free of traps or scary holes. Thanks to Beth Anne, he had all he could ever want—good food, a comfortable nest, and, best of all, love.

In only one moment did Gus ever experience the dread humans tolerate on a daily basis. That was the afternoon when Beth Anne purchased a baby's playpen for him to enjoy grass and fresh air outside without getting into trouble or getting hurt. Beth Anne and Michelle, her roommate, carted the octagonal playpen into the yard behind the apartment. Cars flew beyond the sidewalk just twenty feet away, so Beth Anne was relieved the pen would keep Gus safe.

Once the playpen was set up, Beth Anne lifted Gus from his car carrier and set him on the playpen's floor. "There you go, Gus Bunny." Then she turned around to ask Michelle a question. When she turned back to the playpen, Gus was gone.

"Gus! Gus! Where are you?"

Beth Anne was frantic. No sooner had Beth Anne put him inside the playpen than he had vanished.

They searched around under the blanket in the playpen. They looked *under* the playpen—no Gus.

Michelle poked her hand through the slit. "He must've gotten out here in the corner where the sides attach."

They ran to the front yard and the busy street beyond. No lump of guinea pig lay in the street. Then Michelle ran to the side of their apartment. There, huddled under a pine tree, was Gus. "I found him!"

Gus's teeth were chattering, and he was shivering. Away from his house, away from his owner, under a huge smelly thing with stickers, he was scared witless. When he saw Beth Anne, he ran to her calling, *"Re-ee-ee-eep! Ree-ee-ee-eep! Ree-ee-ee-eep!"—"Help me! I'll never run away again!"*

Since the playpen obviously failed to offer a solution to Gus's apparent boredom while Beth Anne attended classes, Beth Anne brought home a tunnel for pet mice and rats. Gus ran into the tunnel but never came out the other end. Instead, he sat inside chewing on the plastic and spitting the pieces out.

So Beth Anne threw out the tunnel and replaced it with an exercise wheel, which Gus totally ignored. She took that out, then threw in kitten balls, thinking he might like to chase them, but he didn't like them either. Finally, she brought him a gigantic ferret house with three different levels he could climb and gaze from. Gus's reaction to the ferret house was to climb to the third level, back his butt tight-up against the bars, and let fly a turd.

With this new toy, Gus had transformed into a furry BB gun—backing up, taking aim, and firing.

Blam! A tiny turd flew onto the carpet.

Beth Anne yelled from the kitchen, "That's not nice, Gus. Stop that."

"Phr-r-rt!" Another one shot out his butt.

Beth Anne pleaded, "Come on, Gus!"

As Gus backed into the bars again, Beth Anne scooped him out of the ferret house. Then she chucked the house into the incinerator.

Gus never expected he'd have to entertain himself by using a mindless exercise wheel or any other contraption. He was most content to be with his human mistress. When Beth Anne came home just in time for *General Hospital,* they sat together, and he had the run of the living room, race-waddling back and forth for treats. He knew Beth Anne would hold him on her shoulder in front of the TV and stroke his back until he fell asleep.

He followed his princess everywhere, especially to the refrigerator, whose door he could hear opening from his glass house in her bedroom. Then he began to chirp and shriek, *"I want something, too!"* and Beth Anne ran to set him free. He would hustle-waddle after her down the hallway and stand attentive at the refrigerator door until she made him a bowl of fruit and carrots.

Gus died in 1997.

To Gus' credit, Beth Anne found his companionship so special and endearing that she decided she couldn't live without guinea pigs in her life. In fact, she wanted another white, scruffy-haired pig that looked just like Gus.

****

Gus's Memorial

For an animal usually given no more credit for intelligence or affection than a bar of soap by most humans, Gus proved himself a worthy, loving pet. The guinea pig conversed with his mistress by chirping in different tones, depending on the situation or his level of sensitivity or anxiety. He followed her throughout the apartment. He listened attentively when she cried, accepting the burden of her problems like the kindest dog.

Their relationship was reciprocal. Beth Anne could count on Gus because he was always there for her, and not simply because he was confined to his glass house. He was there by her side watching TV, or while she studied, and whenever she ate dinner. He became her loyal companion, a being whose sheer presence and happy demeanor was value enough. For such a small, seemingly negligible animal to fall in love with, play with, let himself be rubbed and held by a comparatively large human, he proved himself a brave, generous, accepting friend, and his loyalty, as grand as he was small, thrilled Beth Anne. His total contentment with her awed everyone—his sitting in her lap speaking "guinea" amused her and her friends. He taught her the most valuable lesson, more valuable than any of her college courses—how to exist purely in the moment.

Gus offered, without any kind of expectations or rewards or paybacks, what we humans call unconditional love. Content to just hang out with his human companion, Gus was happy to just be a guinea pig. He aspired to nothing except that and looking forward to his next cherry tomato or sitting with Beth Anne through the next segment of *General Hospital.*

His needs were the simplest, the purest. And when he was eating a sliver of carrot in the shelter of Beth Anne's lap, he was the happiest.

****

When one local pet cemetery informed Beth Anne that her dear Gus's burial would cost $850, she had to decline. So she called the Dixon Street Humane Shelter in Allentown, PA, and asked if she could bury her pet guinea pig there alongside Chip, the family dog. They generously offered Gus a spot by Chip's grave. Beth Anne felt relieved knowing Gus would be with one of their other family members.

So Beth Anne set to work.

With all the love she could afford, she designed and built a tiny coffin to fit Gus's body. Measuring him from head to toe, she sawed pieces of birch plywood, nailing the sides together with finishing nails. Then she stained and lacquered the outside of the little coffin. Once she found a stencil of a rabbit, she cut out its ears so that it resembled a guinea pig and stenciled the creature on the outside of the coffin with "Gus Bunny" written on it.

She lined the box with maroon velvet and sewed a pillow for Gus's head. Then she carefully arranged Gus's body inside, putting him in his usual sleeping position. The little coffin went into a Tupperware container, and then she drove Gus to the humane cemetery on Sixth Street.

Gus's name was engraved on a bone-shaped headstone alongside Beth Anne's old dog, Chip.

Chapter Fourteen
The Crew

Species: Guinea Pig
Names: Leroy & Squeaky
Both born: 1997
Died: December 22, 2001; December 23, 2001
and
Names: Soda & Whiskey
Born: January, 1999, November, 1998
Died: September 13, 2002; July 1, 2005
Human Companion: Beth Anne

Beth Anne missed Gus so much she vowed to adopt a Gus look-alike. At the time, no punked-out white guinea pigs were available, so she did the next best thing—she bought a black-and-white pig, Squeaky, whose frizzled hairdo came right out of a vampire movie and an all-white, smooth-haired pig named Leroy. Mathematically figuring, Beth Anne had her Gus back in the equation—Leroy, who was totally white, plus Squeaky, who was scruffy-haired, together equaled the white, scruffy Gus.

While Gus had lived alone with Beth Anne, Leroy and Squeaky had each other from the start. Leroy the Lovelorn attempted being "frisky" with Squeaky, but Beth Anne discouraged his amorous advances by thrusting a paper towel insert between the two during their playtime. She loved guinea pigs, but she didn't want a whole house full of them. But Beth Anne needn't have worried. Squeaky tolerated his jumping on her back to a degree, but when the feisty devil got too rough, she refused him. Faced with unrequited love, Leroy forgot his love interests and learned to foster a platonic relationship with Squeaky, chasing her down the halls, lying beside her on Beth Anne's bed, and talking to her about their favorite foods. When Leroy stopped playing the love-stricken Romeo, they got along together—two garlic cloves in a knot.

Leroy and Squeaky weren't always as agreeable as Gus had been. For instance, when Beth Anne opened the kitchen junk drawer to get out their toenail clippers, both pigs ran as though chased by a wildcat—having one's nails clipped was tantamount to being eaten alive. Before they darted beneath the couch, she captured one. "Ah-hah! I've got you, you bad little piggie." As Beth Anne held Squeaky by her back in the palm of her hand, Squeaky's little feet were still running, running for that couch from which she had, only minutes before, been hopelessly snatched.

Just as Gus had been as laid back as a '60s hippie, Leroy had a feisty, busy-busy, Type A personality that sometimes even Squeaky found hard to tolerate. He was also a superior athlete, as far as guinea pigs go. Whenever he had the chance, he exercised like an Olympian before the big event—race-waddling beneath each chair, churning the dust-bunnies up as he spun like a tornado for corners unknown.

In contrast, Squeaky, never as active as Leroy, seemed content to snuggle in Beth Anne's neck. Together Squeaky and Beth Anne watched from the couch as Leroy charged the TV set, ducked beneath a chair, headed for the nether parts of a bookcase, and rounded the corner like a furry go-cart.

Beth Anne had Leroy and Squeaky for only a short time before the local humane shelter called asking her to adopt two formerly abused guinea pigs. When Beth Anne saw how frightened they were of people, she couldn't refuse, so she adopted them, too. Both females, Soda, mostly black and caramel with an orange racing stripe, and Whiskey, a reddish-caramel with black patches, needed some time to acclimate before they could come out to play. So Beth Anne set up their aquarium with food and water in the furnished basement, the quietest part of the house. In time they would adjust.

In the meantime Leroy and Squeaky, unaware of the additions to their family, honed their old tricks. Annoying Beth Anne's cat, Barney, quickly became a fascinating game. To prevent Barney from snatching one of the guinea pigs from her bedroom, Beth Anne rigged a large screen in front of her open bedroom door. The screen allowed air to circulate in the summer months, yet it kept the pigs safe from the cat, who, for hours, stare-threatened the pigs through the screen, just waiting for the right moment to pounce.

But Leroy and Squeaky weren't intimidated by Barney the Brute.

Squeaky, as was her fearless nature, often tormented Barney by sitting just on the other side of the screen. The pig stared at the cat and nonchalantly chewed pieces of wood so that she could spit them at the cat like a gangster spitting a cigarette butt. Rough-tough, no-nonsense Squeaky did all that and more to tease the cat peering from the other side. A few times Squeaky lunged at Barney, then hopped from the screen far enough that Barney felt frustrated. Sometimes Squeaky's mock-attack scared Barney, and the scaredy-cat flinched, losing his balance and tumbling over his haunches.

One day while Beth Anne and her parents were having Sunday dinner, a horrendous shrieking riveted the air. Even rooms away, the sound was deafening. Beth Anne was the first out of her chair, flying to the rescue—surely a pig was in trouble. Barney had broken into Beth Anne's bedroom and was sitting *inside* Leroy's aquarium. From under his wooden hideaway Leroy shrieked at the top of his tiny lungs, the guinea pig's equivalent of *"Help! Help me! There's a monster in my house!"* Beth Anne snatched the surprised Barney away and barricaded him outside the bedroom.

Back in the quiet of the warm, living room basement, Beth Anne dreaded cleaning Soda's and Whiskey's house, for they were still scared and defensive. When Beth Anne reached inside, Soda charged her hand. Before Beth Anne could react, for none of her other pigs had ever tried to bite her, she had a bloody can opener's V mark on her hand.

No sooner did Beth Anne yell than Soda backed away and stared hard at her human. Without doubt she expected being hit, as was the habit of her previous owner.

Beth Anne had to know whether the bite was deliberate or unintentional. "Let's try that again. How about you, Whiskey? Would you like a piece of carrot?" And with that Beth Anne reached inside, a carrot slice between her thumb and finger.

Whiskey, too, attacked her hand, but Beth Anne whisked it away before she could sink her teeth. Beth Anne felt sad. "Whiskey! Soda! What's the matter with you girls?"

Sure their reactions had to be pure coincidence, she tried again. This time both pigs charged her hand, then stood firmly together like an armed vanguard. Many an owner would have returned such ferocious guinea pigs to the shelter or had them put to sleep, but not Beth Anne. She didn't recycle pets. The pigs only hated people because of how mean people had treated them. For the next several days, she first put a paper towel cardboard insert into their house. If the pigs didn't attack it, then she carefully, slowly handed them a carrot slice.

Another tactic she used was acclimating them to Leroy, a male who was capable of amusing any other female. Beth Anne hoped that when Soda and Whiskey realized how affectionate Leroy was toward Beth Anne, they might cozy to her. Leroy immediately became enamored with Whiskey, and before Beth Anne knew it, the three of them began playing and talking on the carpet. Still, whenever Beth Anne reached for them, Soda or Whiskey either backed away or stood their ground and chattered a warning.

Though Soda and Whiskey really liked the taste of kale, they refused anything else except an occasional carrot. Their previous life must have resembled hell. All the evidence proved they had been starved, they had been physically hurt, and they had never had the opportunity to taste anything but pelleted food. What they weren't accustomed to, they didn't like, and their defensive behavior was fear reaction to physical abuse.

Soda's and Whiskey's behavior caused Beth Anne to really think about what animals, in general, must feel. What kind of coward could a human be to pummel a tiny, harmless creature that weighed less than a pound? She concluded it wasn't inconceivable that all animals, therefore, could feel intense fear and anxiety in the company of humans. She felt, likewise, that farm animals raised in the cruelest of farm factories and then transported under horrific conditions to the slaughterhouse, where their death was anything but humane, also felt intense fear and anxiety, too. With that thought, Beth Anne only became more resolved to continue her vegetarian lifestyle along with caring for her guinea pigs.

Within a few weeks of slow and steady kindness, however, Whiskey and Soda began to change. Soda, a true nightmare in the beginning, morphed into a shy little pig who just wanted love and attention. And Whiskey, also a former holy horror, became as kind as Leroy, though she stayed introverted and reserved. Even their tastes changed. Beth Anne tempted Soda and Whiskey with delectable treats, ones even they couldn't resist. In time they learned it was safe to accept apricots and pieces of watermelon from Beth Anne.

Together Leroy and Squeaky and Soda and Whiskey enjoyed a few short years of life and love with their human companion, Beth Anne. They learned to enjoy snuggling in her neck, giving her kisses, chasing her down the hall, and traveling back and forth from school to her parents' house where her mother learned to appreciate them, too.

****

Leroy's,   Squeaky's,   Soda's,   and   Whiskey's

Memorials

Before Christmas of 2001, Beth Anne wrapped up Leroy and Squeaky and took them to Cloud Nine Pet Services, run by Kevin Zerwick—the most understanding and compassionate person to have ever run the pet cemetery in its history. What's more, the burial fee for her two loving guinea pigs was far less money than that quoted when Gus had died.

So, with much care, Leroy and Squeaky were buried, their tombstone engraved with their names, their photos, and a few loving words from Beth Anne's heart. Such a memorial was only fitting for two friends who carried, in their own individual ways, the tradition begun by the loving Gus.

****

Soda's death is notable for the good it speaks for human redemption, and, moreover, for the capacity in animals to forgive and love one of a species whose capacity for evil and unkindness is not unknown in the animal kingdom.

Soda had developed a lesion in the back of her throat, making it impossible for her to eat on her own. Beth Anne devoted three months to nursing Soda, using a syringe to feed her baby food. Soda could neither lick food nor take it into her mouth herself. With the help of Soda's compassionate vet, Doc Terry, Soda sustained a few relapses from which she recovered through the veterinarian's ingenious use of a Tupperware container fitted as an oxygen tank.

After months of Beth Anne's pureeing Soda's food and feeding her five times a day, Soda's condition worsened. Doc Terry called Beth Anne to say there was nothing more he could do for Soda.

When Beth Anne and John arrived at the vet hospital two hours later, she ran in to where her scared guinea pig struggled for breath. "She hung in there until you got here to say goodbye, Beth Anne. Go ahead and hold her for a while, and then put her back into the oxygen tub."

Beth Anne undid the lid and scooped Soda into her arms. With a sudden burst of energy, Soda climbed up Beth Anne's shirt, snuggled her little muzzle in Beth Anne's neck, and abruptly died.

****

The only reason the author has chosen to include this moment of passing is to reveal the big-heartedness, the forgiving capacity, the true love demonstrated in Soda's last moments. So often humans give credit to the more intelligent creatures, as elephants and whales mourn their mates' and friends' deaths, for instance. Dogs who lose their partners die from broken hearts. Horses who have lost a herd mate wither away. Pigs die, too, from grief. But seldom do we give credit for that same capacity for love, suffering, and grief to a guinea pig or rodent. Yet, clearly, Soda's behavior proved her deep connection to her human companion in her fear-filled moment of death. In those final moments of suffering, Beth Anne's reassuring love, her presence, brought the little guinea pig comfort and contentment enough to slip away to the Rainbow Bridge.

****

Others of Beth Anne's guinea pigs:
Names: Ralph & Adelaide
Both born 2002
Died: June 9, 2002; December 1, 2002
and

Names: Althea & Rosie
Born: December, 2001; unknown
Died: July 18, 2005; November 8, 2004
and
George
Born: September, 2001
Died: 2007

.

In the ensuing days, Whiskey suffered Soda's absence. The guinea pig fell into a depression—again, a psychological state only credited to "higher" species, not to guinea pigs. Whiskey refused to eat. So Beth Anne spent extra time with her and got her two playmates, Althea and Ralph, who helped brighten Whiskey's days.

Althea, a Gus look-alike with white, punked-out hair, eventually developed diabetes, and, thanks to Beth Anne's giving her diabetic medication twice a day and Doc Terry's excellent vigilance, she lived to be four years old, long enough to develop a lasting friendship with George, a rescue pig. But George, a medium-haired, white-brown-and-red pig, looked a little silly next to his girlfriend, Althea, because he was three times bigger than she and weighed in at a whopping four pounds. Giant George became Althea's special friend and both guineas accompanied Beth Anne to the QVC outlet after visiting Doc Terry for their checkups, and they also accompanied Beth Anne to the bank and to the mall.

Years passed, and Beth Anne married, but part of their marital agreement was that Beth Anne could keep her guinea pigs. Her husband loved her pigs.

Beth Anne acquired her next guinea pig as a by-product of human unkindness. While Beth Anne was on nursing duty at a local hospital, a co-worker mentioned she had a guinea pig out in her car in the parking lot. When Beth Anne asked her why she had a pig in her car, she explained with a deadpan face, "It's for my snake—his supper."

Beth Anne stopped her short. "What!" Her face grew red. "You're taking a guinea pig home to feed it to your snake? Over my dead body! I want her! You're giving her to me, not your snake."

The nurse was so flabbergasted by Beth Anne's outburst she agreed without hesitation. With no more than a little shame, she told the other nurses she would just have to feed her snake cat food for the evening.

When Beth Anne took the scared guinea pig home, she reached into the cardboard box and smiled. "Your name is Rosie."

****

Ralph and Adelaide, both sweet, gentle souls, lived less than a year, but in that time they confirmed the love and kindness Beth Anne had first seen in Gus, then Leroy and Squeaky and Soda and Whiskey. Though their lives and the tiny lives of Althea, George, and Rosie were as short as guinea pigs' lives are, they had a happy life with Beth Anne, and they made a kind and loving impact on a hard, unforgiving world.

****

Ralph's, Althea's, Adelaide's, George's, and Rosie's Memorials

Ralph, Althea, Adelaide, George, and Rosie have their photos and loving words written by Beth Anne engraved on their tombstones. They are buried at Cloud Nine Pet Cemetery.

****

Cloud Nine Pet Cemetery is run by Kevin Zerwick: 610-285-2720, www.cloudninepets.com. It is located at 9923 Old Rte. 22, Breinigsville, PA 18031.

Chapter Fifteen
My Dragon Wings

Species: porcine—pot-bellied pig
Name: Reggie
Born: February 26, 1993
Died: November 5, 2007
Human companion: Rebecca DiNolfi

Rebecca's eyes flickered open. "Where in the world am I?" She peered down the long expanse of white covering her body. At the end of the bed stood a person in uniform. Becky tried to speak, but a thick pipe filled her throat, silencing her. Her eyes grew wide—she was in a hospital bed with a breathing tube down her throat. She must have had another heart attack.

The nurse went to Becky's side where she lay, eyes frozen awake. "It's okay, Rebecca. It's Monday, July 26, 1992. You're at Einstein Medical Center in Philadelphia recovering from your catheterization procedure. Don't try to talk. I want you to relax and let this machine do your breathing for you. As soon as we think your heart is stable, we'll remove the tube so that you can breathe on your own and be more comfortable."

Becky closed her eyes.

She remembered her cardiologist had sent her to

Einstein Hospital days ago after she suffered her second heart attack on July 18. With symptoms similar to those of her first attack in 1991, her local doctor advised she seek medical help in Philadelphia, where a catheterization could determine the point of blockage. Now, here she was, hocked up to miles of plastic tubing, the air alive with *bleeps* and *boops* from multiple monitoring equipment. Something must've gone terribly wrong with the catheterization.

The next day the nurses removed her breathing tube, and Becky's friend Joyce was allowed into the room. Joyce's smile was strained. "We almost lost you, kiddo." She took Becky's hand—it had no grip. "Your main descending artery in your heart collapsed after the catheterization. Your heart stopped." Suddenly the smile tore apart, and tears rolled down Joyce's face. Becky reached down her leg with her other hand. She frowned.

"It's a pacemaker. And before you feel what's on your other leg, a balloon is sewn in there, just in case your heart plans to pitch a fit again and they have to do another cath."

"Did I die?" Her lips were dry. She tried licking them, but her tongue was too swollen and limp.

"Yeah, hon. You left us for quite a while. The doctors worked on you for three and a half hours and were just about ready to pack it in when they heard a faint heartbeat."

Becky parted her hospital gown and peered at her chest. Her breath caught at all the burn marks before she whispered, "There's gotta be thirty burns here." She struggled at the sight of herself. "And my left rib cage hurts like hell. My God! I did die."

****

Two weeks later, Becky's husband brought her home, along with a suitcase full of prescriptions. Becky could hardly rest as the doctor had ordered; she was a prisoner to her medication schedule, consuming twenty-seven pills daily—to treat a bleeding ulcer, high blood cholesterol, depression, and unrelenting anxiety attacks. At home, after her husband left for work, Becky felt tied to the clock dictating the hour to take her fourteenth and fifteenth pill. She felt like a jailbird, shackled to her ailing body and her pillboxes. And she was hesitant to leave her house for fear of having another heart attack or a panic attack, which came upon her like some banshee from another dimension. In all, she felt as though her former life, and her spirit, had imploded.

The only thing partially able to distract from her health problems was her love of reading, particularly books about pets and animals. After she read *Lowell: The True Story of an Existential Pig,* a book about pot-bellied pigs that revealed their keen intelligence and devotion to their owners, she asked her husband if she could get one. To her surprise, he said, "Yes."

For the first time in almost a year and a half, since her first heart attack, Becky could concentrate on something other than keeping herself alive. After combing the local newspapers, she finally found a breeder selling a litter of pot-bellied pigs. Wasting no time, she called—one little black female was left.

At four weeks of age, the female piglet was no bigger than a can of baked beans. Becky picked up the tiny black pig. "You're absolutely precious." Holding a piglet was so different from a cat or dog. The piglet had heft—solidity—with a body of pure muscle. Becky gazed into the piglet's face with its dark, wide, human-like eyes and an energetic, curious nose.

When Becky picked up the piggy, the animal didn't squirm or squeal, as most piglets do when their feet leave the ground. This little female must have had a lot of playtime with people because she enjoyed resting in a person's arms. Then Becky felt drawn to cuddle the tiny animal to her face. When she cupped the piglet under the butt and brought her to her chest, the piglet climbed higher, finally snuggling her head under Becky's chin. That gesture sealed the deal. So Becky went home to ready her house for a new pet.

****

Becky's favorite athlete was Reggie White, and even though the piglet was a female, "Reggie" became the piglet's name. At six weeks of age, Reggie sat in Becky's lap for the long trip home where she found a sturdy playpen awaiting her. From the beginning Reggie hated being confined to the playpen, squealing to be free in order to shadow Becky through the house. All day the pair worked together as a duo. At night Reggie went to bed with her human family, Becky curling her arms around her before they fell asleep, face-to-face.

Immediately Reggie became Becky's constant sidekick. The two bonded like Velcro. Becky took the little porker everywhere—to the grocery store, the drugstore, the park where Becky walked Reggie on a tiny harness and lead. And they toured the bank, as well as the shopping mall. When Reggie heard Becky's car keys rattling, the tiny piglet bulleted into the kitchen and stood still as moss while Becky put on her harness and attached the leash.

On a daily basis, Reggie sat in Becky's old Lincoln Continental's passenger's seat on a pile of blankets, her front feet propped on the dashboard, her snout pointed straight ahead, intent on the road. When cars passed on the right, people went crazy. "Look! A little pig! A pig's riding in that car!"

Becky and Reggie spent every hour of every day together, and Becky discovered within only a week or two that Reggie was extremely intelligent. So Becky began teaching her tricks commonly taught to dogs— standing up on her hind legs, kicking a ball into a net, walking a figure eight through Becky's legs. Soon Reggie walked an "S" around a set of cones, rang a bell, played a plastic organ with her nose, and blew horns lined up on a rack. Reggie's repertoire included over thirty tricks.

One day as Becky set out the kiddy organ for Reggie to practice her tunes, she clutched her chest. "Oh, my God!" she yelled. Her husband came running, and Reggie stared up at her mom.

"What? Is it your heart?"

Becky looked amazed. "Yes. It *is* my heart, honey. I haven't given it any medicine yet today because all I've been doing is playing with Reggie. I've forgotten to take all my morning pills. And, come to think of it, I forgot to take most of them yesterday, too."

****

Becky's cardiologist yelled as she lay back onto the examining table. "You got a what?"

"I got myself a pot-bellied pig. Her name is Reggie, and she's my soul mate. I'm so smitten by her I keep forgetting to take most of my pills. And I've never felt better. Reggie has cured all my anxiety and my depression. I've not had a panic attack since I got her. I have energy. I'm happy. I can't wait to start each day. I've taught her tricks—over thirty of them. Ya know, Doctor, she has given me my life back. So do you really think I need all those pills?"

The doctor examined her and reviewed each of her prescriptions. "Your pig apparently has been the *best* medicine for you. You need only take two of these drugs anymore. Throw out the rest. You look good, and your heart sounds fine. See you back here in six months."

****

One day while Reggie was performing her tricks, Becky sensed something was wrong. The little pig just didn't seem as happy nudging out notes on the organ and tooting her horns. "What's the matter, Reggie?" Becky laid a hand on the pig's back. Reggie looked back at her, but her eyes weren't sparkling as usual. Reggie walked over to a horn and blew one single blasé "toot" then went back to Becky and curled quietly in her lap.

"You don't like these silly dog tricks anymore, do you, Reggie?" Reggie looked with soft, sad eyes at her human. "Well, then—we'll get you something to learn that won't bore you to death."

Becky began teaching Reggie the alphabet, using oversized flashcards. She also took Reggie to pot-bellied pig shows at various fairs and festivals. Reggie loved showing off in classes such as the Waggiest Tail Contest, the Snag-the-Donut Contest, the Watermelon-Eating Contest, and the Pretzel-on-a-String Contest. On the final evening of the fair, the pot-bellies dressed in costume for the annual piggy pageant—the girls in gowns and the boys in black satin cummerbunds and bowties.

At public events people went wild seeing Reggie decked out in her signature outfit—a necklace of plastic yellow Black-Eyed Susans, sunglasses with Black-Eyed Susans along the rim, a Black-Eyed Susan on Reggie's tail, and on her head a hat with the front brim pinned up with a yellow Black-Eyed Susan. Adorned from snout to tail, people begged Becky to touch and hold her pig, the size of a loaf of bread. Children, especially, were drawn to Reggie's magnetic and charming personality. With her diminutive upturned snout, she looked as though she wore a continuous grin. If that weren't enough to charm even the most jaded onlooker, Reggie began to perform—tooting the horns, carrying a basket of Black-Eyed Susans balanced on her nose, and leaping through hoops.

Mornings at home, however, were devoted to Reggie's schooling, including practicing the alphabet and learning to differentiate between numbers and colors. In a week's time Reggie had learned to distinguish thirteen of the letters from each other. Reggie found the educational moments intense and was an exceptional student.

In addition to going to festivals, fairs, and various community events, Reggie excelled at therapy work. She made world-worn, nervous people calm and anxious teens laugh with her natural sense of timing, and, for those severely depressed, she coaxed a smile. During therapy work, Reggie's people skills shined— she stood quietly so that people could pet her, staying calm if a dish clanked onto the floor and even if one of the residents pulled her tail.

Reggie loved older folks, so her popularity at Pine Run Nursing Center in Doylestown, Pennsylvania, came as no surprise. Escorted to the community room, Reggie and Becky found themselves in the center of a large room surrounded by dozens of elderly folks in various states of disrepair.

At first sight of a pig dressed in a Black-Eyed Susan costume, the oldsters became suddenly energized, sitting straight and expectant. Frowns disappeared, replaced by grins and bright eyes. A few rolled their wheelchairs right over to Reggie, who didn't flinch at the cumbersome, scary-looking object rolling toward her. First one wrinkled hand, then a couple other thin, parched hands rubbed her head, tentatively at first, then harder, feeling the pig's hair coat—so much rougher, more bristly, than the typical cat or dog that usually visited.

After Reggie let all the residents pet her, she performed her dog tricks, which she hadn't practiced at home for quite a while. Though doing her tricks bored Reggie, she accommodated when she was out in public. The elder crowd, clearly amazed by such a talented animal, clapped and cheered as Reggie finished her thirtieth trick and bowed to the crowd.

Back home, Becky concentrated on teaching Reggie letters of the alphabet. First, Becky flashed a card and pronounced the letter. Reggie stared at the flashcard—concentrating. Becky taught Reggie five letters at a time—all ones that sounded different, so Reggie could distinguish the sounds with the different shapes of the letters. Then, Becky tested her, holding two cards. When Reggie nudged the wrong card, Becky held both cards still. "No, try again, Reggie." Then Becky asked again for the letter, and Reggie nudged the other flashcard, for which Becky rewarded her with a Cheerio.

In a few weeks Reggie had mastered the entire alphabet, even so far as spelling entire words. Becky asked her to spell her own name. "Spell 'Reggie,' Hon." Then, Becky held out the "R" flashcard along with an "N" card. "You want the 'R,' Reggie. Reggie stepped forward and nudged the "R." Becky kept showing Reggie two flashcards at a time, one of which was the next letter in her name. Making no mistake, Reggie spelled her own name in under two minutes.

Reggie delighted in her mother's ecstatic reaction when she got her letters correct. And Becky often marveled how it seemed Reggie actually was thinking—pausing after being asked to pick out a letter, then stepping carefully forward and touching the correct flashcard with her snout. Soon, spelling names became Reggie's signature skill during nursing home visits.

During the hot and humid summer, Becky hated to take Reggie out into the heat for therapy work, so she and Reggie stayed inside where they rehearsed numbers and colors. Summer also gave Becky time for making Reggie's numerous costumes, sewn or hot-glued, with feathers, flowers, sequins, and plastic "jewels"—for Valentine's Day, Memorial Day, St. Patrick's Day, and all the different seasons.

Summertime also found Reggie's family camping at Ringing Rocks Campground every weekend. Often, when her parents weren't watching, Reggie sneaked off to other parts of the camp, intent on making new friends. When Becky discovered Reggie missing, she ran to the campground's office and had them announce on the loudspeaker for all kids on bikes to form a posse to find a lost pig. But Reggie was hardly lost. She was busy "talking" somewhere to any and all campers— *"Hi. I'm the pig here. Nice to meet ya."*

One time Becky adorned Reggie in a hula skirt and lei to protest a pig roast at the campgrounds. Reggie wore a straw skirt and a T-shirt that read, "We are not the other white meat!" Weekends at Ringing Rocks Campground passed all too soon, and once the hot weather broke, Reggie and Becky were back on the road visiting the nursing homes, libraries, public schools, and hospitals.

****

One particularly memorable moment occurred on a visit to an adult day care center. After performing her dog tricks and spelling a couple of the residents' names, Becky and Reggie were set to leave and head to McDonald's for Reggie's favorite treat, French fries.

On their way out of the adult center, they passed a man sitting in an adult high chair. He was slumped over his tray. Reggie stopped at his high chair, and Becky tugged on Reggie's leash. "Come on, Reggie. We're going to McDonald's now." But Reggie wouldn't budge. She stood before the catatonic man in his high chair, his eyes closed, his head down. Becky tugged again, but Reggie refused to move.

Soon a nurse stepped up to them. "Joe has cataracts. Though he still can see, he never opens his eyes when he's inside the building. He *never* opens his eyes."

Becky pulled on Reggie's leash again, but Reggie

stood firm. Reggie poked the man's thin ankle with her snout. No response. Becky pulled on Reggie's leash. No response.

The nurse leaned toward Joe. "Joe, there's a pot-bellied pig here to see you. Open your eyes and look at the pig." But Joe refused, sitting stolid, impenetrable.

Reggie nudged his leg again and let out a loud grunt. Finally, Joe sat up, opened his eyes, and looked over his tray at the floor. Reggie looked up, and when he saw the little black pig wearing her Black-Eyed Susan sunglasses, he started to laugh and laugh and laugh. He laughed so hard tears poured down his cheeks. The nurse marveled that it was the first time Joe had ever opened his eyes inside.

Not only did Reggie startle Joe out of his blind stupor, but she also performed a couple of other miracles during her therapy travels. At the Woods School, a live-in facility for the severely disabled, one blind and mute male resident whose depression made him nasty and difficult to handle always looked forward to Reggie's visit. Each time Reggie saw Stan, she stood up on her hind feet, her front feet on his knees, and let out a loud grunt-greeting. In that moment Stan instantly morphed from an unsociable, almost sociopathic personality into a friendly one. The nurses always commented how Stan was so much happier and so much more agreeable after Reggie's visit.

While Reggie treated the severely depressed and the elderly by day, by late afternoon and evening she was back studying her flashcards. In between visits to nursing homes, studying, and visiting schools, Reggie managed the time to earn $15,000 for a charity in a Kiss the Pig contest. Libraries, too, asked for Reggie's services, and Becky, with Reggie's help, began putting on educational shows.

Each show began with Becky introducing Reggie to her audience. Like the good, attentive pig she was, Reggie always greeted her audiences by lifting a front leg and waving her hoof. Then as Reggie waited, wearing one of her many outfits—bunny, Valentine's Day, Tina Turner, clown, or elf—Becky explained where Reggie came from and what she did as a therapy pig. Becky always varied Reggie's performance to prevent boredom.

As Reggie performed, Becky taught children and adults the history of the pot-bellied pig as well as reading them scientific documentation on their intelligence. She dispelled the myths about pigs being dirty, slow, and slovenly. Last, she advised her audience how the pot-bellied pig made a fine companion animal. She described her efforts to remove the pot-bellied pig from livestock status in towns' zoning laws and, instead, be accepted as a companion pet. She urged audiences to support laws allowing pet pigs companion-animal status.

The most amazing feat Reggie ever accomplished was not only identifying numbers from her flashcards but adding and subtracting them, too. Unbelievable though it may seem, Reggie, given two flashcards, could add them or subtract them. Becky herself couldn't believe Reggie began adding and subtracting, but it happened by accident one day while they were practicing Reggie's flashcards in the living room.

"Do you think you can add two numbers, Reggie?" Becky held up a 1 and a 2. Do you know what 1 and 2 add up to?" Then she held up two flashcards, one with 3 and the other with 9. Without being given any cues, something Becky never did anyway, Reggie paused, then stepped toward the 3 and nudged it. Pure coincidence, Becky thought. Surely a pig couldn't add numbers, so she tried it again and again. Only a few times did Reggie make a mistake.

Once Becky discovered Reggie could add and, later, even subtract, she included those talents in Reggie's performances. Her ability to do simple math problems stunned her audiences. Becky reminded folks that since pigs had the intelligence of a three-year-old child, perhaps it wasn't all that miraculous that Reggie was able to do math. "But Reggie really hates doing fractions," she said, laughing.

During another performance, Becky walked into the audience, leaving Reggie on stage, and asked a child to pick out a flashcard printed with a giant colored crayon. After the child picked out one color from the stack, Becky showed the card to the audience and took that card, along with one other, back on stage where Reggie waited. Becky warned the youngster-audience, "Now, don't say the color's name out loud." Everyone was dead quiet. Could Reggie read minds? Then Becky held the chosen color out alongside a card with another color. "Pick the color your friend Cindy and the audience is thinking of, Reggie."

At first, Reggie hung back, not too anxious to commit herself to a color she couldn't even see. Becky chuckled to herself. She believed Reggie was searching for vibes from the audience. A minute passed, and the audience began whispering, for they could see Reggie concentrating, too. Then, as Becky held the two colored flashcards at Reggie's nose-level, Reggie stepped forward and hit the blue card. The little girl in the audience jumped up, squealing, her hands cupping her mouth while the audience clapped and cheered.

By 1995, Becky began fighting Pennsylvania's city councils' ordinances against keeping pigs, considered livestock, as companion animals in city homes. So afraid was she of losing her own Reggie to an outdated town law that she became an avid activist for allowing pet pigs in households. So while Reggie's main work as a therapy pig and an entertainer continued, she also supported, alongside Becky, the fight against the pot-bellied pig being considered not a pet but only livestock. The more people saw how civilized a pig could be, the more inclined town council members would be to pass laws accommodating pigs as pets.

Despite Reggie's good-natured personality, she was no pushover, neither at home nor in public. At home she could be a brat if she didn't get her way. If Becky didn't arrive home promptly to give Reggie her dinner, Reggie, in no subtle way, informed her of her displeasure—she began flipping the dining room chairs and rearranging the furniture. If Becky was talking on the phone and Reggie discovered her water dish empty, she began rubbing her snout on something, making a loud rasping noise, almost like chalk squeaking on a chalkboard. When Reggie opened the back sliding-glass door to go outside to relieve herself, she never closed it, letting in scores of bugs and, one time, a squirrel. Becky's friends and relatives all knew Reggie could be a "pistol" when she wanted.

Even when she was in public, she wasn't fawning or submissive. Though she loved most folks, she approached them with porcine dignity, her head held high, almost aloof. For sure, Reggie knew she had a higher purpose and that she was special in many ways. She loved every minute of her interaction with people, but she would have no silliness and disliked any tone of voice sounding like mockery.

On a couple of occasions, after Becky dressed Reggie in her signature Black-Eyed Susan costume and sunglasses, Reggie would rush against a wall, trying to knock off her glasses. Then she picked them up in her jaws and bit down, breaking them in half. Reggie was pissed off, but Becky didn't know why. After Reggie destroyed six more pairs of glasses, Becky finally called the animal communicator. The communicator came to Becky's house and "talked" with Reggie. She revealed Reggie hated the glasses because she looked so silly in them that people laughed at her. From then on Becky never made Reggie wear glasses again.

In 1995 the mayor of Philadelphia, Ed Rendell, judged a pot-bellied pig beauty contest in honor of the opening of the Broadway show "State Fair"—a show about a pig winning first place at the fair—at the Merriam Theatre on Broad Street in downtown Philly. The swiners, all costumed, paraded down a red carpet, and Mayor Rendell judged each for the best costume. Reggie was dressed in her finest—a sequined gown with a fur stole.

Becky also hoped that, by introducing Reggie to the mayor and showing him how well-behaved and well-mannered she was, he might influence change to the antiquated livestock laws in Philadelphia. This meeting triggered Becky's becoming an activist for families cited for breaking the livestock laws simply because they chose a pot-belly as a pet.

After their meeting with Rendell, Becky, with Reggie in tow, climbed the City Hall stairs to the top floor where they "crashed" the City Council meeting. With Reggie representing the pot-bellied pig community, Becky intended to convince council members that pot-belly pigs make great pets. But no sooner had they stepped inside the council chambers than Becky and Reggie were escorted away. A crew from TV Channel Seventeen had been filming the council proceedings and followed Becky and Reggie out into the hall. There on Philly TV, alongside Reggie dressed in her signature outfit, Becky made the case for removing the pet pig from livestock laws.

Becky's cause eventually took Reggie to a Shelton, Connecticut, courtroom in 1996 for a zoning appeal hearing in which a decision was handed down to uphold the existing livestock laws, thus forbidding pet pigs as companion animals. The defendant, who was willing to go to jail to keep her pet pigs, lost her bid against the city livestock laws and was fined $25,000 for having two pot-bellied pigs. Because she was unable to pay the fines, a lien was put against her house. Though Becky and Reggie were escorted out of the courtroom, a photographer took their photo standing proudly on the courthouse steps, a photo which later won the journalist a first-place award in photo-journalism. And the TV news documentary show *20/20* featured the Shelton, Connecticut case in a segment on "Bad Laws in America." Weeks later, Reggie appeared on the TV show *America's Greatest Pets*.

For the next several years, Reggie continued her therapy work and entertaining in elementary schools, hospitals, and nursing homes. Every night, exhausted from such a heavy schedule, Reggie fell asleep, as usual, in her mom's arms, their noses touching. And every night Becky thanked Reggie for all she had done to change her life and inspire other people.

Though pigs may not have wings, Reggie gave Becky wings that allowed her to soar in so many different directions, all of them positive and beneficial to both herself and humans. Scott, a good friend, once commented, "Reggie is the dragon, and you are her rider." Indeed, Reggie was Becky's Earth Angel, who protected her and let her ride until Becky could manage alone.

Not only did Becky and others benefit from Reggie's inspiration, but Reggie earned many kudos for herself. In 1997 *Life Magazine* paid her a special tribute in their *Celebrating Our Heroes* Collector's Edition by acknowledging her as a world hero. One out of 2,000 animals to earn the Delta Society's Animal Therapy designation and for being one of twenty-eight animals nominated for the 1996 Therapy Animal of the Year Award, Reggie took her place beside both human and animal heroes of all time. Among others in *Life Magazine's* special edition, Reggie shared her award with human heroes—Abe Lincoln, Eleanor Roosevelt, Colin Powell, Amelia Earhart, John Wayne, Mother Teresa, and Tecumseh. And among other animal heroes, Reggie shared the limelight with the head sled dog Balto, deliverer of life-saving diphtheria antitoxin to victims in Nome, Alaska; Binti Jua, a gorilla who saved a three-year-old who fell into the gorilla exhibit at an Illinois zoo; GI Joe, a carrier pigeon that flew a valuable message to a U.S. airbase in WWII; and Scarlet, a calico mother cat who carried each of her five kittens to safety from a fire.

Becky always credits Reggie with having inspired her to be an activist against livestock laws. Without Reggie she may not even have lived to realize that dream. Though she doubted the abilities of people to read animals' minds, she studied the practice herself and considered herself an animal communicator. Without Reggie, Becky claims, she would have been a rather ordinary person.

Reggie died November 5, 2007.

****

Reggie's Memorial

Becky's entire house is a memorial to Reggie.

Reggie's portrait festoons the walls in Becky's home. Her picture is displayed everywhere inside in various poses—looking up at the mayor of Philadelphia, peering from the driver's side window of her Lincoln Continental, sitting in her mother's lap, participating in a kissing contest, lying amongst the wildflowers, taking a snack from Becky's hand, Reggie and Becky parked at the drive-in movies, and many others.

Tucked into a corner of Becky DiNolfi's living room is a memory spot with many, but certainly not all, of Reggie's mementoes and awards. Behind her box of ashes sits the photo of her *Life Magazine* hero honor— her leaning over a barn Dutch door wearing a smile as wide as the door opening itself. Various stones and a pyramidal crystal surround her box—all meant to protect and help her spirit transition into the next world. And a rose quartz stone, signifying love, is one of them.

On another table sit several photographs of Reggie wearing her Black-Eyed Susan hat and necklace, along with photos of Becky hugging Reggie. Her black harness with her registration medal from the Delta Society, which she earned on January 1996, sits next to the cremains box, and next to it, a sculpture of a pig with wings. Nearby sit Reggie's flashcards with a ceramic book and plaque Reggie received on two different occasions as Random Acts of Kindness awards.

Among all the awards and accolades Reggie received during her lifetime, the most meaningful, perhaps, is a poem Becky wrote in Reggie's honor, entitled, "The Touch of Love":

As I lie on the couch my hand drifts down to feel the rough bristles on my

Potbellied

Pig Reggie.

She is the scratchy feel of love and companionship that only we can share.

My Reggie and I have passed through many trials and tribulations over the years

She has taught me so much about the real meaning of why we are here on this planet.

She asks nothing in return for all the love and laughter she abounds.

She is my Guardian Angel in a little chubby, black, bristled body,

So even though she is not soft and furry,

Her heart sure is.

It's about what we gave, not what we got.

****

In the dining room hangs an oil painting Becky painted of Reggie in the same pose as the *Life Magazine* photo. In the bathroom sit various pig figurines, and in the bedroom hang photos of Reggie doing her flashcard tricks during the Fourth of July show at Big Bass Lake in the Poconos, as well as photos of Reggie peering out from Becky's decorated pig mobile, the car they used for traveling to pig events. Also, in the bedroom hang photos of Reggie dressed in her beauty pageant gown and meeting Mayor Ed Rendell again.

Reggie's entire life—her accomplishments, her personality, her socializing skills, her intelligence, her love of her mom and other people—is memorialized on most every wall of Becky's home because Reggie, a pig who gave Becky her life back and offered disadvantaged and not-so-disadvantaged people moments of happiness, deserves a tribute of no less magnitude.

****

Of Reggie, Becky wrote, "She made me who I am today and gave me the courage to persevere under extreme circumstances that I thought would end my life. She gave me a reason to live and get out of bed every day. We lived an amazing life together. She brought me in contact with the most wonderful friends anyone could ever hope to have. I am so grateful she was sent to me to share my life even if it was for such a short time. She taught me so much.

"I have been able to accept the gifts she brought to me. She was definitely my soul mate. She taught me what is really important in this life and time. She taught me unconditional love, acceptance, patience, guts, courage. She taught me to laugh, but, most of all, she taught me how to live my life out loud."

****

Rebecca DiNolfi died in 2016. I am sure she and Reggie are cuddled together beyond the Rainbow Bridge. My tribute to both these exceptional beings appears on my blogsite:

www.adventureswithanimals.blogspot.com.

Chapter Sixteen
Feline Felicities: Memoirs from the Windowsill

Species: feline—domestic shorthair
Names: Greta & Hildy
Born: Greta, April 19, 1992; Hildy, July 10, 1996
Died: Greta, 2007; Hildy, 2005
Human companion: Marcia Lauf

On a cold rainy day, Marcia decided to visit a Chicago animal shelter and adopt a feline companion. Most of the kittens she talked to crawled, frightened, to the back of their cages Off in a corner, however, a kitten sat alert and eager at the front of her kennel. She watched Marcia as she peered into each cage. Marcia went over, stooped down to the kitten's level, and began to talk to the mostly white kitten. The second she bent down, however, the animal went ballistic, spitting and clawing at Marcia through the cage bars. Marcia retreated, glanced around at the other shy cats and kittens, then back at the white kitten, who was still hissing. She called an attendant over. "I want a kitten with personality. I'll take her."

Marcia learned from the shelter people that when she was a month old, Greta had been plucked from the jowls of a German shepherd and barely survived. In addition, Greta's history revealed moments of being abused and kicked, so it was no wonder Greta was hardly a loving cat when Marcia brought her home. In fact, Greta was downright nasty, charging from behind a dining table leg and leaping, like a wild thing, at her legs. She played offense like a celebrity football player—her take-downs on target. In fact, Marcia couldn't even dress for work *inside* her house. If Greta was in one of her nasty moods, she rushed her, clawing big runs in her hosiery. So every day before work Marcia pulled her pantyhose on in the car.

Anyone else would have taken Greta and her inhospitable temper back to the shelter, but not Marcia. Despite Greta's aggressive temperament, Marcia treated her with kindness and love, asking her to sit in her lap, which, of course, Greta wasn't ready to do, and offering her treats and catnip toys. Greta, however, wouldn't be bribed. She would allow Marcia to cozy with her only when she was good and ready.

For the first six weeks Marcia needed a medieval suit of armor when dealing with Greta, for the cat ran after her, her front paws splayed, ready to slice and dice her legs like a cut cantaloupe. Greta resembled a manic can opener, but Marcia's evasive tactics worked. She scooted sideways, talked to Greta, and laughed at her until the cat decided to lighten up. Though Greta barely tolerated Marcia's attempts to pet her, she *did* like the warmth Marcia's body emitted while she slept. So, each night after Marcia scurried under the covers and fell asleep, Greta jumped up on the bed and curled up next to Marcia's legs.

All too often, however, Marcia was stabbed awake by Greta sinking her teeth into her human's calves and feet. Marcia tolerated Greta's biting her feet and legs only a few times before she had had enough. So she got out the heavy artillery—her old cowboy boots. From then on Marcia's bedtime routine changed. She took a shower, donned her nightie, brushed her teeth, put on her cowboy boots, and slid under the bedcovers. No matter how hard Greta tried to bite, she couldn't sink her teeth through the tough leather.

When Greta reached nine months of age, she began to trust Marcia more, though she still didn't allow Marcia to pick her up. She was an independent spirit, and though she enjoyed a warm lap from which to watch television, she accepted that lap on her own terms. Finding a friend in the species that had abused her was hard-learned.

Little by little, Greta began to forgive. She sat with Marcia as she ate her cereal, sitting patiently next to the breakfast bowl while Marcia finished the last flake. Then Marcia tipped the dish for her to lap the rest of the milk. If it was a weekend, Greta sometimes jumped into Marcia's lap for a marathon television viewing. And she always slept with Marcia, which her mom didn't mind, even though Greta became a blanket hog. If Marcia moved toward the edge of the bed, Greta moved tighter against Marcia's legs. Depending on the night and how many turns she made, Marcia found herself clawing the edge of the bed with Greta hogging three-quarters of the bed for herself.

Despite Greta's growing trust, she still was wary of people. For instance, one evening Marcia rushed her to the veterinary emergency room because she thought Greta had something stuck in her throat. In the vet's waiting room the two sat amongst five burly men attached to their equally burly dogs—a shepherd, a Rottweiler, a pit bull, and two mixed breeds. A veterinary technician came out to the waiting room, picked up Greta, who was wrapped up in a blanket, and took her to an examination room. Marcia, a bit squeamish about medical issues, had decided to wait out in the room with the logging crew and their macho dogs. In a few minutes, the technician came back to the waiting room with Greta blanketed in her arms.

Greta was wearing a muzzle.

The guys snickered. "Gads, I thought my hundred-pound dog would be the one wearing a muzzle. I can't believe they had to muzzle a little cat."

Marcia laughed, taking the muzzled Greta into her arms. "Yeah. She can be pretty feisty. I was wondering who was going to draw blood first—the vet or Greta."

****

One night, in order to protect the hand she'd had operated on, Marcia decided to sleep downstairs. So she strapped on her cowboy boots and went back downstairs to the living room sofa, where she drew the afghan up to her chin. She had just about fallen asleep when she felt Greta jump onto the couch. Marcia opened her eyes and watched as Greta, in the twilight of the night, began to creep between Marcia's legs. Then she very slowly slinked up Marcia's body, circled once, and curled up on her chest. The whole night Greta slept on Marcia's chest. Marcia was thrilled—the barrier had finally given way.

****

When Greta was four years old, Marcia's veterinarian had delivered a litter of kittens from a feral mother cat. He called her, begging for help with raising the kittens. He was going to spay the mother and let her be released back to the wild as part of the "Trap and

Release" Program. So Marcia decided to help out. She and another volunteer took turns bottle-feeding the babies. Even while the babies were only two days old, Marcia already knew she had to adopt the only female in the group. And at five weeks, she brought Hildy, whom she named after her mother, home to share company with her and Greta.

Hildy, an all-black kitten with a white speck beneath her chin, was an immediate hit with Greta. Greta had someone of her own to talk with instead of the neighbors who passed below her bedroom window each morning and evening. Hildy, too, took to the older Greta who, no doubt, surely thought Hildy must be her natural daughter, for all the fussing and licking Greta made over Hildy's jet-black coat.

One of the first things Greta showed Hildy in her tour through the courtyard building's apartment was the bedroom windowsill where Greta spent hours gazing into the tenants' back yards. From her windowsill she watched all eighteen neighbors come and go from their back porches. During the summer Greta was her neighborhood's furry rooster, waking everyone by six in the morning with her deep-throated *"yeow-ow-owl."* From twenty feet below Greta's window, the neighbors conversed with her—scolding her for awakening them or wishing her a good day or asking what she was planning to do that afternoon.

Though Greta loved to talk, she could never persuade the more reticent Hildy to join her in cat conversation. Though Hildy, too, learned to enjoy the view from the bedroom windowsill, she didn't have Greta's vociferous personality. Because Greta was so loud, a concerned neighbor even asked Marcia's veterinarian whether there was something wrong with Greta. The vet, knowing Greta and Marcia well, assured Marcia's neighbor nothing was wrong with Greta other than she was a talker and one spoiled kitty.

While Greta was the loud independent feline in Marcia's home, Hildy remained speechless, preferring to bat around her favorite ball and chew on a catnip-stuffed toy rather than sing out the window screen and be the talk of the neighborhood. But Hildy was curious and longed for her place on the windowsill. Soon two sets of eyes peered twenty feet down at Marcia's neighbors. One neighbor shuddered. "Those eyes give me the willies." One could only imagine how creeped out the neighbors felt when Greta shrieked in her "murdered woman" voice.

Hildy was, by far, the more loving cat, always curling up next to Marcia for an afternoon of television. Because she protected Marcia, licking her neck clean and head-butting her as is the way of an affectionate feline, Marcia always helped her retrieve lost balls and stuffed toys from under the furniture. Hildy the Demure guarded Marcia around the house when she wasn't sleeping with Greta or gazing down from the windowsill onto the courtyard below.

The human and her cats safeguarded each other. In the dead of winter, with five inches of snow on the ground, Marcia, wrapped in a Victorian rose comforter and scruffy slippers, stood on the back porch, smoking her cigarettes. Several times a day her neighbors saw her on the porch taking another drag. Bundled up outside, she looked cold and miserable, but her bad habit forced her to muster the courage against the elements. Mr. Loo, a neighbor from across the courtyard, asked why she always stood on the back porch to smoke her cigarettes. He knew she didn't have any other family members living with her. "I can't smoke in the house. My cat has asthma." And he laughed, thinking she was silly, but Marcia didn't think herself silly at all. She would do whatever she had to do to help Hildy's asthma.

Marcia always marveled at how the two very different cats formed an immediate bond. While Greta became Hildy's surrogate mother and protector, Hildy taught Greta some things, too. Hildy, along with Marcia, taught Greta that good humans could be trusted and befriended. She taught Greta how to love and accept a human. She taught her that sometimes humans redeem themselves with kindness.

Greta died in 2007. Hildy died in 2005.

****

Greta's and Hildy's Memorial

Marcia Lauf sneaked around the corner of her dining room buffet to snap a photo of her two cats cuddling each other atop their cat castle. Greta, the larger of the two, had her arm draped over little Hildy's shoulder. Obviously the two cats loved each other, found comfort in each other's presence, and cherished falling asleep in each other's arms.

After Greta died, Marcia decided she wanted to pay her two girls the highest tribute—cast them in an art form that would portray their sense of family and love. So she took the photo of the cats in their cat castle to a tattoo artist and had him render that photo as a tattoo on her arm.

Marcia remembers her decision to tattoo her upper arm with Greta and Hildy. "The picture depicts not only their love for each other, [but] it also shows our relationship as a family. Happy, secure, and loving. I had the tattoo made because I want[ed] to keep that feeling and honor two cats who were totally different, yet brought me such joy."

Today, wherever she goes, Marcia has her two cats with her—wherever Marcia is, wherever she goes.

Marcia paid another tribute to her cat Hildy. After Hildy died, Marcia, with permission of her priest, took Hildy's ashes to her church's cemetery where Marcia's mother was buried. Marcia had named her cat after her mother, so when Marcia knelt at the grave with Hildy's ashes, she told her mother she was putting on her grave the ashes of her only grandchild named after her. In Marcia's church's cemetery, the two Hildys lie together in peace.

Chapter Seventeen
On a Hosta High

Species: feline—domestic shorthair
Name: Ebee
Born: August 1986
Died: January 22, 2002
Human companion: Sharon Lilla

Ebee came into Sharon's life by accident. When Sharon first lived in a country cottage in the cozy town of Lyons, fourteen miles from Lake Ontario in upstate New York, she periodically spied a black-and-white male cat scouting her property. Sharon, who had loved cats as a child, found Tough Guy, as she named him, fascinating. He walked her four-hundred-foot driveway as though he owned the place, yet he was, at first, tentative when she called to him. Such a Sumo cat should have had an equivalent ton of courage, but, in fact, Tough Guy was shy and wary of people. Still, every morning, according to his internal "clock," he strolled up the driveway after probably having spent the night alone and hungry in the old dilapidated barn across the street. And every morning he found a dish of tuna fish awaiting him.

On the third day as Sharon saw Tough Guy crest over the hill, she waited. As he padded closer, she crouched down and whispered for him to come over and talk with her for a while. And, as though he knew exactly what she was saying, he marched right over and rubbed against her hand. Tough Guy wasn't feral—he was just a lost soul in search of a home.

So she and Tough Guy talked about his day, what he did last night, and if he had caught a mouse to eat lately. He looked her in the eye, tilted his head, and then let out one high-pitched *"Re-ow-ow-ow-ow!"* While they chatted, she offered him three small pieces of chicken, which he devoured in three gulps. After a week of breakfast outings, Tough Guy became a semi-resident at Sharon's home, appearing early in the morning for his breakfast, hanging around all day, and then disappearing as dusk blanketed the land.

Tough Guy was hardly a tough guy. Once friends, she discovered he was more of a gentle giant. With his big, round, sweet face, he proved himself a pussycat in so many ways—cozying up to Sharon on the porch swing, rubbing his forehead against hers, and licking her hands. What she found particularly enchanting, too, was the way he conversed with her. On any morning, she set his dish of cat food before him and then asked how his evening had been. Then Tough Guy answered, murmuring and muttering in cat language, *"Myum, myum, myum"* and *"Re-ow, Re-ow, Re-ow."* Whenever she asked if he was hungry, he said in soft, short bursts, *"Ow!—ow!—ow!"* He had an answer for everything. Still, for all the intimate conversation and offers of food, every evening he walked back down the driveway to sleep in his abandoned barn.

One early summer afternoon while Sharon was outside snipping stalks of Russian sage for a bouquet, she saw Tough Guy walking up the driveway, another cat in tow. She stood up and called to him, and he marched right up to her, his girlfriend fearless by his side. Taking her courage from Tough Guy's cue, the female cozied immediately to Sharon, and she, too, lapped up a dish full of cat food.

For weeks Tough Guy and Wanda made daily breakfast trips to Sharon's cottage. Each time Wanda ate as though she hadn't eaten in days, and Sharon thought, considering the size of her belly, that she should cut back on the amount she was feeding the two cats. One day Tough Guy came by without Wanda. Worried, Sharon bent down. "Where's your woman, Tough Guy?" He murmured something that sounded as though he had things completely under control. Later that day when Sharon went out to sweep her front porch, she found her answer. There, in one of the Adirondack chairs, Wanda had had a litter of kittens.

All five kittens looked like Tough Guy—black and white—and because early summer could fashion cool nights, Sharon retrieved a cardboard box and blanket as a nest for Wanda and her brood. Several times a day Sharon visited with the babies when they weren't sleeping. She talked to them and held them close to her face so that she could smell their sweet breaths. As the weeks went by, Wanda, Tough Guy and their kittens became Sharon's feline family.

When the kittens were one month of age, Sharon put them and their parents into pet carriers for a trip to the veterinarian to get physicals and shots. During the exams Sharon was devastated to learn that both Tough Guy and Wanda tested positive for feline leukemia. Sharon's eyes brimmed with tears when the vet told her no cure existed for the lethal disease. Only treatments with interferon and anti-virals could extend a Fe-leuk-positive cat's life for four to seven years. The vet smiled, despite the diagnosis. "The good thing is that none of the kittens have it. The adults will probably live for a while until the disease catches up with them."

Sharon eventually found homes for three of the kittens but kept two for herself—Ebee, a solid black kitten with a little white under her chin, and her sister, Abbey, who looked more like her calico mother. Ebee's personality most closely resembled her gentle giant father, Tough Guy. Just as he was a lover boy and luxuriated in having the backs of his ears scratched and his chin rubbed, so did little Ebee, stretching out her neck to make it easier for Sharon to rub.

Sharon's life with Ebee and Abbey was tranquil. The cats became her tonic after a hard, fast-paced day at work—their laid-back attitude rubbing off on Sharon. Abbey wasn't quite as affectionate as Ebee, who loved cuddling and being held, so Sharon often scooped Ebee up and paraded her around the yard, showing her the clusters of impatiens bordering the maple trees and the rows of Echinacea. Sharon even found some wild catnip Ebee drooled over. During their garden walks Ebee settled back into Sharon's arms as though she were lying in a hammock and stared into Sharon's eyes with a tranquil gaze. On some days Sharon walked Ebee below the cottage along Ganargua Creek where the sound of the trickling water mesmerized Ebee. In Sharon's arms Ebee personified peace.

Unfortunately, one day little Abbey was attacked by a feral tomcat. Sharon saw no wounds; otherwise, she would have rushed her to the vet. In a few days she suddenly became listless, and on the way to the vet, she died. Without her best feline friend, Ebee became even more attached to her human friend.

In six months Ebee was firmly entrenched in Sharon's household, and Wanda and Tough Guy were still making their daily trips up Sharon's driveway. But one day Tough Guy came to breakfast alone. Sharon thought he looked a little thin, and when she set his bowl of food in front of him, he was less than enthusiastic about it. Without finishing it, he walked back down the driveway, muttering and murmuring to himself as he went.

The next day Sharon worried when Tough Guy again walked alone up her driveway. In fact, Sharon never saw Wanda again. Days later Tough Guy came staggering down the driveway. He was weak and bone-thin. Sharon rushed him to the vet, who said the leukemia was finally killing him. Cradled in Sharon's arms, the gentle giant, Tough Guy, talked to Sharon as she tried to console him through her tears. He murmured to her in cat whispers until the vet injected the euthanasia solution. Then his voice fell silent.

****

Ebee perpetuated her father's chatty, kind disposition. Ebee was a loving spirit and Sharon's best friend. Everywhere Sharon went, Ebee accompanied her—to the kitchen, to the toilet, into the dining room where she shared Sharon's dinner, on the couch in front of the TV, outside in the flower gardens. While Sharon raked and picked sticks fallen during the winter, Ebee sat close—watching, muttering she would help if Sharon had a shovel just her size.

Whenever Sharon gathered her hoe and hand trowel, Ebee grew excited—she loved gardening. When she knew they were going outside, her eyes sparkled, and she did pirouettes, urging Sharon to *Hurry! Hurry! We're going outside!* Then she raced for the creek where she looked intently at the water and then, very carefully, raised one paw, dipped it into the water, and licked it, savoring the taste of the pure liquid. At the water's edge Ebee played for hours, scouting for bugs and stalking butterflies until she heard her mother calling.

Once in the gardens she darted from one bush to another. With her body low to the ground, her claws digging the earth, she raced under the porch, then out the other side, where she stood huffing and puffing and smelling the air. When a large bug buzzed past, its wings laboring under its own weight, Ebee danced after it, leaping four feet into the air as it tried to escape. Though Ebee was a cool, calm kitten inside the cottage, content to lie in her mom's lap, outside she became a *premiere danseuse*, spinning and flipping, leaping and laughing, a mischievous elf of nature.

Six months later Sharon loaded Ebee into the car for their move to a house on a hill overlooking Sodus Bay and Lake Ontario. Thrilled with the lure of adventure, Ebee peered from the car window as they drove through forests of pine and oak. Ebee couldn't believe her eyes and her nose. The smell of the pines was soothing, the air crisp, and the smell of the lake cool and pure.

Ebee loved her new home, especially the pine-scented trees. And she could climb them nearly as fast as any squirrel. A natural athlete, she could leap from the ground and land five feet up a tree, hopping, pulling, and stretching herself onto a particularly inviting branch. Most of all she loved her new deck, from which she protected her mom from intruders like rabbits, moles, and butterflies.

At some time Ebee discovered a special place where she could have the best of all worlds—be close to Sharon, be protected from animals larger and stronger than she, and still have a full view of the bay and lake. She found a large hosta plant to make her own. On days Sharon puttered in the garden, Ebee directed the day's activities from under her hosta. On days when Sharon was away, Ebee cherished the tranquility found beneath the hosta's big shady umbrella leaves.

Not only did Ebee love to help Sharon with outdoor chores, now that they had moved to an even more remote property, but she also loved watching Sharon get ready for work each morning. While Sharon showered, Ebee curled up in the sink and waited for her mom to finish. Then Ebee followed Sharon into the bedroom where she watched her dress. When Sharon went back to the bathroom to dry her hair, Ebee trotted behind, for this was the best part of the morning ritual—the hair dryer.

At the sound of the dryer's motor, Ebee leaped onto Sharon's jeans, all four feet clinging to the fabric. Not unlike a lumberjack scaling a tree, Ebee had built-in spikes in her "shoes." The first time Ebee jumped on Sharon's leg and started crawling up her torso, Sharon worried about being scratched, but Ebee was careful not to let her claws hurt Sharon's skin. Soon the trick became a habit. With the roar of the hair dryer, Ebee leaped, sticking like Velcro to Sharon's pants leg. Then she ran up the Sharon-tree, hooking her claws into

Sharon's sweater and pulling herself toward Sharon's shoulders. Most people wouldn't have tolerated such boldness from a cat, but Sharon was used to it—liked it, in fact, because of how it would all end.

After Sharon turned off the dryer, Ebee, already clinging to Sharon's chest, continued north. Once at Sharon's head, she wrapped her arms around her neck in a grand kitty hug. Then Ebee tucked her head underneath Sharon's chin, and, in that position, Sharon walked her best feline friend around the house—their good-bye dance until Sharon came home from work.

Just as Ebee craved closeness with Sharon before work, so she felt the same way at bedtime. At bedtime Ebee was hardly content to sleep at the foot of the bed or by Sharon's side. She had to be snuggled against Sharon's head. Because Ebee insisted on sharing Sharon's pillow, Sharon found herself without much support for her own head. Ebee was a "pillow pilferer." So Sharon bought Ebee her own head rest.

Ebee loved having her own pillow, and each night after Sharon lay on her back to fall asleep, Ebee jumped onto the bed, walked up alongside Sharon, went up to her own pillow right behind Sharon's pillow, and curled around several times, scrunching the pillow with her paws, kneading the lumps from it. Finally, she lay on her properly adjusted pillow, heaved a big sigh, and stuck out her paws, settling them atop Sharon's forehead. Every night unfolded the same ritual—Sharon lay on her back, Ebee curled up, Ebee rested her paws across Sharon's forehead. Then they both fell asleep.

In the morning Ebee was always famished because sleeping was serious work for a cat. If Sharon didn't get up promptly, Ebee gave the weary rester no peace.

Already curled at Sharon's head and with her paws draped across her forehead, she first slapped Sharon's forehead with one paw. If Sharon didn't respond, she reached her paw out, stuck out a claw, hooked it gently at the edge of Sharon's nostril, and tugged on it. Sharon knew, then, to wake up, for Ebee's next signal would not be nearly as subtle.

Two things Ebee loved besides a timely breakfast were being vacuumed and being blow-dried. Whenever Sharon vacuumed the carpets, Ebee followed, anxious for her vacuum-bath. She lay on her back, her feet in the air, and Sharon took the small head of the cleaner and let it suck her body and back all over. No doubt Ebee felt much as though she were being given a massage because she extended her arms and legs in order for Sharon to reach easily all the hard-to-reach areas. Each weekly carpet cleaning ended with Ebee's being suctioned by the vacuum.

So, too, did she enjoy being blasted with the blow-dryer though she didn't care for air blown in her face. Of course, the blow-drying happened after the big hug and parade around the bathroom and bedroom. Sharon warned her before turning it on, and then when she heard the machine roar, she knew she was in for a treat. Her fur flew, whipping this way and that as the warm air hit her body. Then she lay on her back on the bathroom counter, her legs extended, her chin up and back, her lips cranked back into a smile as Sharon directed the warm air over every nook and cranny.

Life with Ebee at the edge of Lake Ontario was idyllic. Ebee was all about friendship and love, and she was affectionate with other people, as well as Sharon, though her all-time fave was Sharon. One year Sharon left home for a month, so, reluctantly, Ebee roomed with one of Sharon's friends in upstate New York. Sharon missed her sweet ebony-furred buddy during her time away, but thirty days passed quickly. As Sharon drove home, she just hoped she would be coming home to the same loving, quirky cat she had left.

When Sharon pulled into the friend's driveway, she called out Ebee's name. No Ebee. As Sharon hurried toward the house, suddenly a black bullet came speeding around the corner of the house. It was Ebee. Just as she had done every morning while Sharon dried her hair, she leaped onto Sharon's legs and climbed her body to her face. When she arrived at Sharon's chin, she wrapped her arms around her neck and laid her head under her chin. It was the tightest hug Sharon ever felt from her feline soul mate. For several minutes she walked around and around her friend's yard, with Ebee clasped around her neck, purring and purring, muttering and murmuring in her father's fashion, so happy was she to have Sharon home.

Back at Sodus Point, Ebee ecstatically explored the woods surrounding their home. She headed down the hill to check rocky crevices and the neighbor's gardens for critters to play with and toss in the air. Her mom's garden of Echinacea and daisies was blooming, but somehow the neighbor's overgrown bushes and towering hollyhocks and delphiniums made for a more secretive place from which to hunt.

Sharon always laughed when she called Ebee to come home from the neighbors down in the valley. When Ebee heard her human calling, she hunkered down—so that she'd have less wind resistance, no doubt—and charged up the hill, her little belly swaying back and forth with each bound. *I must hurry home.*

The years passed rapidly, and as Ebee grew older, she still loved going out each morning to explore the neighbor's gardens. In her latter years she did far less hunting, content to lie on Sharon's deck or sleep in her special place beneath the towering hosta plant.

Ebee died on January 22, 2002

****

Ebee's Memorial

Though Ebee's tiny urn of ashes shares a prominent place on a bookshelf filled with great American literary artists such as Faulkner, Fitzgerald, and Twain, the urn's cremains are no less dear to Sharon than the works of the great literary masters. Ebee, in her own right, was an artist as well, because Ebee danced through life, each day performing pirouettes through the garden, around her hosta plant, and to the edge of the creek. In her grace, her style, no less artful than a classical ballerina's, she represented, in feline form, the embodiment of happiness and pure devotion. Sharon decided to memorialize her with a stone that truly reflected Ebee's unique spirit.

Each winter Ebee's memorial stone sits safe from the elements in the garage underneath an iron rack holding a snow shovel and push broom. In spring when the flowers begin blooming at Sodus Point, Sharon prepares for the Placing of the Stone—Ebee's stone. She tidies Ebee's favorite spot in the flower garden off the back porch. Then she carefully picks up her black stone, etched with a stylized version of Ebee's face and the words "Ebee's Spot" etched beneath, and places it, with personal ceremony, in what had always been

Ebee's favorite napping place overlooking turquoise Lake Ontario—beneath the umbrella-leaves of the giant hosta plant. The memorial site is restful and as still and beautiful as the water below.

Chapter Eighteen
Cosmo Dog

Species: canine—mini dachshund
Name: Lady
Born: 2001
Died: 2013
Human companion: John Forrest

When the Great Recession hit in 2008, most Americans were affected negatively in some way. Many people's lifestyles changed almost in a nanosecond—luxuries became forbidden in such an age of financial and economic decline. Few pockets hid extra money to buy giant barbecue grills, to book fancy vacations to Europe and the Caribbean, to invite friends over for dinner, or enjoy a restaurant. The middle class floundered amid the poor financial climate, and it seemed only the wealthy had money enough to thrive while the poor muddled by as usual, day-to-day, by virtue of their monthly government checks. Those caught in the middle, however—small business people, factory workers, retail workers, secretaries, managers and such—suffered real misery.

During that time, which will forever go down in history as one of the saddest times in United States history, a man of fifty-six years of age, named John Forrest, and his once-lucrative small business became vacuumed up in the maelstrom of the times. His landscaping and yard furniture business in Eugene, Oregon, crashed along with the stock market. Despite employing every marketing trick available and even expanding his business to include indoor wares, he lost his home, his wife of twenty-eight years, the comfort of his grown kids, and his upper middle-class lifestyle. With no decent job opportunities in their small town, he set out to California where employment was rumored to be better. With no more than change and a few bills in his old faded jeans, he left behind everything dear to him—his wood duck collection, his trumpet he had cherished since third grade, and his Gramma's Christmas decorations from Germany. Material possessions hardly mattered—he needed a job. The only thing of value he could take with him to California was his dachshund, Lady. While the financial crisis had robbed him of his career, home, and family—he vowed it wouldn't take his dog, too.

So, with no car and no financial means, he and his dog set out on an arduous trip, a both literal and figurative life-altering journey. On the long bus ride from Eugene, Oregon, to Cayugus, California, John and Lady sat beside each other for hours watching the landscape unfold before their eyes. Lady could vaguely smell the Sierra Nevadas as they sped down Highway Five. He patted Lady's back to assure her all was fine. "It's all right, girl. Everything's going to be okay. I promise." She looked adoringly at him, and he regretted the lie. Nothing was a guarantee anymore, not after his life had blown up in his face.

When Lady wasn't seated next to her human, she lay in her soft-sided kennel under the bus seat in front of him. The tedious hours passed—the bus was moving, but time itself had stopped. Every few moments Lady sniffed her dad's legs just to make sure he was okay. As long as he was near she felt fearless.

After many hours the bus stopped at a small beach town—their destination. John and Lady stepped into the streets of Cayugus and stared at the ocean. "Here we are, Lady. We are at the ocean, and nobody's gonna stop us now." Lady jumped up, her front paws on her dad's leg. She seemed to agree.

Transitioning from a fairly wealthy life to one of poverty would be a hard task for anyone, especially devoid of one's family, relatives, and all one's possessions, but finding a job that would mark the beginning of the recovery could be even harder. John, even though he had been a business owner and employer, was willing to accept any job to support himself and Lady. So, after the hours-long bus ride, John and his canine sidekick walked again as many hours searching the streets of Cayugus for Help Wanted signs. At the end of the day, John was forced to carry his mini dachshund because she was road weary, exhausted. It was almost as frustrating as what it had been in Eugene. No one needed help—not for painting houses, not for cleaning vacation homes, not even for grocery store clerking.

After hours of inquiring about work at local businesses, John set Lady on a park bench. "We gotta keep going, gal—gotta find a spot to lay our heads down tonight." Lady tucked her paws under her chin and blinked a look of concern. "Come on, girl. We must find somewhere to stay." The middle-aged man got up and began walking, Lady following closely alongside.

A neon sign flashed a few doors down—a pet grooming shop. Lady followed John inside. After a few minutes of conversation, the owner recognized the special relationship John had with his dog. He liked the well-spoken, friendly demeanor of the older man who could be an asset to his business. Bill didn't have to think long—he offered John a job as a pet shampooer. After Bill learned that John and Lady were new to town and in need of a room to sleep, he offered them one at the back of the shop. The two could stay until they found more permanent quarters.

So John and Lady spent their first night and several more in the back of Sudsy Tub pet grooming shop. The space was small and spare, but it would only be temporary. The next day at work John didn't disappoint—he proved he had a knack with dogs and even the cats—he was a sort of animal whisperer. The animals immediately took to John's comforting touch and his lighthearted personality. Just as they felt soothed by his low, quiet voice, so did they enjoy the massage-bath and blow-dry experiences.

Lady also took her job at the grooming shop seriously although she earned pay only in dog treats. Immediately she became the shop's greeter—the hostess. She walked around the shop greeting the dogs arriving to be newly coiffed and primped. She loved her job, too, because her dad worked right beside her. Nothing was ever daunting as long as he was nearby. A couple of weeks passed, and John and Lady had made many new friends, animal and human, and Bill enjoyed having them working alongside him in the shop, too.

When John and Lady weren't working at Sudsy Tub, they took long strolls on the beach. Lady loved the ocean. As the waves chased her up the sand, she whipped around, barked, and ran after them as they retreated in fear. No wave intimidated the little black dachshund. John and Lady walked miles along the beaches around Cayugus. And while Lady adored all the sights and smells along the way, she pitied other dogs tied to their owners by leashes. She never needed a leash, always sticking close to her dad, who would protect her from anything. As they walked, she sniffed the clean sea air and turned her muzzle into the wind, her ears lifting and falling with the ocean breezes.

What Lady loved most of all about the beach, though, was the rich, cloying smell of rotting things. When she found a pile of dead seaweed or a dead crab, she couldn't resist rolling in its perfume and showing her dad how wonderful she smelled. Since rolling in nasty things was Lady's only vice, John tolerated it because he'd later sanitize his odiferous dog back at the shop.

Lady accompanied John not only to the beach but everywhere he went in Cayugus, including apartment shopping. Cayugus was a dog-friendly, artsy town with many gift shops and small eateries in which dogs and their companions were always welcome. In their free time when they weren't at the beach, John and Lady walked around town, stopping in at various retailers. The shop owners quickly cozied up to Lady, to whom they offered treats and water. It wasn't too long before all the townspeople and business owners knew John and his Lady. The two became a fixture in Cayugus and everyone's favorite couple on the beach.

Although Lady was always a gentlewoman with dogs coming into the shop to be groomed, she was no pushover with unmannerly, pushy canines she met outside the shop. Size didn't matter to Lady since she viewed herself as massive as a German shepherd. If any dog challenged her, and her dad wasn't right there to straighten things out, she growled a warning and stood, her four legs splayed, ready to defend herself. Lady felt as imposing as the biggest dog, and she had a personality to match. She would take no shit from anyone.

In a few weeks Lady and her dad rented a studio apartment within walking distance to Sudsy Tub. It wasn't much and certainly wasn't accommodations even remotely close to what they had had in Eugene, but their only choice was to adapt. As long as they had each other, they didn't need anything fancy.

The man and his dog shared a symbiotic relationship that soon revolved around life at the grooming shop. While John anticipated Lady's daily needs, including potty breaks, play, and treat time, the dachshund reacted to John's every gesture, his body language and facial expressions, and every voice command.

The mini dachshund understood her human companion better than any other person ever had. With that ability came her recognition of many words. Of course, she knew all the commands like "sit," "stay," "come," "no," and "good girl." She especially liked "good girl" because her dad always smiled and looked in her eyes when he said it. And she understood more complicated expressions like "out of there" when she wanted to roll in something disgusting. When she needed water, John asked her, "Are you shirshy?" before she lapped up an entire cup of water.

She reacted to his mood reflected in the timbre of his voice. "It's been another long day, hasn't it, Lady? Are you tired? Would you like a boney?" And Lady smiled widely as John slipped a smoky bone into her mouth. Another phrase Lady recognized was "Wanna go car-car?" That was one of her "happy phrases" but she hadn't heard it for a long time, at least since the "shrinking of the world" happened in 2008.

But one day she and her dad walked a long time to a strange place—a hard, black-floored place with rows upon rows of car-cars. And in a couple of hours, John jiggled the keys to an old beater. He grinned at Lady. "Wanna go car-car, Lady?" And she leaped onto the front seat of the 1989 Chevy Lumina. And every day after that, Lady got her daily "car-car" ride.

Nothing is easy recovering from bankruptcy, but John was determined to overcome that total shock to one's system—he had gone from comparative riches, complete with a home with an outdoor kitchen, no less than three new vehicles, four TVs, and a pampered wife, to complete destitution. In the space of a year and despite trying to keep his business afloat, his life as he knew it had dropped out from under him. One day he had it all. The next he had nothing—except Lady—his constant.

One of the things he missed most about his former life was his vegetable garden. Having a tiny studio apartment allowed for no space on which to grow even one tomato plant. John missed digging in the ground, smelling the good earth, patting seedlings that would grow strong and yield lots of fruit. He could never understand people who didn't like gardening. Why wouldn't a person enjoy a hobby that was fun, fulfilling, and could actually produce wonderful things to eat?

Likewise, John's "Shrudy," as he sometimes called Lady, delighted helping in the garden. When he slung weeds, she flew after them and bit the ground where they landed, tearing out the dirt and flinging them with a growl into the air. The weed became her prey. After an hour of weeding, Shrudy stood, happily tired, a mouthful of dirt smearing her gums and lips. What she really savored from the garden were peas, her favorite treat. She raced her dad at harvest time to eat more peas than he could pick. Perhaps, sometime in the future, Shrudy and John would have a garden again where she could chase weeds.

Once John had a car, he and Lady traveled everywhere together when they weren't working. On weekends they took the car-car to visit his four grown kids. Lady had always been a good car traveler, but now she had to grow accustomed to riding for hours from Cayugus to Oregon and Washington. She rode for hours and hours at a time, her head on John's lap, his good scent reassuring, comforting. Riding in this "car-car" was far different from the traveling she had done before the "baddie." In a plane she would stay quiet in her soft kennel under the seat. Once at the airport, John would let her loose and she walked quickly, deliberately, alongside him, to the next gate. People had marveled at the little dog who seemed unfazed amid the noise and bustle of a busy airport. One time Lady had even strutted through O'Hare Airport on her way with her dad to a hardware convention. Nothing bothered her as long as she was with her human.

Her past life, along with her present one in

Cayugus, had made her a dog wise to the world, a cosmopolitan canine. Surely she had visited more states, both by car and plane, than most dogs and many people had, too. Of course, she and her dad drove Route 1 along the Pacific coast where his kids lived in Washington, Oregon, and California. She had toured Reno and Vegas for vacations. The landscapers' conventions had taken them from Chicago to LA to New York City. Lady had become a world traveler, just like her dad.

One day Bill had some good news. "I have a wealthy friend who won't be using his condo for the next year. He'd like someone to stay there and keep an eye on things. Interested? A condo—rent free." Lady stood smiling silently at John's side.

John looked at Lady. "Wow. That would be terrific! Did you hear that, Lady?"

Lady grinned.

Bill looked away. "Uh, ...Lady's a problem. The guy won't allow a dog in his place—that's the only caveat—otherwise, you can have the place for free. Place has nice hardwood floors and stuff he doesn't want ruined."

John looked down at his smiling dog. "I can't do it. You know me, Bill. I won't leave Lady behind."

"Surely you can find a nice family to take her."

"Nope—not doing it. Lady has been a loyal, devoted dog. I owe her the same. I don't care how skimpy my living arrangements are here—Lady and I are a team. Had it not been for her company every day and night, I don't know if I'd have made it through the financial mess. She comforted me. I owe her no less. Nope—we stay together."

****

After a few years working for Bill, John had an opportunity to move to the East Coast, so he and Lady packed a bag, said a sad farewell to Bill, and drove cross-country to Pennsylvania where awaited a strong, pretty woman who owned a horse farm. And she fell in love with Lady at first sight. After a few weeks of dating, the two decided to make things permanent. Lady thrived in the Pennsylvania countryside where she and John kept a garden again, where the three rode a very different "car-car"—a golf cart—every day, where she developed other friendships with cats, horses, pigs, chickens, and even a peacock. She knew not to chase the chickens because her dad used the phrase again she hadn't heard since before "the fall"—"Don't chase chickens!"

Instead of feasting on garden peas, however, Lady grew to love Pennsylvania sweet corn. When her new mommy gave her a piece of a freshly cooked cob, it became Lady's habit to parade it around in her mouth before settling under a redbud tree to chew off the kernels. Nothing tasted better to Lady than freshly-picked sweet corn.

With acres and acres of farmland on which to run and play, John reminded Lady of the hamburger game. John bought a plastic hamburger and squeeze-squeaked it. "Where's your burger?"

Lady danced around in circles and laughed, eager to play her burger game. Then, John threw it into the grass, and Lady went into hunting mode. Though the burger was clearly visible, and though she absolutely knew where it was, she pretended to be on the hunt—dog detective. *Sniff...sniff...sniff...*she played, circling, searching for the escaped burger. Round and round she trotted, all the time John and his human lady laughed and encouraged her to "Find the burger." Then, after the dog had paced the yard for five minutes, suddenly she threw herself upon the plastic burger, scooped it up in her mouth, and clamped down until it squeaked for mercy.

That burger accompanied Lady wherever she went. She took it in the car-cars and on walks where it hung from the side of her mouth. She even took it with her to go potty, not letting go of it for one minute while doing her business. Her protection of her burger was clearly understandable—years ago she had put her burger down one day, and suddenly it disappeared...for years. She wasn't going to risk losing it again. Everyone laughed at the little black dachshund with the burger dangling from her mouth.

When the three weren't playing the burger game or gardening, they drove in the real car-car to the Poconos or to Philadelphia or to New York City where Lady sat, her lips cradling the plastic burger, in the other lady's lap. The three spent many days outside tending chores on the farm, and Lady came to love the woman of John's dreams almost as much as she did John.

Lady died at Thanksgiving 2013.

****

Lady's Memorial

John had had many dachshunds throughout his life, and he loved them all. But it was Lady, in particular, who stole his heart. He refers to her as his Cosmopolitan Canine—cosmopolitan in spirit as well as experience. His was a dog who had survived many extremes, as had John himself—a rich lifestyle, a poor one; a large family, a family of one; having a worldly well-traveled life, being isolated in one place; living a life on the West Coast, living one on the East Coast. Just as John found himself surviving such a roller-coaster life of highs and lows, so Lady's life "before it went down" compared to "after it went down" demonstrated life at its extremes. But people and dogs can win against extremes by taking comfort in each other, and that was exactly what happened to Lady and John.

Lady, when John woke up to nothing one day in 2008, offered her human unending loyalty, positivity, trust, strength, and devotion. John, in the same way, offered her his dedication, loyalty, love, and trust. The two supported each other. To this day John credits Lady with saving his life by just being there with him—being present every day, every hour. She became his best friend, his most loyal companion, and the truest love of his life.

****

John's dearest dog is buried—with her burger—in the woods on her farm in Pennsylvania beneath a bench amid acres of pachysandra and wildflowers. The woodland nature around her mirrors Lady's soft nature and strong dedication to those people she loved. Lady is reflected in the soft fluttering of the leaves, the sweet smell of the flowers, the earthiness of the ground above her. Her strength of character and ability to weather the extremes of life is reflected in the strength of the sixty-foot trees themselves, in their ability to survive super-storm winds, extreme heat and cold, and bone-numbing blizzards.

Alongside her pachysandra-covered grave stands a

metal gravesite marker bearing a tile plaque with a picture of Lady lying on the ground beside John. In the photo the man and his dog lie amidst the zinnias and tomatoes in their Pennsylvania garden. Each is a survivor, tired and world-weary, but ecstatic in the arms of the other, complete knowing their real home was never in any one state or at any one property. Their home was *wherever* the two of them were together.

Chapter Nineteen
A Sweetheart in a Swine Suit

Species: pot-bellied pig
Name: Bo Jackswine
Born: May 3, 1991
Died: June 19, 2007
Human companion: Janie Finck

Janie's elderly father hung on to the door handle in the back seat. "We're gonna be pulled over by the cops! We're gonna get arrested, for Christ's sake!" Gloria, Janie's mother, raced their SUV down the road at seventy-five miles an hour after just leaving the pot-belly rescue center in Seminole, Florida.

That morning Janie's terminally ill father had begged to go along as a diversion from his weakening, relentless condition as well as respite from boredom. And the ride to the pot-bellied pig farm had been pleasant enough. The trip home, however, amounted to no less than a flight out of Hades.

Janie grimaced, clasping her new pig to her chest. "Can't you go any faster, Mom?"

Her mother pressed the gas pedal even harder, her face up against the windshield. "I'm going as fast as I can."

All three were anxious to get home to St. Petersburg to escape the vehicle in which they were hopelessly trapped. Inside the echo chamber of a car their ears endured the shrieking of a terrified pig. From the bottom of his powerful lungs the little animal yelled, his screams excruciating, achieving a decibel level rivaling a jet engine's. Neither Janie nor her parents could tolerate the din within the vehicle for much longer.

Suddenly Janie's mother stepped on the brake, the car skidding to a halt under a stop light. The abrupt stop silenced the pig all of about ten seconds. Then the piglet sucked in a deep draft of air and blew it out again through the strongest vocal cords in all of Florida.

The squeal filled the car like air filling a balloon—to a breaking point.

Janie's father yelled almost as loud as the pig. "My God, can't you do anything? I'm telling ya, if anybody hears this, they're gonna tell the cops we're murdering a woman. I'm telling ya—we're gonna get arrested."

The light turned green, and Gloria tromped the pedal.

Janie's face was red. "I've tried everything, Dad." The pig's short, staccato shrieks ricocheted off the inner walls of the vehicle, boomeranging, reverberating off the metal and accosting their eardrums. Janie held the tiny pot-bellied piglet to her chest, patting his back, but he would have nothing to do with this woman's kindness. He was being *pignapped.*

Gloria's face was up against the steering wheel, her eyes bugged, her mouth clenched. Janie and her father, however, sat nearly catatonic.

The tiny breadloaf-shaped piggy screamed. *"Vree-ee-ee-ee! Vree-ee-ee-ee! Vree-ee-ee-ee!"* Janie pleaded with Bo, her new pig-son, to shush, but it was no use.

She covered him with a blanket.

He screamed.

She pushed him into his little car carrier.

He screamed.

She held the piglet up to her face.

He screamed.

She held him in the crook of her neck.

He bit her.

"Yeo-ow! He bit me!" With that, Janie scooted the frightened animal into his carrier and pulled the visor's mirror down to check her neck. Four little teeth marks were engraved and growing red and fiery under her chin. At least there was no blood. "I think I adopted a vampire, not a pig!"

Suddenly, as their car flew over the road like a toboggan down an ice flow, a heavy quiet descended on the car. Janie's mom looked puzzled—silence. The piglet had quieted.

"Thank God." Her father sighed from the back seat.

Janie looked down at the pig in the carrier. "Bo, are you okay?" She turned the carrier to make sure the piglet hadn't keeled over from pure fright. Then, just as quickly as the cacophony stopped, it started up again. A whimper first, then a whine, and then a full-blown shriek. Janie's father rolled his eyes, and his hands flew to his ears. The ride home couldn't end soon enough.

****

Once Janie brought Bo into his new home, Janie placed the bellowing creature into his brand-new playpen complete with his own bed, dishes, blankets, and toys. No sooner had she put down the screeching pig than his mouth shut like a trap door.

Eyes glazed over, Janie gazed down at her new buddy. "Thank goodness." In a few minutes the little pig was calmly checking out his little playpen, and he even ate a few carrot treats from his dish.

After dinner Janie tiptoed into the living room where Bo's playpen had center stage. Unfortunately the pen blocked the TV set so that her husband Bob had to peer around it. Janie bent to her knees beside the pen. When she peeked over the edge of the playpen, the tiny pig whipped around and stared, his eyes bulging, at the human head that, to him, was surely decapitated. He let out one loud shriek. Then Janie stood up, reached into the playpen, grabbed Bo around his waist, and lifted him into the air.

"Vree-ee-ee! Vre-ee-ee! Vreeeeee!" His voice was deafening. Immediately Janie put him back on his playpen blanket.

Silence.

Again the apparition appeared—bodiless. He stared at the head peeking at him from the side of the playpen and grunted a warning.

Janie ran for the phone and dialed the rescue center. "Rhonda, what in the world am I going to do with him? He's scared to death of me. I'm the worst boogey woman he's ever seen."

The pig rescue director contemplated the situation. "Try not to pick him up too much. Sows never pick up their young, unlike mother cats. The only things that ever pick up a piglet are predators—wolves, dogs, and stuff. Bo thinks you're going to eat him. Give him the night to get used to his pen and his surroundings. Feed and water him, and let him see you and your husband coming and going. Let him realize you have no interest in tasting him. Tomorrow, take him out and start offering him bits of carrots, trying to coax him into your lap. It's going to take some time until he trusts you."

****

For the next month Janie put the tiny piglet into a routine. He was served breakfast by eight a.m., his pen cleaned by nine a.m. Then Janie played with him and began his training session until ten a.m. During each training session, Janie sat with him, talked with him, and asked him to come closer. With the help of carrot and grape peace offerings, Bo slowly learned to approach and take treats from Janie's fingers. Then she coaxed him closer, and he followed, snatching a piece of carrot and then running two to three feet away where he stood munching, always one eye intently focused on Janie.

Bo's training sessions gradually improved, and finally, after about a month, the two reached a turning point. After Janie put Bo on the floor, he turned around, snuffling behind the couch, nudging the carpet with his snout. As he investigated a fuzzball, Janie sat on the floor several feet away, her legs crossed Indian style.

"Whatcha doin', Bo?"

The pig ignored her, intent on a spot whose scent from a food spill probably years ago was still detectable, and, to Bo, delectable. Bo's keen sniffer tracked down the fruity smell.

"Don't you want to play with mommy?"

Bo turned toward her. Then he turned back to the carpet. But Jane could see that as he was nudging and sniffing, he had one eye on her, an eye that resembled a human's eye.

"Well, if you're going to ignore me, then I'm just going to lie back on the carpet here and take a nap." Janie leaned back as though ready for sleep.

With that Bo stopped, turned, thought for a moment, and trundled over to Janie's side. In the next instant he jumped onto her thigh and stepped gingerly over her stomach and up to her chest where he lay down, his snout against her chin.

Janie was ecstatic, gleeful—what a transformation! But she stayed calm, her eyes closed, feigning sleep. Slowly she raised her arms and cradled the little pig's back. Together they lay on the floor until Bo fell asleep. Janie, however, was too thrilled to doze. This was the solidifying moment—Bo had accepted her as his own.

In the next few months Bo grew like an onion bulb, and within a few months he was the diameter of and half the length of an Electrolux vacuum. And at about six months of age he usurped the position of the family dog, Mindy, a fifteen-year-old Golden Retriever/ Samoyed mix to whom he had initially paid obeisance. Now that Bo was stronger and more influential within the household, he decided he was boss, so their friendship morphed into a love/hate relationship. During snack time, play time, nap time, and when vying for the softest chair in the house, Bo challenged the easygoing Mindy.

In one battle over Mindy's rubber bone, Mindy growled when Bo picked it off the carpet. Bo did his dominant-pig thing—dancing sideways, raising his mane so that he looked larger and more intimidating, and chomping, his jowls flapping while chattering a not-so-empty threat. Finally, Mindy retreated, and Bo enjoyed his new toy.

From the family's cats, however, Bo felt no threat. In fact, Miss Pat, Scotty, Rebel, Midnight, and Slim liked Bo well enough, crawling into his blankets alongside him. On cooler evenings, four-year-old Moose, the kitten, climbed aboard Bo's back, kneading himself to sleep on the pig's rump. By the time Moose had finished making his "bed," Bo, too, had fallen asleep.

In 1993, when Bo was just seventeen months old, Janie adopted Bo's half sister, Barbie. The two pigs became fast friends though Bo remained king pig of the household. Bo had been the runt of his litter and was bottle-fed, so he never grew up with a pig's consciousness. Instead, he was certain he belonged to the homo sapiens' species rather than the porcine one. To further solidify his humanness, after being spoiled at the rescue center, he went to Janie's home where, from the beginning, his human mom cut up his food and hand-fed him carrots, grapes, bananas, celery, lettuce, and broccoli.

In contrast, Barbie had been raised by her natural mother and taught piggy behavior, so she acted much more piglike than did Bo.

Bo was a person in a swine suit. While a normal pig didn't care how his dinner was served, just as long as it *was* served, Bo had definite hang-ups when it came to food. He demanded all his vegetables and fruit be washed and cut up into bite-sized pieces, or he just refused them. After all, he knew he would hardly starve in Janie's care. He just had to wait until his mommy caved.

His finicky eating habits became even more obvious when all the pot-bellied pigs from the local club met at the strawberry-picking patch at the end of strawberry season. While everyone else's pig tore from the car at the first scent of rotting and fresh berries, burying their heads in the vines and munching with enthusiasm, Bo stood at the end of Janie's leash wondering what all the fuss was about. Even seeing Barbie buried up to her ears in strawberries did nothing to titillate his appetite. It was obvious the whole affair seemed very uncouth to Bo.

So that day Janie began to pick strawberries *for* Bo, slicing them with a knife borrowed from the picking shack and feeding the tiny pieces to Bo one at a time. Bo only agreed to eat the cut-up fruit because that's what he was accustomed to. While Barbie and the other pigs disappeared into the strawberry patch, devouring every morsel and snorting and huffing in ecstasy, Gentleman Bo Jackswine accepted only those strawberries that Janie had washed, sliced, and delivered to his most delicate lips.

Similarly, Bo rejected Janie's gummy bears and pizza crust. While Bob and Janie always discouraged Bo and Barbie from begging at the human supper table, Janie thrilled at seeing their pigs' reactions to different foods. So on Friday pizza nights, Janie saved her crust for Bo and Barbie. When she proffered it, Bo sniffed and looked up as if to say, *"You're not going to cut it up for me?"* Then, no sooner had Bo walked away, his tail arched in superiority, but Barbie snatched the crust, running with it to her dog bed. The same happened with the gummy bears—Barbie gobbled each candy while Bo watched with disgust. Barbie loved their jellylike sweetness while King Bo, snout up, categorically rejected them.

Eventually Bo discovered the cloying sweetness of a gummy bear. Once he dropped the superior facade and acquiesced, there was no stopping him. Thereafter, Bo and Barbie wrestled and pummeled each other in the presence of one gummy bear. And Bo soon became a fierce sweet-thing addict.

The birthday party held for one of Bo's piggy acquaintances was as much a failure as the trip to the strawberry patch. Janie admits that, in trying to befriend Bo when he was younger, she turned him into a one-person pig who could be as spoiled and cantankerous as he could be loveable. Just like a human mommy's boy, Bo resented strangers invading his home and stealing his beloved mother's attention. So he became defensive at sight of an interloper. Bo challenged visitors, standing sideways, raising his mane, and chomping his annoyance. And Janie's friends had no choice but to cower until Janie escorted the resentful Bo to his room.

Because of Bo's jealousy, Janie had warned the young man who volunteered to pig sit Bo one weekend to avoid the pigs' bedroom once they went to sleep inside their camping tent. Apparently, a refrigerator loaded with beer and soda shared the pigs' bedroom, and though Bernie knew he was forbidden in that room once the pigs were asleep, he thought he could just sneak inside and steal a beer without the animals' waking.

Quietly, slowly, Bernie turned the doorknob to Bo's and Barbie's bedroom. Not a sound came from the door as he opened it just enough to let himself inside. At sight of the refrigerator, Bernie's mouth began to water. He tiptoed into the room, Bo's and Barbie's camping tent standing four feet high in the center, eyed the refrigerator against the far wall behind the tent, and headed toward it.

Both pigs were sound asleep, heavy snoring emanating from the tent. Bernie slid quietly across the floor, put his hand on the refrigerator handle, and pulled. *"Msh-sh-sh."* The door sucked open.

"Vropp! Vropp!" A pig-bark broke the dark silence.

Bernie ignored it—the beer was within reach. He grabbed a can and opened the crisper box for other goodies. When he turned around, arms loaded with snacks, Bo was standing behind him.

Bo stood his ground. *"Vrapp!"*

Bernie turned and headed to the door.

"Vrapp! Vrapp!" Bo leaped at the intruder.

Bernie reached for the door, but it was too late. Bo grabbed him by the pants leg and tore a hole in his jeans. Bernie escaped with his beer, but he dropped the apple and banana chips, and his jeans were hopelessly ruined.

****

While Bo's challenging strangers at home embarrassed Janie, when she took him to nursing homes or to her middle school where she taught, he became Mr. Personality. At the nursing homes he became an expert schmoozer with the old folks and, to their delight, nudged their frail, wheelchair-bound legs. When he went to school, he paraded up and down the classroom rows, accepting pats to the head and enjoying conversations with children who loved to play as he did. Bo especially loved the sixth graders as they read *Charlotte's Web* out loud. They all sat in a circle, Bo in the center, of course. The afternoon passed quickly for the kids as well as Bo, delighted by so many little hands stroking his belly.

In fact, when Bo visited Janie's school on different occasions, the kindergarteners begged him to visit. The class learned that Bo didn't stink at all, which ran contrary to everything their parents ever told them about pigs. Then, when they saw him do a pirouette and sit, they knew they were in the presence of a special, very intelligent creature. Mr. Bo Jackswine quickly was dubbed the school's mascot and became the subject of a scrapbook displaying umpteen photos of himself alongside his adoring children.

Kids weren't the only humans Gentleman Bo Jackswine impressed. When Janie petitioned Pinellas County city council to change their anti-swine ordinance and make the ownership of pot-bellied pigs legal in St. Petersburg and the entire county, Janie dressed Bo in a black cummerbund and red bowtie and brought him to the city council chambers. To the amazement of the council members, Bo proved a pig could be as intelligent, as outgoing, and as entertaining as a dog. Bo demonstrated his repertoire of tricks—sitting up on his back legs, pirouetting, and putting a basketball through a hoop. The council persons thought Bo and pigs like him worthy of pet status, so they voted unanimously to allow miniature pigs as household pets.

Bo wasn't nearly so impressed with his veterinarian, however. Bo hated having a pedicure, and he hated having his tusks trimmed even more. Being flipped onto his back like a beached whale didn't jive with his self-image as a sophisticate. So when Janie scheduled the visiting veterinarian for Bo's and Barbie's hoof trims, she had to devise a ruse. To lure

Bo into the bathroom/exam room, Janie would offer him gummy bears.

With Bo unaware and watching TV in the front living room, Janie ushered Dean, their young burly neighbor, and Bo's veterinarian into the tiny downstairs bathroom. After much strategizing, in a few minutes both men stood plastered together in the shower stall, the glass door shut. The two 235-pound men stood, staring, bug-eyed, into each other's faces, their bodies compressed into the shape of the shower stall.

The two, pressed to self-consciousness, stood embarrassingly silent, breathing each other's breath, and endured the seconds until they heard the bathroom door open—Bo's appearance.

Janie spoke in a high cloying tone of voice. "Good boy, Bo. Here's your gummy bear, Honey." Then they heard the door close again.

Both men tensed, ready to spring. On cue the vet nodded, and Dean burst from the shower. He grabbed the unsuspecting Bo around his waist and flipped him into the air and onto his back.

"Re-ee-ee-ee-ee-ee!"

Bo's objections were jet-engine ear-splitting. Surely the neighbors thought a woman was being torn limb from limb.

Bo roared. *"Bla-a-a-a-ah! Ra-ah-ah-ah-ah!"*

Stuffed inside the tiny bathroom along with the two large men and Bo, Janie winced, but she knew there was no other way to trim his feet than to flip him. Since pigs can die from anesthesia, immobilizing a pig by flipping it onto its back is the only safe way to work on one.

Janie kneeled by Bo's head, talking to him and

rubbing his cheek, and she steadied his sides as the vet took his pony nippers to his feet. One after another, shards of nail flew into the corners until the vet finished one foot. Bo shrieked, furious—his mouth foamy, opening and closing with each inhalation and squealing exhalation. The din in the tiny room was excruciating, but the humans had prepared for Bo's high-pitched bugling—each wore a heavy woolen cap to protect their ears.

Fifteen minutes later Bo's nails and tusks were trimmed down to size. Finally, Dean rolled Bo over onto his side. Once released, he jumped up, grunted a warning, and shot through the open bathroom door.

Though Bo hated strangers during his yearly veterinary visits, he loved them during the holidays. In fact, Christmas became his favorite time of year because Janie planned many excursions at community functions in which he played Christmas characters. One year Bo dressed as an angel, the next as a tree decoration, and one year he awed everyone wearing his Father Winter snowsuit.

Most of all he enjoyed visiting Janie's beauty parlor. Women in every stage of beautification filled the salon around Christmas time. Bo, dressed in a Santa suit and wearing a headband with reindeer antlers, strode grandly amongst the beauty chairs. Bo enjoyed his role as greeter but found nothing particularly inviting in the smells of hair dye, sprays, nail lacquer, and defoliation creams. Some of the women reached a hand down to pat his head; others laughed and wished him "Merry Christmas." Others told him he looked rather silly, and some ignored him—being neither in a pig nor Christmas frame of mind. Finally, after Janie paraded him through the entire shop, she sat down and offered Bo his reward for being a good Santa pig, vanilla yogurt—one spoonful at a time. Bo long ago had decided he could endure such embarrassment and follow his mom anywhere for a few spoonfuls of yogurt from the shop next door.

****

Reindeer Bo loved his yogurt, for it satisfied many needs. First, the different, sweet kind of deliciousness cooled his mouth and throat. Second, the heaping spoonfuls satisfied his craving for his mom's attention. All was fine in Bo's world.

What Bo relished most about Christmas, though, was his Christmas tree. When Bob hoisted the blue spruce through the door, Bo stood back in awe. He knew what was coming—the brilliant crystal balls, the tinsel, the sparkly garland, and the smell of pine in the air. As was his custom, Bo lay down in the living room, watching the flurry of activity as Janie and Bob pulled out the ornament boxes and began to trim the tree.

Once the tree was fully decorated and Janie and her husband stood back admiring it, its lights aglow, Janie nodded to Bo, who had been patiently waiting for this moment. "Okay, Bo. It's all yours." Then Bo stepped towards it, lifted his face to a branch, sniffed the piney scent, and smiled, his lips drawn back, his snout taut. As he did every year, he bent down, scrunched himself underneath the tree, and slept there until supper. And after supper he walked back to the tree and basked beneath it, looking up through the branches at the pretty lights and sparkling balls. He simply loved his Christmas tree. Never did he take an ornament off, nor did he ever chew at the branches or lick the tinsel. He just enjoyed lying under *his* tree, the colored lights glowing all around him, the glass balls shining and tinkling when he nose-nudged them.

For the next month, every evening Bo squeezed himself under the tree, but finally the day came to take down the decorations and his tree. For several days after the tree was removed, Bo mourned. He walked into the living room, stood for a few minutes where the tree had been, then slowly turned and walked back to the family room. Bo realized he would have to wait for a long time, as he had done every year since he could remember, until his tree would appear again.

****

Bo Jackswine was a sweetheart in a swinesuit. He was Janie's best friend, her confidante. At home he became the protector of his human family, Mindy, and the cats and his sleeping partner, Barbie. Gentleman Bo Jackswine redefined the usual image of a pig. Though pigs are known to be clean and intelligent, Bo took those qualities to a higher level, insisting on having all his fruit and veggies washed, cut up, and placed neatly in his bowl. And he didn't eat just anything—he tasted it first. He never gobbled his food, unlike so many swine.

Bo Jackswine regarded himself a person from the time Janie brought him home. Though the two different species had a rough time adjusting to each other, Bo soon learned to love his human mom as much as she loved him. And when Janie took him out, he morphed into a social butterfly, entertaining school children, the elderly, the ladies in the beauty parlor, and impressing a city council enough to change their anti-swine laws.

Bo Jackswine died June 19, 2007.

⋈ * * *

Bo Jackswine's Memorial

After Bo died, Bob commissioned an artist friend to paint a picture of Bo for Janie's birthday present. But Bob had to find just the right photo of Bo, one that reflected the pig's strong, noble personality.

On days Janie went to work, Bob rummaged through boxes and boxes of Bo photos. All seemed nice to him, but, after a while, they all began to look alike. Finally, one picture struck him as particularly Bo-dacious. He drove it over to Rick Whalen's house. Rick examined it. "It's perfect! This photo captures his personality the best. I'll sketch it up, and if you like it, I'll start painting."

After about five sketches, during which time Rick and Bob discussed the little nuances of Bo's face—the deep wrinkles around his mouth, his almond-shaped eyes, the white blaze which ran down through the center of his snout and onto his chin—Rick was almost ready to paint. But he wanted to make the pig come alive in the painting. The "catch" was in Bo's face. The blaze was always Bo's most fetching feature—it looked as if a cone of vanilla ice cream had been dumped on his head, dribbling down his face and off his chin. Finally, Rick got the drawing right. Then he began to paint.

Rick's painting of Bo was as close as an acrylic painting ever gets to being interactive. Because Bo never shed any of his bristles, unlike most pigs who, during the hottest months, lose all their hair in the space of two weeks (pig people call it "blowing their coats"), his bristles grew to a whopping eighteen inches long, an unheard-of length except in African bush pigs. So Rick decided to use a putty knife to paint, instead of a brush, so that Janie could not only recognize the lush thickness of Bo's hair but could walk up to Bo's painting and actually pet him, feel the long hairs that had become Bo's trademark.

At sight of Bo's painting, Janie wiped her eyes. "Oh, my God! My Bo Jackswine! He looks as though he's going to jump right out at me. I love it, Bob. I have my Bo back. What a wonderful birthday present this is!"

Bo's painting is the image of the real Bo—his royal expression, his commanding presence, his total swiney uniqueness. In the painting, Bo lives again.

****

Addendum: When Bo died, Janie insisted Bo's University of Florida Gator afghan be cremated along with him. He had never been without that blanket during his life, and he would certainly not be without it in death.

Chapter Twenty
Country Born 'n' Bred

Species: canine—Chinese pug
Name: Choy
Born: May 16, 1985
Died: August 5, 2000

Species: equine—spotted walking horse
Name: Tonka
Born: May 16, 1991
Died: August 4, 2000
Human companion: Mary Ann Kennedy

The little girl sang as she galloped her red sorrel mare along the woods' edge, the weeping wild cherry trees lean-sheltering her path. "I was bo-o-orn to ride. I was bo-o-orn to ride. I was bo-o-orn to ri-i-i-ide." The ebony-haired ten-year-old, Mary Ann, and her copper-colored Quarter horse, Suzie, flew past the trees, the passing world in slow motion, her ponytail flying, the wind rush-singing through the horse's mane.

"Come on, Suzie. Faster. Run faster. Fly." Mary Ann rode fast, inhaling the cool, pure Wisconsin air. "Fly—like a bird is born to fly." The rangy youngster leaned and curled her hands into her horse's mane, the reins loose. "Go, Suzie." And she bent into the horse's speed. Leaving the woods behind, Mary Ann and Suzie danced over the fields—two spirits unified. Suzie moved with the grace of a deer, moved like the rhythm of poetry. Riding her horse under clear blue skies swept Mary Ann to a different place and time. There she didn't have to think, didn't have to follow rules. She could just ride her pony like a petal on the wind and be free again.

When they arrived back at the dirt path to the barn, Mary Ann pulled up on the reins. "Whoa-oa, Suzie." Suzie stopped, and Mary Ann slipped to the ground and drew the reins over Suzie's head. "Let's walk back to the barn." The two walked down the old farming path toward home. Suzie was a good, healthy mare—so slick and round. "Good Suzie. I love your horsey smell. It's my favorite perfume." Suzie looked at her diminutive owner and nickered, and Mary Ann kissed the mare's cheek.

****

"Miss Kennedy, wake up! I don't know where you are, but you certainly aren't participating in this history class! So answer the question, Miss Kennedy." The teacher frowned, hands on hips.

"I'm sorry." Mary Ann shook the daydream from her head. She tried to recall what her teacher had been discussing. "I don't remember." The other fifth-graders turned toward her, their mouths agape as though experiencing their first solar eclipse.

"No, it's not that you *can't* remember." Mrs. Worthington's voice was shrill. "You didn't *hear* the question—that's what. Where is your mind, Miss Kennedy?"

The teacher marched over to Mary Ann's desk.

"What do you have there? Move your arm away

from your notebook."

The girl slid her arms under her desk and bowed her head.

Squinting, Mrs. Worthington leaned over the girl's desk. "What's this stuff you've written? I knew it! Read it out loud. We all want to hear what you're obsessing about when the rest of us are discussing history."

The class was anxious, sorry for their classmate's predicament, for each one of them had had times of inattentiveness. Yet they were excited to hear what surely must have been a love note to some boy in the class.

Mary Ann picked up her notebook and cleared her throat. "I'm really sorry, Mrs. Worthington. Must I read…"

"Read it!"

The small girl cleared her throat and slowly read from her notebook. "I wish I had a horse of my very own. I'd name it Tonka." A couple of giggles erupted from the class. The teacher shushed them and walked back to the blackboard.

"Horses again. It's time you put your mind to things that matter—like history. Your punishment is to outline this chapter. Have it to me by tomorrow morning."

Mary Ann put the notebook down. "Yes, ma'am."

****

Mary Ann learned a lot during her childhood, but the most important things she learned didn't come from her school books. On the contrary, the little girl learned all the things that truly mattered in life from her animal friends—things like honesty, respect, and loyalty. Lady, her first dog friend, attended wherever Mary Ann ventured, always protective and vigilant. Together they scoured the woods for wildflowers, then tree leaves, then insects required for school science projects. At night Lady slept in Mary Ann's bedroom, barking a warning at any unfamiliar noises or movements, and when Mary Ann cried, Lady nuzzled her face.

Lady wasn't Mary Ann's sole guardian animal, however. Whenever Mary Ann rode Suzie down the dirt path, her horse took care of her—neither spooking nor leaping sideways. Even Mary Ann's parents trusted Suzie's sensible nature enough to let her take their ten-year-old out for a ride alone. Suzie taught Mary Ann courage and the power of endurance—living each moment to the fullest, running hard, playing hard, and searing the landscape with speed. But the most important thing Mary Ann learned from her dog and horse was that an animal could love a little girl in much the same way as her parents could—completely and without conditions.

Next to her love of horses and other animals, Mary Ann's second love was music. When Suzie was busy grazing on pasture and Lady was asleep on the porch, Mary Ann pretended to be a rock star. Using two sturdy sticks from an oak tree, she danced around the wraparound front porch and beat out a syncopated rhythm on the railing. When school started, Mary Ann begged her parents to let her study the saxophone in school. That opportunity helped pave her way to music heaven, but it wasn't heaven for Lady, who had to endure Mary Ann's practice sessions.

Mary Ann frowned, putting the sax down. "You could at least listen to me, Lady. I'm not *that* bad." The dog lay in a corner of the youngster's bedroom, paws over her ears. "Well, I know I'm not that good yet, but I'm also not that bad. I have to practice to get better." And Mary Ann blew another ear-splitting note.

A half hour of saxophone practice was almost too much for Lady and her parents to bear, but the worst was the next half hour's practice on the drums. Sitting behind her trap set, she beat out a rhythm on the snare and bass drums. But when Mary Ann smashed the hi-hat, two cymbals on a pole controlled with a foot pedal and a stick, Lady took off running.

****

As the years slipped by, Lady and Suzie both died. Mary Ann missed her dear animal friends who had taught her about love, honesty, and how to say "good-bye." Though she didn't have her animals to protect and love her, she had her music for comfort. In a move that Lady would have appreciated, Mary Ann laid aside the saxophone and picked up a different instrument—a guitar.

Her finesse with the guitar came as naturally as her riding skills had. After years of daily practice through high school, Mary Ann earned herself a role in a family band, The Country Cousins, in which she sang, made up songs, and played the drums and the guitar. After graduating from the University of Wisconsin, she continued to sing and write songs for country and pop bands. She also taught junior high school choral music. But what she had always loved about her connection to music was the creativity, the songwriting, the actual singing that came right from the heart. So she sold the horse her parents bought her for graduation, packed up Mits the cat, and moved to the heart of country-western music—Nashville.

Living in Nashville alongside country artists and being in the thick of the music-writing and producing business felt right to Mary Ann. As luck had it, in 1981 at the age of twenty-five years, Mary Ann Kennedy's big break came when, with the group Calamity Jane, she wrote the song "Ring on Her Finger, Time on Her Hands," which was nominated for a Grammy and later hit the top of the charts with Reba McIntire.

With this success Mary Ann secured a foot in the country music scene. Nashville felt almost like home. The only thing missing was a bevy of animal companions. So as soon as she had some extra cash, she went out and bought herself a beautiful black walking horse named Dolly and a couple of dogs.

In the early eighties Mary Ann signed with Almo Irving Music and found a songwriting partner in Pamela Rose, a singer whose musical spirit touched her heart. They developed a totally unique sound and style, and in no time, she and Pam were nominated for a Grammy for their song "I'll Still Be Loving You" by Restless Heart. Soon after, Emmylou Harris signed them on as background singers and instrumentalists, and Kennedy-Rose began touring as Harris' harmony singers.

One day in 1985 a friend came to Mary Ann's house carrying a basket. Mary Ann and Pam had been rehearsing a new song they had just written, and in a few days she and Rose would be on tour again with Emmylou in her Ballad of Sally Rose tour. Time was precious. When she invited her friend inside, Phyliss handed her the towel-covered basket. "I have something for you."

Mary Ann peeked inside. Looking up at her was a tiny puppy so dirty and scabby with mange it was difficult to tell its breed.

Mary Ann stroked her head. "Oh, the poor thing. What is it?"

"She's a Chinese pug, Mary Ann. She's been terribly neglected. I had to buy her and get her out of that crummy pet store. She needs you and would fit right in with your other animals. Please take her."

"Look, I just can't." She bit her lip and wrung her hands. "You don't understand—I'm slammed right now. I've got to get this song under my belt, and we're getting ready to tour."

The dirty, patchy-haired pug pup looked up at her from the basket, a strained look in her eyes. Mary Ann reached inside the basket and took the puppy to her chest. "You poor thing. Who could treat an animal this way?"

"Please take her. You need each other." Mary Ann's friend smiled.

"Okay, but I can't take a puppy on tour. Promise you'll take care of her while I'm away?" With Phyliss' promise, she took the basket and set the pup in a chair.

The next day the first thing Mary Ann did was take her new puppy, now named Choy in the spirit of her breed's origins, to the vet. The vet told her Choy's mange could be easily cured with topical antibiotics, but Choy had another problem.

"She's blind in one eye—probably an infection she got at the kennel. Her eyesight's gone."

Mary Ann stroked Choy's tiny head, no bigger than a tangerine, and Choy looked up as if to ask if everything was okay. The vet explained that though she wouldn't have good depth perception, she'd still be a fine house pet.

****

Weeks later, when Mary Ann came home from the Harris tour, she rushed to Phyliss' house to pick up Choy. The first thing Mary Ann noticed was how happy and fat Choy had grown. She hadn't realized how much she had missed her pup.

Though Mary Ann had other dogs at her western-style ranch in Nashville, including Pal, a black lab mix, Choy became her special friend. Everywhere Mary Ann went, Choy accompanied her—hustling, bustling to keep up with her busy human mother. Choy's happiness was evident in her attitude. She was a ball of cyclonic energy wrapped in dog skin. By the time she was a year and a half old, she owned the ranch, taking inventory of the animals and the chickens, bossing Pal and the other dogs, fast-walking the property with her front legs slightly bowed, her plump rear end swinging from side to side, and her tail beating its own rhythm.

Choy quickly usurped Pal's position as the farm manager. In the barn Choy helped Mary Ann brush Dolly. She lay atop an old rusty chair on a saddle pad in the barn aisle while Mary Ann picked Dolly's feet and curry-combed and brushed her. While Mary Ann mucked horse manure, Choy, running ahead and yipping, directed her human to push the wheelbarrow to each horse stall. She barked when the grain man came, and she nipped the heels of the sawdust delivery man.

Choy especially liked being in the barn with Mary Ann when it rained. A Tennessee summer rain obviously felt special, cozy, to Choy. With the sound of the rain pattering on the tin barn roof, and Pal and the other dogs, chickens, Dolly, and the cats taking shelter in the barn, Choy must have felt so safe with her family. The rain pouring outside the barn doors felt like a soft blanket enveloping them all together. Even when the southern sky brewed black with thunderclouds, and Mary Ann raced to get Dolly in from pasture, Choy loved everyone's excitement—her mom's and the barn help—running to secure doors and windows before the rain and lightning hit.

Another of Choy's favorite things was sleeping in Mary Ann's bed. When she was on tour, Choy went along, as she had on the *Austin City Limits* show in Texas. When the concert ended late at night, and Mary Ann flopped into bed, exhausted, she always remembered to hoist Choy and put her at the bottom of the bed. By morning, however, Choy had squirmed under the sheets, her small, chunky body warming her mom's side like a hot water bottle.

One morning while on tour, Mary Ann laughed as she shared a cup of coffee with Emmylou in her tour bus. "Choy scared the livin' you-know-what out of me this mornin'."

Emmylou wiped a long silvery stray hair from her face and took another sip. "What in the world happened?"

"Well, last night when I went to bed, I put Choy on top of the comforter at the bottom of my bed where I always put her.

"When I woke up this morning and opened my eyes, I was staring straight into her big bulgy eyes—like an inch or two from my face. I yelled bloody murder. Thought some old man had crawled in beside me. Choy's head was right there, against my face, her big ol' eyes starin' at me. She has this little wrinkly face. Looks like an alien. Really freaked me out."

Emmylou laughed. "She simply *adores* you, Mary Ann. You're her mama."

On tour with Mary Ann, Choy had the run of her tour bus, which she and Mary Ann shared with Pam Rose. During the day when Mary Ann took a break, she took Choy with her for a walk backstage and around the concert grounds where workers prepared the stage for the evening's performance. Choy visited with them all, helping to clean the stage from last night's show and barking as to where to set up the microphones, the lights, and the special effects equipment. Mary Ann watched proudly as Choy trotted, directing the men here, ordering them there with her huge bark, so many times larger than Choy herself. She bossed everyone. *"Here, that's right. Set the stand there."* Then she darted after another of the stage crew setting up the lighting equipment. *"Yes, that's right. I approve. Good—okay—let's get on to something else now."*

Choy was nearly as busy on tour as her mom. One time while Mary Ann was readying her outfits for the night's performance, Choy escaped the bus. Mary Ann found her having a snack and conversation with Emmylou Harris. Similarly, Choy met other renowned country singers—Lacy J. Dalton, Rosanne Cash, LeAnn Rimes, and Gail Davies. The ladies Choy preferred over the men singers, but she really liked Hank Williams, Jr. and John Berry, 'cause they played rough.

Her favorite celebrity, however, was Emmylou. Choy gazed, transfixed, in Emmylou's lap as the singer told Choy what it felt like to be a famous singer and how hard it was to leave one's family and her animals for months at a time. Just like Emmylou, Choy preferred being home, too—she had more room to run.

So when Mary Ann's tour bus pulled into their driveway in Nashville, Choy leaped down the steps of the bus, ran to the barn, traced a couple of frantic circles, and barked furiously to let Pal and all the other dogs, the chickens, ducks, and Dolly know she was back home.

Once home, Choy couldn't wait for Mary Ann to saddle up Dolly so that she could ride along with her mom. Sitting upright as all good equestriennes do, Choy took her place in front of Mary Ann, just behind the Western saddle horn, where there was just enough room for a tiny dog butt. While Mary Ann walked Dolly carefully along the trail, she always had a hand on Choy's back, and Choy knew to keep quiet so as not to upset Dolly.

To a bystander, Choy looked as though she loved her horse rides, feeling the rhythmical back and forth of the horse's flat walk, smelling the good odor rising from Dolly's skin. And Choy must have found the Tennessee landscape, with its lush grasses and foliage, with its thick stands of woods, delightful from the back of a horse.

In a few weeks, though, the rides ended because Dolly became pregnant with her first foal. Soon after, one fall day in 1990, Choy overheard a phone conversation Mary Ann was having with Sting's manager. "Yes, Pam and I would love to open Sting's tour. I can go anytime, but I must be home by May. My walking horse mare is going to foal the middle of May. I've got to be here."

Choy listened attentively, her head cocked. She saw her mom nod. "Okay, it's a deal."

Unfortunately, Choy wasn't able to accompany

Mary Ann on her Sting tour. She had to be content living with the ranch's farm manager and her husband while her mom was away. When the gigantic black tour bus pulled up to take Mary Ann and Pamela Rose to their first gig with Sting, spinster Choy ran out to the front porch, her tongue lolling from the corner of her mouth, her big eyes sad. She had seen her mom off on so many occasions she couldn't have counted them on two paws. Friends helped load the last of the luggage, two guitars, a mandolin, the kalimba, the hand drum and tambourine, the dulcimer and the bouzouki into the bottom of the bus.

Just before the bus was ready to pull away, Choy barked from the porch. Suddenly Mary Ann popped from the bus and ran to Choy, hoisting her into the air. "I wouldn't forget about you. Mommy'll miss you somethin' terrible, Choy. You behave yourself, and don't boss the chickens around so." Choy looked into Mary Ann's face, and she panted with a furrowed brow.

"Now, don't you worry. You've got to take care of all the animals, Choy. Make sure they're happy—especially Pal, 'cause he's gettin' old. Oh, and most of all—take care of Dolly. If you see anything wrong, run and tell Sarah. I love you, sweetheart."

****

The following months passed slowly for Choy. She missed her best human companion, but she distracted herself with hunting sprees with Pal, sleeping under the cedar tree, directing the chickens and guinea hens, and checking on Dolly out in pasture.

Every few days Mary Ann phoned home to check on things. When Choy recognized her mom's voice from across the living room, she blew past all the other sleeping dogs, jumped over the sleeping Pal, and stood on her hind legs at Sarah's side as though demanding to speak with her mother. Then Sarah lowered the phone to Choy, and the little pug listened intently as Mary Ann described to Choy her life on tour. Mary Ann whispered into the phone, "I miss you, Choy. I'll be home in a few weeks, darlin'. You take good care of Dolly now, you hear? Mommy loves you very much." And then, to Choy's disappointment, her mom's voice went silent.

****

At two a.m. the morning of May 16th, 1991, Mary Ann's phone in the tour bus jarred her awake. It was Sarah. Mary Ann sat upright, afraid of some terrible news. "You've got a beautiful black-and-white colt, Mary Ann. Dolly gave birth about an hour ago—no problems. I knew you would want to know as soon as it happened. Everything went fine, and Dolly is being a good mother with him. I'll get the vet out in the morning to check him out."

Mary Ann sniffed back happy tears. "He's black and white! My first foal! And he was born on Choy's birthday—May 16th!"

"What are you going to name him?"

"I'm going to name him Tonka."

****

Two days later, Mary Ann's bus pulled into the driveway. All her friends had come out to welcome her home, but first she wanted to see her new foal. Into the barn she ran, and there, in the foaling stall, standing behind Dolly, stood the two-day-old foal.

She opened the stall door slowly, reminding herself not to shriek out loud in her excitement. Mary Ann patted Dolly on the shoulder. "Good girl, Dolly. You are one special lady." Then she peeked around Dolly's side for a good view of the colt. Her breath caught in her throat, and she could only speak in a whisper. "Oh, oh…my goodness, Tonka. You're absolutely gorgeous! Let me touch you."

The colt turned toward her, his long-lashed eyes blinking to bring his human owner into focus. Mary Ann bent down to his level and put out a hand. Tonka reached out and placed his tiny muzzle in Mary Ann's palm.

"You're so soft, my handsome boy. Look at you. Your mommy's so proud of you. She made the most gorgeous little colt I've ever seen." The colt sniffed Mary Ann's fingers, and Mary Ann giggled at the long white whiskers on his muzzle. "You look like a little old man. You have a beard." So Mary Ann walked quietly to a corner of the stall, sat in the clean straw, and watched while Tonka ducked his head under his mom's belly. As she heard the quiet, comforting sounds of Tonka nursing, she said softly, "Happy birthday, sweetheart."

Suddenly Choy appeared at Dolly's stall door, her little alien-wrinkled face uncertain. She had never seen a baby horse before. When her mom spoke, though, Choy's tongue fell from her mouth, and she looked anxiously from Mary Ann to Dolly's baby, then back to Mary Ann. "Come 'ere, Pumpkin. It's all right. Come and watch our Tonka with me."

Choy walked slowly, tentatively, into the stall, and as soon as she reached her mom, she leaped into her arms, lapping her face and wriggling all over. "Happy birthday, Choy." Choy's body shook, so happy was she to see her mom. Talking in a low voice, Mary Ann petted Choy calm, whispering how much she had missed her, and soon Choy turned around and sat down in her lap, her face turned adoringly to her mother. Together, Choy and Mary Ann sat in the clean straw while Tonka took good, deep sips of Dolly's milk.

****

The next morning Mary Ann led Dolly, with Tonka following closely behind, from her stall to the pasture. Tonka, at only a few days old, was a naturally gaited horse—he had a God-given way of moving at a running walk, a smooth, four-beat gait specific to the walking horse breed, and he followed his mother everywhere through the lush grass, dancing circles around Dolly as she grazed. When Tonka became brave enough to wander over to a couple of chickens passing through the field, Dolly whickered to him to come back to her circle of safety.

As always, Choy slipped under the fence to make her daily inspection as she had grown used to doing when Dolly was pregnant. Tonka came running, stopping just a foot short of the little dog. Then the two touched noses, and Tonka charged back to his mother for reassurance and a milk snack. Satisfied that all was right, Choy trotted back to the barn.

The summer months passed by quickly. Mother and baby hung out daily in the pastures except on rainy days when they stayed in their stall. With every day Mary Ann watched Tonka filling out and growing taller. He had been very amenable to his halter training, and already Mary Ann had started sacking out the little colt—a trainer's term for running blankets and other objects over a young horse's body in order to desensitize the foal to the smell and the touch of manmade stuff. Sacking out a horse was part of the preliminary training for breaking a youngster to saddle.

That fall when Mary Ann wasn't busy writing songs for a CD with Sting, she took breaks from her music to run with Tonka, newly weaned from his mother, in the pasture. The two romped together, the colt running toward Mary Ann and Mary Ann running toward Tonka. One chased, the other ran. Mary Ann kicked Tonka's beach ball, and Tonka tore after it, kicking his heels high above his head. At first he accidentally kicked the ball with a front hoof, and it sailed into the air. That thrilled the little colt, so he kept after it, nudging it with his muzzle, walking after it, then stubbing it with a hoof. When Mary Ann tried to horn in on his game, he leaped into the air and went after the ball, surely not wanting to be outdone. Finally, the playtime ended with Mary Ann popping a couple of baby carrots in his mouth.

In weeks Mary Ann and Pam Rose were set to finish writing and producing two CDs, *Hai Ku* and *Walk the Line*, on Sting's Pangea record label. That day in the recording studio, with Choy sitting at attention on a metal fold-out chair, Kennedy-Rose belted out their first song in the glass-lined studio. The engineer mixing the songs in the control room gave them a thumbs up— it was a seal. They sang the next song, which needed a couple of re-takes. Then they got the signal that it had recorded well. They took a break, drank some coffee, and began the next production session.

When they began the second session, the engineer indicated something was wrong with the playback. Mary Ann couldn't understand what sounded so weird.

"Play that back to me one more time, and turn down the volume." The engineer piped the song into the sound room, and Pam and Mary Ann strained to pick out the foreign sound.

Pam strained to her. "What *is* that noise?"

Suddenly Mary Ann began laughing. She pointed to Choy, who had fallen asleep in her chair in the corner. "It's Choy—snoring. Play it back again, boys." And after another playback, there was the proof—between the notes were the sounds of Choy's luxurious nap, almost in rhythm to the song itself.

****

Back home on the ranch, Mary Ann devoted herself to taming Tonka. She had long ago halter-broke the colt. Tonka, since the second day of his life, had been imprinted by Mary Ann much as he had his own mother. To Tonka, the human was simply another relative horse who just smelled a bit different. That "horse with two legs" ran in the pasture as he did, kicked around a ball as he did, and whinnied to him just as his mother did. She fed him as his mother did, though not milk. The human horse gave him carrots, apple pieces, and lots of molasses-laced grain. And she groomed him as his mother sometimes did, too.

Though Choy was getting a little old to be running from the pastures to the barn, she still sat with Mary Ann while she brushed and saddled Dolly. She didn't enjoy the rides as much anymore. So Choy contented herself with watching Mary Ann from the sidelines—sitting atop a saddle pad while his mom brushed Tonka and picked out his hooves and listening to the country songs softly playing on the radio. Though Mary Ann didn't notice it, Choy's watery snores sounded like a drain emptying. The loud gurgling was worrying to the wide-eyed Tonka standing cross-tied in the barn aisle.

Choy loved being with all the animals at the ranch, but she seemed jealous of all the attention Mary Ann gave Tonka. So in an effort to include Choy in her horse-training sessions, Mary Ann yelled for the pug to join her in the pasture. "Choy, come here. Watch this!" Choy, trotting slowly to the fence because of her arthritis, heard her mistress and forgot about herding the chickens.

Choy watched from beyond the fence. Mary Ann stood beside Tonka, rubbed her hands all over his body, rested her weight, which wasn't much, on his back, mindful that the young colt could get scared and gallop off. She tested Tonka's back again to see if he would react, but he stood as calm as a stone, turning his head to his side to see what she was up to.

"Now watch, Choy." With that, she pulled a mounting block over to Tonka's side, stepped up three steps, and very quietly slipped onto his back. Choy watched anxiously, her tongue lolling from her mouth. What was her mom doing?

Tonka had no reaction. He just stood still. Turning his head to look at his back, he didn't seem to mind that Mary Ann sat aboard him. Then she slid off. "Good boy, Tonka. That was the next step in your schooling. In a year of our practicing that, you'll be ready to graduate to first grade. Then you'll be off to a trainer when you are two years old."

****

For the next few years Mary Ann's life of music and animals filled every day. She had cut two CDs for Sting, went on tour with him, and wrote more songs with Pam Rose. Choy accompanied her on most tours while Tonka went and came back from being broke to ride. Tonka had grown into an obedient, smooth-gaited walking horse, levelheaded enough to be ridden bareback even at such a young age.

Though he was well-mannered under saddle, Tonka was a horse in clown's clothing. Had he been born small enough to sit in Mary Ann's lap as Choy always did, he would have because he was a lap horse, always wanting to be cuddled, played with, stroked, and brushed. He much preferred the company of his human mother to that of his equine mother, and loved playing ball with Mary Ann in the field, letting her ride bareback and without a bridle in the pasture.

Tonka had, ages ago, tired of the beach ball, and it had deflated to the flatness of a flake of hay anyway. Mary Ann replaced it with a good, long-lasting soccer ball, but even that he grew bored with. As most human kids become bored with their Christmas toys, so Tonka was always on the lookout for something new to satisfy his curiosity. When Choy happened into the pasture or when a couple of chickens ventured into Tonka's field, he ran to them, asking them to play, but Choy, who used to run and bark, now dived under the fence railing to safety on the other side, and the chickens scurried beyond the fence, too.

Finally, after standing on his toes and stretching his neck to twice its length, Tonka was able to grab the end of a lead rope draped over a fence rail. He pulled it into his pasture, and while he had the snap end in his mouth, the rest of it hung down between his legs and curled at his feet like a snake. Tonka probably wondered what it could be. Would it roll like a beach ball? Could he eat it? Would it run if he dropped it? Could he chase it down the pasture?

Dropping the rope to the ground, Tonka stared at it. It was dead, he surely thought. Not to be deterred, however, Tonka picked it up in his mouth, and with it he ran the length of the pasture. Round the pasture Tonka flew, the end of the six-foot cotton lead rope in his mouth, his head high, the rope flapping alongside him. He ran past his mother, and Dolly's eyes went wide as the flying rope whipped past her in a blur. Down the other side Tonka galloped, the rope undulating in the wind. Then he stopped, stood up on his hind legs and, with his mouth, tossed the rope around in the air like a cowboy wielding a lasso.

Mary Ann saw all this clownish activity unfolding from her window where she and Pam had been polishing their last song. Mary Ann stood at the window and put down her guitar. She laughed. "Damn horse. He's such a character. Never had one so playful like him. Most horses just like to stand and eat grass all day, but Tonka's always lookin' for trouble. And if it doesn't come to him, he'll go lookin' for it."

Pam joined Mary Ann at the window. "He's some animal. He's your kind of horse. You've always owned horses, haven't you, Mary Ann?"

"Yep, ever since I was a little girl with my first sorrel mare, Suzie. I never outgrew 'em. And I never will. On the day I die I'll be lovin' 'em still." She sighed.

Pam thought hard. "Hey, those words would make a good song. Come on, let's finish and take a break."

****

For the next five years Mary Ann wrote music for

EMI. After she became co-owner of Gila Monster Music and Dreamcatcher Music, she began developing other songwriters and singers. When she wasn't working or touring, she was expanding her horse farm, acquiring other brood mares and geldings, and riding Tonka along the hills and through the woods surrounding her ranch. And Choy was always there— gentle by her side.

****

Tonka died unexpectedly on August 4, 2000. He was 9 years old

Choy died the next day on August 5, 2000. She was 15 years old.

****

Choy's and Tonka's Memorials

The passing of her two best animal friends within a day of each other put Mary Ann into a grief-stricken tailspin. Her work came to a standstill. Her bed felt empty without her dear pug by her side, and the pasture looked empty without Tonka kicking up his heels. Her world felt dead. The day Choy died, Mary Ann, tears flooding her eyes, looked at the sky. She would forever swear two clouds formed right there in the shape of hearts—one a small heart, the other a larger heart.

Her Choy, who came to her out of the blue, a mangy, flea-bitten rescue, inspired her with her unconditional love and adoration. Just as Choy followed Mary Ann everywhere—to the barn, to bed, on tours, to every place Mary Ann went at any time of the day, so did Mary Ann realize that the true meaning of life was bound in one's devotion to another being and that, though career and happiness in one's job is important, it pales in comparison to meaningful relationships offering uncritical love as Choy's and hers had exemplified.

Choy was Mary Ann's best friend, her teacher—about life, love, and innocence—and her hero.

****

Tonka was a little fifth grader's dream realized in flesh and blood. Tonka, like Choy, delivered a large dose of love and acceptance. Trust comes slowly between a horse and a human, but when Tonka was only one year old, he had trusted Mary Ann enough not to buck her off when she crawled onto his back. And when he was older, and she rode him over the fields and through the woods, he trusted her to take him to safe places and over solid terrain.

****

Both animals balanced out Mary Ann's hectic life. At times she was overwhelmed with the music business, with its share of competitiveness and fast-paced demands. She loved most of her associates, but bad, untrustworthy people existed in the music business as well as in all businesses. Away from home she pushed paper and pens, and the red tape never ended. When the stress turned her smile into a frown, she confided in her friends that she needed some horsin' around. So when she came home from a tour, ragged and worn out, she fell into the loving folds of Choy and Tonka, their love, their acceptance, their trust, their honesty and their goodness refreshing her spirit, making her brand-new again.

Choy's and Tonka's passing inspired a whole new development in Mary Ann's career. She began by working out her grief in songs about her animals. When she shared the new songs with Pamela Rose, they recognized a uniqueness to her music that was totally different from her previous musical work. This music, they said, was from Mary Ann's heart and her soul. This music was about her and her relationship with animals. In her music about her dog and her horse, she was living herself, being true to herself.

****

Today Mary Ann says that Choy and Tonka are her angels who, she says, are "not really gone." And, to be sure, they may be physically gone, but their life forces, their innocence, their spirits live on in her music. Besides the two songs "Choy's Song" and "I Wish I Had a Horse," both of which she wrote in their memory and produced in her first CD, *The Trail Less Traveled*, she is now devoting herself to songs related entirely to the human/animal bond. She writes, in particular, about horse-related activities—mucking out stalls, taking in hay, Jack Russell terriers, barn cats, riding green horses, and riding in the evening with fireflies. Her songs speak to animal lovers, horse enthusiasts, and riders of any style of riding. Most of all, her CDs speak to the spirit of our animal friends.

****

To listen to the memorials for Choy and Tonka taken from her CD *The Trail Less Traveled*, go to www.maryannkennedy.com. You will be directed to www.cdbaby.com where you will be able to access Mary Ann's album *The Trail Less Traveled* and listen to "Choy's Song," "I Wish I Had a Horse," and "Goodbye."

Chapter Twenty-One
The Purr-fect Moment

Breed: domestic feline
Name: Cynthia
Born: 1992; adopted July 15, 1994
Died: January 27, 2006
Human companions: Tod and Connie

Vet tech Sherry laughed when she put the big, foofy-tailed, black-and-white cat on the counter. "We all call her Poochy-Cheeks." Connie smiled as the homeless cat perched on the edge of the counter, obviously content in a high place, as most cats are. Her face was distinctively round, like a cherub's. Her cheeks protruded like little mounds of vanilla icing—she had the charm of a big-cheeked baby. And the rest of her was as equally striking, with her long, glossy hair, her tail resembling the bushy, ringed tail of a raccoon. Connie's breath caught in her throat at such a commanding presence.

Then Sherry's face went sad. "Abandoned."

Connie patted the top of the cat's head. The cat shot her a look—*I'm not happy with strangers invading my space.*

"Who could do such a thing?" Connie stroked the cat's long, lean body.

"When the new owner moved into his house, he

found two cats inside with empty water and feed bowls. I found the other one a home. This girl needs one now."

"I can't stand people."

"I know. We're a throwaway society. People even throw away their animals when they're finished with them."

Again Connie stroked the cat's head, and this time the animal leaned into Connie's palm. She hadn't been touched by a person in a long time.

"I'll take her home with me, Sherry. Right now. I think she likes me."

****

As soon as Connie set the carrier down on the living room floor, Tod walked over and raised it to eye level. "Hello, kitty."

"You should see her." Their other cat, Willie, observed from several yards away while Tod carefully opened the top of the cardboard carrier.

"Yeoooow!"

The big, bushy-haired cat burst through the slit like fireworks through a tube. Tod leapt back. The cat went airborne and landed right next to the surprised Willie.

Tod wore a look of incredulity. "Wow, seems you brought home a spitfire. But she sure is pretty with her long fur."

"Her new name is Cynthia Ann—Ann for "anniversary." Connie planted a kiss on her husband's cheek. "Happy twenty-fourth Cynthi-anniversary, dear."

****

Their old cat Willie was used to being king of the condominium, so he didn't appreciate the living, breathing anniversary present. He stared at the intruder, who sat perfectly still on the floor, neither attempting to hide from him nor going into a submissive position. Most cats would have surrendered the moment they laid eyes on Willie's hugeness, his bulk, but this one had been fending for herself for months, living off rats, bugs, and whatever else she could find in the abandoned house. A big-haired orange cat didn't intimidate her in the least.

Willie had always been shy, using his size as a shield against any feline competition. He'd never met a cat who reeked with attitude like the one sitting with perfect calm before him. He shivered.

As Tod and Connie watched, Willie creep-slinked toward the sitting Cleopatra, her poofy cheeks and regal posture making it clear she was in no mood to tolerate any crap from anyone. Willie took another step. *Careful, testing—*

"*Yeooow!*"

Cynthia erupted like Mount St. Helens. She charged, spitting and spraying Willie with indignant vitriol, her toes spread, claws raking the air. When she landed, Willie had already raced for the basement. What monster had invaded his home? Tod and Connie felt sorry for Willie, but they couldn't help laughing. Cynthia looked so pleased with herself, so smug.

****

The next day Cynthia, perched on her favorite ottoman, guarded the living room from higher ground. When Willie creep-moused into the room, he cast her a sidelong glance. *Is the bitch going to attack?*

In slow-mo Willie made his way carefully, slowly, past the ottoman whereon the queen was enthroned. Monitoring Her Highness, Willie trod lightly on tiptoe, setting down one slow, deliberate paw at a time. Cynthia shot him a look. Willie turned and slinked, padding quietly out of the room.

Whenever Willie crept past Cynthia's perch, the highest point, wherever it might be, in every room, she simultaneously stared at him and through him. Then, when he peered up at her, she rolled her huge eyes. *Don't give me any shit, or I'll nail you.*

Cynthia terrorized Willie until she commanded his total subservience, but she adored Connie. In the evenings when Tod and Connie watched television, Cynthia, perched on the back of the sofa, rose up on all four legs and walked the tight wire back of the couch over to Connie's head where she let out a high-pitched, stringy, *"Bree-ow-owl"* to which Connie responded with her own version of "Hello, dear heart." Then, just as natural and unremarkable as a mother's and daughter's kiss, the two would bang heads. Head-butting is a cat's way of expressing affection, and Connie always butted Cynthia in turn. It was their love butt.

All cats live in the moment, but Connie knew that one of Cynthia's most intriguing attributes was her living in the *perfect* moment—be it lying in the kitchen sink, guarding the living room from the stairs' landing, ruling from the ottoman, or play-dancing with Connie.

Cynthia clearly valued sharing each perfect moment with Connie. In particular, she loved curling up for a nap in the cast-iron kitchen sink. Each night while Connie scrubbed the dinner dishes Cynthia waited, perched above the sink filled with hot bubbly dishwater. Connie or Tod hurried to finish the dishes because Cynthia demanded the sink.

"Okay, Cyn-Cyn, I'm going as fast as I can." Connie swirled her dish rag, soap suds flying—quick rinse, into the dish rack on the other side of the sink, pick up the next plate. Hurry up, Cyn's getting impatient. Cynthia watched the tub of hot water and gingerly tapped a bubble with her paw. She glared with an intensity cats are noted for, her eyes huge, her chin drawn back. The only thing that mattered at that moment was her sink. Then she pawed the water again.

"Okay, I'm hurrying already."

Finally Connie pulled the plug, and the water swirled away, a hot sudsy maelstrom. All the while Cynthia stared, and then, after wringing out the dish rag, Connie quickly wiped out the sink.

"Okay, go to it, Cyn. It's all yours."

Cynthia stepped down carefully into the sink, her eyes half closed as she felt the heat radiating from the tub. Slowly she circled once, twice, and lay down, her back against the warm sides, her cheeks puffed all the way out, her lips pulled back into a smile, her chin relaxed. Once curled in the sink, she twisted herself in the middle—all luxuriance—her front arms out and over her head. She was Ingres's *Odalisque with the Slave.*

Another perfect moment found Cynthia as the sous chef. The second Cynthia heard a big celery stalk thud onto the cutting board, she jumped onto the kitchen counter. For the next fifteen minutes Cynthia sat, her chin tucked under, cheeks puffed out, lips pursed, eyes mesmerized by the ceremonial *cutting of the vegetables.* The moment was indeed perfect, contemplative—personal time with her human.

Seeing Connie's hands working so quickly, with

such rhythm and precision, Cynthia crept closer and closer to the action. Connie watched Cyn from the corner of her eye, not saying a word—just watching. *Chop-chop-chop-chop-chop* went Connie's knife. The bits of celery hopped around the cutting board, and Cynthia followed each piece as it fell. By the time Connie picked up a carrot, Cynthia was practically on top of the cutting board. *Carrots—heaven!*

After Connie finished the carrots and onions, and all the vegetables had been dropped into the cook pot, Cynthia closed her eyes and sighed. The deed was done. Connie decided she looked like someone who's had a massage—renewed, refreshed.

Much as Cynthia loved her perfect moments such as lying in the hot sink, helping Connie cut vegetables, playing sentry from the highest place in every room, she disliked other things, such as being held captive in Tod or Connie's lap when she wasn't in the mood. Though Tod still worked as a chemical engineer, Connie had retired from biological research and greeted each morning with exuberance, her day filled with fun things to do, her morning relaxing. Coffee and sticky bun in hand, she headed to the back porch to luxuriate in the bird songs and the beauty of the morning. In her quiet ecstasy she sometimes scooped Cynthia up into her lap—for Connie, the perfect morning moment was a cup of coffee with a side order of Cynthia.

But the morning quiet didn't last very long. After approximately thirty seconds and two sips of her coffee, a low guttural rumble sounded. *"Brrl-rrl-rrl-rrwl!"* Like thunder after a lightning strike, it was all so predictable. Connie took another sip. This one was accompanied by a vibration issuing from her lap, followed by a louder growl. Connie sipped again, smiling. A hissing intake of breath was followed by a growl-yowl. Connie put her coffee cup down just in time before Cynthia burst from Connie's lap, landed with a thud on the porch floor, turned around, gave Connie The Look, and headed to a patch of sun in the grass.

The Look, as Connie and Tod referred to it, was Cynthia's version of disdain—disgust blended with detachment, irritation combined with the ability to render something invisible. Cynthia possessed the uncanny ability to look *at* something while at the same time looking *through* it. The Look sometimes involved a rolling of the eyeballs. Cynthia's head never moved when she broadcast The Look to her humans or to other cats in the family. Whether from one of her command-and-control centers on top of the hutch, the refrigerator, or the upstairs landing, she gave everyone The Look— *"I'm comfortable, I'm ensconced here, and I don't intend to move. Disturb me at your peril."*

Sometimes, depending on Cynthia's daily agenda, she actually enjoyed lap-sitting. Every evening at supper time she climbed into Tod's lap before the television just as Connie handed him his plate of food. With his plate resting precariously on the chair's arm, he ate gingerly—careful not to disturb Cynthia in his lap—his head and neck twisted to the side, his tongue reaching for the forked food before it dropped off and rolled into the netherworld of the chair's guts.

****

Meghan, a kitten known in the family as the Drive-By Kid, admired Cynthia but was underwhelmed by The Look. Cynthia, having enslaved her new humans

and beaten Willie into submission, was ensconced on
her ottoman and relaxing to her favorite New Wave
music, "Deep Breakfast" by Ray Lynch. She was, in
fact, living a perfect moment. But mischievous little
Meghan had different ideas. Knowing Cynthia was
zoned out in the twilight contentment of the living
room, the little tuxedo kitten began revving up in the
kitchen. Meghan sprang, racing through the house until
she reached the living room where she skidded into the
turn, leapt up and over Cynthia, down the other side of
the ottoman, and out of the room. Cynthia pretended
not to notice at first, but when Meghan streaked through
the living room again and did a brazen leap along the
side of the ottoman right under Cynthia's nose, her
claws making a Velcro-like rasping sound against the
furniture, Cynthia opened her eyes and gave Meghan
The Look, followed by a warning gurgle.

Connie was sitting in the living room enjoying
Meghan's game. Before the second drive-by, the kitten
crept into the doorway of the living room and looked at
Connie—if her human mom disapproved of her teasing
Cyn, then she'd have to stop, but if she was okay with
it, Meghan could keep playing. Connie was smiling.

Again Meghan revved up, this time far off in the
den. Claws raking the hardwood—revving into turbo-
boost—the kitten tore into the living room and did
another side-pass along the ottoman, right under
Cynthia's nose. Cynthia's body stayed perfectly still,
but The Look intensified. Then Cynthia turned toward
Connie and gave *her* The Look. *Aren't you going to
scold the brat?*

With her next drive-bys, Meghan pounced beside
Cynthia's head, leapt onto the floor, and raced back into

the kitchen. After four or five cycles of Evel Knievel's routine, Cynthia had had enough. She flashed The Look, jumped from her ottoman, and sashayed away.

Cynthia wasn't always in stoic control mode. Sometimes she liked to play—when she was in the mood. One game was the Paper Chase. Connie put a piece of paper on the kitchen counter facing Cynthia. Under that paper she put another one, the end of which Connie held from the side opposite Cynthia. When Connie pushed the paper underneath toward Cynthia, she slapped it with her paw. The object of the game was for Connie to snatch the under-paper away before Cynthia could paw-slap it.

In the micro-second Cynthia saw the edge of the under-paper, she hit it—*Slap!* Then, after she thought she'd killed it, out it came again. Her lips pursed, her poochy cheeks stuck out. *Smack!* It was gone—dead, for sure.

Only it wasn't. Again the sheet peeped out from under the top one, and again Cynthia slammed it with her paw. Again it disappeared. Low growls erupted from her throat—Cynthia was a poor loser.

The Cat-titude never lost the Paw-Slap game either. When Connie saw Cynthia's paw out in front of her, whether she was sitting, watching Connie cut vegetables, or just hanging out on her landing to the upstairs, Connie slowly put her hand on top of Cyn's paw. Cynthia immediately slid her paw from underneath Connie's hand and placed it on top of Connie's hand. The game always started slowly but gradually sped up. Connie's hand covered Cynthia's paw. Cynthia's paw rested on Connie's hand—*hand on paw, paw on hand; hand-paw, paw-hand; handpaw, pawhand; hdpw, pwhd; hp,ph.* Finally, *paw-paw-pawpaw*—Cynthia declared herself the winner.

One day Connie made Cynthia a special toy. She took an old black pair of opaque pantyhose, cut one leg off above the ankle, filled the foot with a jellyroll of polyester batting and catnip, tied off the end, and presented the "rat" to Cynthia. All was well if Connie gave Cyn her rat during the day, but if Connie ever made her one at night, she and Tod might be shocked out of sleep by Cynthia's howls and growls as she stalked, swatted, and finally killed the big rat in the house. In the morning the evidence of the kill—guts of cotton batting—lay scattered on the floor.

Cynthia considered certain areas of her body acceptable for brushing—from the shoulders to the head. But the other area, from the shoulders to the tail—absolutely off limits. If Connie brought out the brush, Cynthia gave it The Look so that it would go away just like Willie. Cynthia would allow brushing only on her terms. In fact, in order to remove a hair mat, it took both Tod and Connie in the PYA position—Protect Your Ass—a term coined by Cynthia's veterinarian, the recipient of Cyn's wrath on numerous occasions. In the PYA position Tod scruffed Cynthia's neck and pinned her back legs. He and Connie stood to either side of the cat, arms and hands out of range of her teeth, Connie brushing her as fast as possible lest she swivel her head *Exorcist*-style and bite. Cynthia twisted, writhing against them with jaguar-like strength, trying to snag a hand or at the very least, a tasty finger. Tod and Connie gritted their teeth and held tight while Cynthia screamed, her mouth wide, high-pitched feline obscenities spewing, deep-throated.

"Ah, dear Cynth-ia-ah, you'll look so pretty when we're done." Tod pretended Cynthia was the perfect, most civilized patient. Then he mustered his calmest voice. "My wicked, wicked girl. You are a Cynthi—ah—bitch!" Connie laughed as she pulled a nasty mat from the cat's rump.

Connie made sure the brushing always ended peacefully by putting Cynthia back into one of her perfect moments. After the horrific brushing from the shoulders to the tail ended, usually with either Tod or Connie bleeding, Connie continued with the head. No need to scruff her neck and pin her to the counter, for just as Cynthia loathed having her body brushed, she adored having her head, throat, and ears groomed and rubbed.

The Brushing of the Head could morph the cat in seconds from the Manson-like Cynthia to the calm, Zen-like Cynthia. All of this depended somewhat on Cyn's mood at any given time, but cats are quick to forgive, and when Connie stroked her down to her chin, Cynthia usually stuck out her nether lip—*Yea-ah, that really feels good, and I'm going to make it even easier for you to scratch it.*

Cynthia also went into Zen mode when Connie worked in her garden. From her favorite outdoor chair Cynthia watched Connie scratch out weeds with a hoe and hand trowel. *"Scritch—scritch—scritch—scritch."* Cynthia clearly loved the ground-purrs of the hoe digging dirt. After fifteen minutes Connie looked up to make sure Cynthia was still in her chair. *"Scritch—scritch—scritch-scritch—scritch."* Cyn looked as though she was asleep, but she was actually zoned out as long as the scratching continued without interruption.

If for any reason Connie stopped digging, Cynthia suddenly rose to alert, eyes open, body rigid. Connie knew what came next—The Look. *My moment is being disturbed. I don't like it.*

When Cynthia was young, Connie had decided to put her love of New Wave music and rock to good use. Connie's mother had entered a nursing home in Maryland that had a lounge for watching TV or videotapes relatives sent. Connie set up her video camera on a tripod focused on the staircase landing and cranked up Billy Ray Cyrus's "Achy Breaky Heart." If this act didn't get the old folks laughing, nothing would.

With the camera on and the music blaring, Connie went into action, gyrating, twirling, beating the air in rhythm to the music. And Cynthia, poised on the landing at Connie's shoulder, sashayed parallel to Connie—up the stairs, down the stairs, whirling around the landing at Connie's head. The two were dancing with each other, with Cynthia leading, or so she thought. Back and forth Connie moved to the beat while Cynthia ran, leapt, and jumped next to her. Then, in a grand finale, Connie positioned Cynthia onto her shoulders and the two of them whirled and twirled, Cynthia balancing herself perfectly, loving the screaming beat, the heat of their movement.

****

When Tod came home one evening from work he immediately noticed that Cynthia wasn't at the door to greet him as was her habit. He called in his most melodious voice. "Cynthi-ah-ah! Cynthi-ah-ah? Where are you-ou-ou?"

Nothing.

Very strange. Cynthia always called to them in her mellifluous voice.

So Tod went looking for her. He found her sitting sternal on the ottoman, but something looked off. He picked her up, and she growled but without giving him The Look, and it wasn't a warning type of growl. It was more a growl of distress. Later that evening Tod and Connie discovered that Cynthia had somehow broken her jaw, whether by jumping from the refrigerator and landing wrong or falling from another of her favorite high places.

Despite the vet's best efforts to wire her jaw in place, Cynthia had lost the ability to chew. Thereafter Connie had to tie a bib around Cynthia's neck and hand-feed soft food through a syringe. Considering Cynthia's personality and sensibilities, Connie was afraid she'd find the whole business offensive. But come mealtime, she curled around the refrigerator, her metal-wired mouth grating against the door—Cynthia wanted her meal.

Feeding Cynthia each day, for each meal, three to four times a day for what turned out to be three years, quickly became a ritual—warm the cat food in the microwave, lift Cynthia onto the counter, attach a paper towel bib under her chin with a clip in back, feed her with the syringe, wipe Cynthia's mouth and chin with a warm washcloth, take off the bib, gently set her on the floor. All this Cynthia endured without resentment or complaint. But once her belly was full, she'd had enough of the fussing and ordered Connie to let her clean herself.

Tod and Connie's "Cynthi-ah-ah," as they yodeled for many years, had been their most cantankerous, most playful, most entertaining best feline friend. And though they had to use PYA time and again, Lieutenant Cynthia guarded their house and garden, she danced and played "gotcha" games, and she simply curled up and became loving every night after they climbed into bed.

Sleeping with Tod and Connie was the most perfect of Cynthia's perfect moments. She leapt onto the bed, walked across Tod, took a sharp turn to the right, and lay with arms outstretched on Connie's chest until first Connie, then Tod, and then Cynthia fell asleep.

Cynthia died January 27, 2006.

****

Cynthia's Memorial

When Cynthia died, their vet placed her into a large freezer. Connie and Tod were to pick her up at the vet office on Saturday and bury her later that day. But when Tod came home with her body and laid her aside to start digging the hole, he just couldn't do it.

"She's just too beautiful to put in the ground. There has to be something else we can do for her." He went inside to search the internet.

Tod found a chat room for grieving pet owners and learned that a pet could be freeze-dried. He found several companies that did freeze-dried preservation in the United States, but he was suspicious. Would he be sending their best friend into the arms of a shyster? Would the technicians respect her body? Maybe they'd never get Cynthia back at all, the culprits making off with their money *and* their dead cat. Then Tod found the company Perpetual Pets in Keyser, West Virginia. Tod's dad lived in West Virginia, so he called him.

His father sounded concerned. "How can I help?"

"I'd like you to do a drive-by of this freeze-drying place and tell me what it looks like. You don't have to go inside or anything. At least I'll know whether they're actually a business."

Later that night the phone rang. "I did a little bit more than a drive-by. I had lunch with Sandy, the owner of the place." At eighty-three, Tod's dad was still feisty and gutsy. "You won't go wrong sending little Cynthia to them. She showed me her own cat they had freeze-dried. She looks great—just like she's sleeping. Go for it."

Within minutes Tod was on the phone with Sandy. The scientist in him wanted to know all about the freeze-drying process. He also wanted to be sure he wasn't buying into any procedure that would desecrate Cynthia's body. Sandy explained that during sublimation the animal's body is placed in a chamber containing a refrigeration compressor with a vacuum pump. The pump lowers the pressure inside the chamber to a point that when the ice inside the body is slightly heated by the heating shelves, the moisture under pressure turns directly into water vapor instead of water, which is pumped out of the chamber.

"After ten weeks or so when the process is completed, the refrigeration is stopped, the chamber opened, and Cynthia will be lifted out, looking as perfect and real as when she went in." When Tod asked how long the body would stay intact, Sandy said that so long as her preserved body was kept in an indoor atmosphere, she'd stay dehydrated, free of bacteria and odors, for years and years.

Under Sandy's directions, Tod built the ultimate

shipping container in which to send Cynthia's body from their home in North Carolina to West Virginia. With all the attention to detail required by his job as a chemical engineer, Tod began construction of a container fit for a pet of royalty. From the local hardware store he bought a two-foot-square heavy-duty cardboard box whose walls he lined with polystyrene insulation board. Into the box he placed Cynthia inside a plastic Tupperware container filled with Styrofoam "peanuts" and gel ice packs. Then he took the frozen package to FedEx for overnight-air shipment to West Virginia.

All night Tod sat in front of his computer, tracking his MVP—most valuable package. Cynthia's body had made the plane to Indianapolis, then to Pittsburgh, after which the tracking data said she was on a truck bound for Cumberland, Maryland. At 2:05 the next afternoon, the tracking information relayed the shipment's delivery to Perpetual Pets, and twenty minutes later Sandy called to say she had Cynthia and that she was still perfectly frozen.

****

The process for readying Cynthia's body for the freeze-drying chamber was no different from any of the other animals she had preserved. First, she was thawed and her organs removed to rid the body cavity of excess moisture. Perpetual Pets does not extract bones or flesh, but the body is cleaned, groomed, and the pet posed in the position requested—most often the sleeping position with the eyelids closed. If open eyes are requested, the technicians insert glass eyes of the appropriate size and color.

Once the body is cleaned, groomed, and

positioned, it's put back into a freezer to lock the pose in place. The body is placed in a bell-jar kind of chamber with a hose on the end and the temperature dropped to minus five degrees Fahrenheit. During the sublimation process (like dry ice exposed to a higher temperature that forms a vapor instead of liquefying), the moisture in the form of vapor is removed, but the protein structure does not collapse. Over a course of ten to twelve weeks, the frozen moisture is extracted in a gaseous form and removed. While there is some shrinkage of the body, the form remains mostly intact, except for the nose leather, which looks a bit wrinkled.

When Cynthia's body came back to Connie and Tod several weeks later, they were awestruck. The dead Cynthia looked exactly like Cynthia taking a nap. The only really noticeable difference between the live Cynthia and the freeze-dried version was that she felt considerably lighter. The ten-pound cat finished at three and a half pounds.

In death the preserved Cynthia looks as beautiful as she did in life. Her freeze-dried body has the same fullness and shape it had when she was alive. Her luxuriant fur looks as though she has just been given a shampoo.

With Cynthia's body in plain view, sometimes in the living room, sometimes in the den or their bedroom, Tod and Connie pass her, tell her "Good morning, Cynthia," or they joke, "You really need to find something to do, Cynthia." Having her freeze-dried body lying in a corner feels neither morbid nor grisly to them. On the contrary, over time and once a person gets used to the idea, he or she can even develop a sense of humor about it.

Connie and Tod don't kid themselves into thinking she's alive, but they admit to occasional, almost subliminal thoughts sometimes as they pass her— *Whoa! Did she just move?* Tod says the human brain is hard-wired to think that a sleeping animal might move. The preserved Cynthia is the sleeping cat who delighted them, slept with them, played with them, and ordered them around. It's not so surprising that every once in a while, when Connie and Tod walk past Cynthia, they have to remind themselves that she is, in fact, dead. But usually the sight of her triggers only the happiest memories.

Recently they lost Willie. This time they didn't hesitate—his body was sent to Perpetual Pets to be preserved by freeze-drying.

Anyone interested in freeze-drying services for a passed pet can find out more information at www.perpetualpet.net. Perpetual Pets is now located at 6704 Sinsonte Street, Fort Pierce, FL 34951.

Chapter Twenty-Two
Until They Meet Again

Species: canine—standard poodle
Name: Maggie
Born: 1981
Died: 1994
Human companion: Su Menu

In 1981 Su Menu was a single mom living in an apartment with her two boys, six-year-old Josh and four-year-old Nathaniel. In the apartment below there lived a standard black poodle named Max, his hair cut in the chiseled way of the show poodle, pom-poms on each ankle, on his tail, and atop his head. The first time the boys saw him, they threw their arms around him in bear hugs. His personality was so kind and tolerant, his bearing so impressive, that Su decided her boys should have a dog just like him for their very own.

After much searching through the local newspaper and dog magazines, Su happened upon a breeder of standard poodles in the town of Springville, close to their hometown of Bountiful, Utah. At the breeder's home Su inspected each of the four puppies, holding each to her chest, lifting them into the air, and looking into their faces. Each was adorable and friendly, but when she picked up the fourth puppy and looked into her eyes, she was immediately captivated. The white pup stared at her in such a soft, loving, almost uncanny way.

Su held the pup to her chest and stroked her soft fur. "She wants me. She's the one. I can't describe it, but there's something going on between us—a connection, of sorts, I didn't feel with the others. It's strange, but I almost feel as though I know her from somewhere."

****

Maggie, as Su named the puppy, quickly grew to standard poodle size. She and Max sometimes played together when Josh and Nathaniel took her outside to play catch and walk the neighborhood. While Max sported a fancy, froufrou hairdo, Su chose not to groom Maggie with all the show-poodle frills and pom-poms, preferring to shave her close all over, except for around her ankles and her mustache. And later she decided to remove Maggie's mustache, too. She wanted Maggie to be a more natural-looking poodle. Haute couture was not in Maggie's or Su's personality.

Not only was Maggie the boys' playmate, but she protected them wherever they went in Bountiful. If the boys went on an errand to the local grocery, Maggie followed, always watchful of any danger the boys could stumble into. If any other dogs approached, Maggie stood by her young charges, growling, staring hard, her lips quivering. And she always walked on the outside of the pavement so that the boys couldn't accidentally fall into the street and hurt themselves.

Often Maggie and Su strolled through the town park. After the sojourn each time, dog and human shared a frozen yogurt on a park bench. At the park Maggie watched as the birds busied themselves building nests, tugging at worms, and flying low beneath the oak trees. There, amongst nature, Su found peace and tranquility borne from her best friend and curly-haired sidekick.

Su found Maggie's presence comforting in every way. When she had to run errands on a weekend—to the bank, to the grocery store, to the deli, to the soccer field to drop off her sons for a game or practice— Maggie rode alongside in the passenger's seat, content to stay in the car while Maggie shopped. Maggie's constancy provided Su, in contrast to her hectic workday schedule, much solace. After work Su relished coming home to her Maggie, longing for her serenity.

Though Su didn't think Maggie particularly needed any kind of training because she wasn't a high-energy, curious type of dog, she decided to take her through obedience school anyway. As a two-year-old, Maggie trained quickly, learning to heel and stay, sit, and lie down.

To be sure, Maggie seemed too good to be true. Having no vices such as loud barking, howling, or agitated, frantic behavior, she seemed too perfect, always agreeable, quiet, and willing. In time, however, Su discovered Maggie's only temptation—the church's sprinkler system across the street.

One day Su pulled into the driveway with Maggie, newly groomed, her hair washed, dried, and combed, not a hair out of place. After Maggie was coiffed, she felt particularly proud and spunky with her newly washed coat. She paraded around like a princess, prancing and dog-laughing, so pretty and clean she felt. But on this particular day, Maggie wouldn't feel clean or proud for very long.

"Come on, Maggie. We'll go inside, and I'll give you a treat for being such a good doggie at the hairdressers." Su climbed out of the car. Maggie jumped out, trotted to the front door, and then her perfectly shaved ears perked. She whipped around. The church's sprinkler was on—*"Tck-tck-tck-tck-tck-tck-tck-tck."* Over and over the water sprayed the grass in a diameter of thirty feet. Suddenly Maggie took off at a gallop. Su's heart leaped to her throat as she watched her dog run into the street. "No, Maggie! Come here! Come here!" But Maggie wasn't listening. Laughing and smiling, she bounded into the church yard beneath the water spray.

Beneath the sprinkler she frolicked—twisting, leaping, rolling in the soaked grass—her new hairdo dripping and sagging. Wherever the burst of water hit the ground, Maggie bit the grass, tossing clumps of grass, roots, and mud into the air. She ran after the clumps when they landed, scooped them up in her mouth again, and sent them airborne. Then the sprinkler rained down on her, and she again tore the ground where the water hit.

Across the street Su, Maggie's leash in hand, stood irritated but half-smiling. Maggie had ruined her thirty-dollar hairdo and was soaked and covered with mud. By the time Su leashed Maggie, dragging her from under the sprinkler, Su was soaked, too.

Another day when Su let Maggie out the back door to do her business, Su waited at the screen door. Instead of coming back inside, however, Maggie took off at a trot around the side of the house. Su called and called, running after, but it was too late. Maggie had heard the church's sprinkler system going and was off to play.

What Maggie hadn't noticed in her frenzy to cross the street was a car speeding towards her. Before she knew it, the car was on top of her. The driver swerved and hit the brakes, but it was too late. The car slammed into her. Screaming, Su ran into the road after her best friend. She scooped her in her arms and laid her down in the yard. The driver ran to their side to help.

Luckily Maggie was not dead, but she had a broken back leg. So with the driver's help, Su hoisted Maggie into the car, and they flew to the vet's office. During the operation the vet found the break serious enough to need steel pins to stabilize the bone. Then he wrapped Maggie's leg in a fiberglass cast. Back home, Maggie rested, somber. As Su fed her salami pieces, her favorite treat, she seemed depressed—she knew she had paid a high price for running off.

In the next weeks Su helped her adjust to the ungainly leg cast, bringing her dinner so that she didn't have to walk and helping her go outside when necessary. Maggie's convalescence took six weeks, but her leg finally healed and the cast was removed. Though Maggie walked with a slight limp for the rest of her life, she never again ran across the street to play under the church's sprinkler.

The sprinkler had been Maggie's only vice; otherwise, she was a sweetheart, even with Su's students. Su taught piano lessons, and when her young protégés came to the house for a lesson, Maggie was right there, lying beneath the piano bench, her tail thumping to the rhythm of the music. Even during the recitals held at Su's home, when upwards of thirty people gathered to hear their sons and daughters play, there Maggie attended, the child's steadfast supporter beneath the piano bench. Maggie's calm presence helped ease the children's fear. They figured if Maggie could be the center of attention and not be scared, then they, too, could play without stage fright.

After living in Bountiful for seven years, Su moved her family to Salt Lake City. Su, Josh, and Than found a new life in the bustling city. For Maggie the main attraction was the wooded area behind the capitol. Called City Creek, the woods ran along a creek. A paved road ran parallel to the creek until it diverted from the stream and headed up the mountain. City Creek was beautiful, and Su took Maggie there to walk many times, especially in the morning when no one else was there. Just the two of them, Su and Maggie, walked and walked in the peace and quiet of the woods. In the winter City Creek was particularly dazzling right after a snowstorm, the ice crystals sparkling in the new-fallen snow. On their snow-covered walks, Su and Maggie painted two different sets of footprints—one human, the other canine—two spirits, the sounds of their footsteps snow-muffled in their journey as one.

Soon after Su settled into her new home in Salt Lake City, she adopted a cat from the local humane shelter. Her name was Shura, and she was part Siamese, her eyes the color of a robin's egg. Maggie's reaction to the new addition to the family was welcoming.

Shura took to Maggie like a honey bee to a daisy. She was naturally drawn to Maggie, lured to her curly, soft fur and calmed by Maggie's easygoing temperament. Most days when Su was at work, Shura and Maggie lay together on Su's bed or the couch. Shura constantly groomed Maggie, licking and licking her fur as though she was cleaning another feline. Little

Shura picked Maggie's fur, separating the hairs to look for fleas, licking, nipping along the skin like a monkey grooming a sibling. Most times Maggie tolerated Shura's fascination with cleaning her fur, but sometimes Shura's tedious pulling and licking got to be too much. Then Maggie growled, *"Enough already!"* and Shura would stop licking.

Only one other time did Maggie have a lapse of judgment. For Thanksgiving Su had taken two pumpkin pies out of the oven and set them on the kitchen counter to cool. But she had forgotten to buy whipped cream, so she ran to the grocery store. When she came back, Maggie stood with embarrassment, pumpkin pudding hanging in clumps all over her white mustache and her feet. She had devoured one whole pumpkin pie and had been working on the second when Su came home. At sight of Maggie decorated with Thanksgiving's dessert, Su's first reaction was anger, but as she reached for the towel to wipe Maggie clean, she had to giggle. Maggie, bloated and messy, looked up at Maggie with her big, brown sorry eyes. Maggie never got sick from too much pie, but she never was tempted by the taste of pumpkin after that.

Maggie had been a true best friend and lifelong companion. She was Su's shadow, her protector, her walking buddy, her child-friend. She shared Su's bed, played with her boys, and went everywhere with them. Maggie was Su's true spiritual partner.

Maggie died in 1994.

****

Maggie's Memorial

When Maggie died, Su defied death in the only way she believed was appropriate. The process of mummification, with its spiritual will, guaranteed the two would be together somewhere, someplace, possibly in different forms, but together nevertheless.

****

In death, Maggie, a white standard poodle, has become a work of art through the mummification process. Maggie's bronze mummiform® stands under her human companion's bay window in the living room under a banana plant tree, a schefflera, and a five-foot Norfolk Island pine.

Su Menu often thinks about her reasons for memorializing her best friend through mummification. "After my beloved Maggie died, I just couldn't put her in the ground to be eaten by worms. And I couldn't burn her up, either. I thought that transforming her into a piece of art was the nicest way to thank her for all she brought to my life."

Su carefully weighed all options before she decided to mummify her pet poodle. Besides the fact that she could not bear to bury or cremate her friend, Su had already signed with Summum© to have herself mummified upon her own death. So she wanted her dog in a mummiform®, too, so that the two could share a mausoleum space together one day. She believed mummification was a lasting way to keep Maggie with her, not only in her living room, but also in another life.

The decision to mummify her best friend, however, involved so much more than the simple fact of transforming her dog into a work of art. Mummification, by its very nature and ceremonial process, assures the living participants and their deceased loved one they will meet each other in another form or in another time or place again. They will be reunited again in their next lifetime.

A person not accustomed to such a way of memorializing an animal might think mummification rather primitive and even grisly. After all, what most people understand about mummies comes from television dramatics about the Egyptians' method of mummifying, a few of which use special tools and procedures.

In fact, mummification is not simply an Egyptian practice. From 6000 BC to 600 AD, 400,000,000 people all over the world, from the Egyptians to the Jews to the Chinese to the peoples in North, Central, and South America to those in Europe, Asia, Australia, to the high llamas of Tibetan Buddhists, to Popes, and even to Jesus, who, after his crucifixion, was treated with myrrh and aloes, wrapped, and entombed, have been mummified using different methods (B. Aua, personal communication, April 5, 2008).

In the case of Summum's operations, the barbarism portrayed in horror movies is absent. The body, says Su, is treated with the ultimate respect, and while the organs of the body are extracted and cleansed in the "fluids of purification," the brain is not. And the organs, once treated, are all carefully put back into the body cavity before it is wrapped.

Allowing their clients to meditate or pray as they wish next to their pet's body, Summum allows the living companion to play a part in the creating and the reading of the spiritual will. Most often it is prepared by the animal's human companion. In Su's case, she wrote and participated in the reading of the will because she wanted Maggie to know she was present to help her find her way to the next life and to cross over to the other side. Su wanted to allay her fears in case Maggie's essence or spirit, in its death state, was scared and feeling lost in the next destination. So several times Su went to her side while her body lay in the purification font for seventy-seven days.

The mummification process is multi-dimensional as well as scientific and can take many months until the mummiform®, the metal casing containing the prepared body, is completed. In the preparatory stages the animal is taken to a pyramidal structure said to release calming vibrations. In the center of the pyramid, the pet is placed in a font of liquids which preserve the body. The body is submerged in the covered font for many days, at which time the spiritual will is read aloud over the font over and over again. The spiritual will or transference is akin to a road map that provides directions to lost travelers. It serves as a guide for the deceased, directing the spirit into the next life. A soul, a spirit, an essence, or whatever term a person prefers to call the personality of the lost one devoid of a physical self, needs this kind of guidance in order to stay calm, for a dead person or animal may feel worried and lost in the transitional, unfamiliar world.

In the pyramid wherein Maggie lay immersed in the liquids of the font, Su sat and visited with her dog-daughter of many years. She felt strangely tranquil and complete within the pyramid's walls. Su reminded Maggie, by reading and rereading the spiritual will, that she shouldn't be afraid and that she loved her and would meet her in the future in another life.

Su deeply appreciated the respect and kind treatment both she and Maggie received from the people at Summum during her grieving time. Just as

Summum encourages human companions to bring their pets' personal items to place around the font—a feeding bowl with some food, the pet's toys, or anything else the animal loved so that its spirit would be eased with familiar things—they allowed Su to bring to Maggie's font whatever would ease her dog's fears. Su chose to bring flowers and Maggie's picture.

After many days Maggie's body was removed from the font, and Su petted her for the last time. Her skin was soft, her fur silky. Even her eyes were just as they had been when she was alive. She was not dried up or shriveled at all. It was amazing. She looked so real she could have been alive.

The next part of the process was wrapping the body and forming the clay model. Maggie's body was wrapped with gauze many times to keep the body wet. Then she was covered with a rubber membrane, after which fiberglass material was applied. This resin, when dried, held the body in position. Then, after Su explained to a clay artist that she wanted Maggie's mummiform® standing, he covered the body with a layer of clay, molding the clay around Maggie's facial features and sculpting the clay to resemble her fur. The clay figure then became the mold from which another mold was made and into which the bronze was poured. Because, as the bronze cools, it shrinks, using the clay as a mold is necessary so that the body is able to fit inside the metal mummiform.®

Modern mummification® allows pet owners to have their beloved pets alongside them at home preserved in an artistic metal casing. In addition, the reading of the spiritual will, an integral ceremonial process, insures the deceased animal's essence will be given direction in order to meet his or her human companion again in the next life.

Su Menu wanted to do everything she could to defy the terminal nature of death itself, which, she believed, was accomplished through the spiritual will. In whatever life remains after death and in whatever form Maggie's essence assumes in that life, Maggie will be searching for Su. In turn, in whatever form Maggie takes, Su will one day be searching for Maggie, in whatever form Su takes. The two will find each other and live and love together in another life.

****

All information about Summum's method of and philosophy of mummification and the history of mummification was in the form of a personal communication with Bernie Aua, director of Summum, to Gay Balliet-Perkins on April 5, 2008. Additional information on Maggie's mummification was provided by Su Menu in personal communications from April 2 to 5, 2008.

For more information on modern mummification®, see "Spiritual Will for Animals" & "Mummification—A Philosophical Examination" at:

www.summum.org/
mummification/pets/spiritualwell.shtml

Summum® and Mummiform® are registered trademarks of Summum.

****

Any reader interested in exploring mummification for memorializing a pet or themselves can find information at www.summum.org.

Conclusion
Talkin' 'bout My Girl

Species: feline—Cornish Rex
Name: Wendy
Born: Spring 1999
Died: June 2, 2003
Human companion: Gay L. Perkins

I smiled down at the princess-white cat in my lap. "Wrinky nose! Show me your little wrinky nose." Wendy lay sprawled on her back, her torso curved in a half moon, all four legs splayed like a sunbather on a pool float. She stretched a front leg toward my face, her gesture of adoration. My cat loved me.

Wendy was as white as a snowfall just hours old, her fur as pristine as a newly opened container of dessert topping. Her coat looked as untarnished as the pure-white caps of an energetic sea. Her fur sparkled like the bubbles in my bath water. She glowed like the fullest moon.

And she was mine.

My snowflake-colored cat's affection for me rivaled that of a sister's. Over the four years we lived together, she became my best friend and constant companion—far more forgiving and accepting of my faults than any human friend had ever been. Daily she accompanied me on my house and barn chores, walked beside me through the woods, and sat on a stump with me. With no amount of exaggeration, I felt as though, through understanding Wendy, I had magically grown a layer of feline skin just beneath my epidermis.

At once human and feline, I discovered a renewed desire to play like a child—peek around the furniture at my alabaster friend, to chase and be chased all around the house. I squealed when she raced me to the end of the hall, and I skidded to a stop beside the sofa while she back-pedaled, grinning, through my legs.

Wendy was my comfort and confidante, never questioning my motives, never judging my actions. When I burped or passed gas, she didn't scowl, laugh, or chastise my brutishness. During our conversations, she never interrupted, never gazed off in another direction with eyes glazed over, never disagreed or told me I was foolish. Always she was as attentive as a kindergartener on her first school day. She question-looked, her head tilted, and listened—rapt and enraptured. And then she asked in her cat language if everything was all right—if we were safe.

I assured her we were.

Likewise, I listened to her. She didn't just discuss what she expected on her dinner plate that evening. Though she became most vocal at mealtime, Pussy Gourmand brand was by no means the only topic of conversation. My feline was well versed and gregarious about all things cat and human. In the morning we spoke of the day's activities—what tree she was going to climb, how she might play in the barn loft and hunt for mice, how she could guard my garden from butterflies. And I explained she needed to wear her invisible fence collar so that nothing bad happened should she stray while on a wild-mouse chase. She didn't argue, just meow-agreed, and curled around my legs.

"So show me your wrinky nose, Wendy." As she lay on her back, I stroked her down the center of her belly, and she looked up at me with her wide, kind eyes. Then it happened as it had a hundred times before—the crinkling of the nose. She curved her body to port, never taking her eyes off me because she knew the conversation was meant exclusively for her. She understood my tone of voice as much as any person understood speech. Her wide golden eyes caught mine, and she tilted her head again, her eyes turning to contented slits. Then, almost imperceptibly, I saw the little parentheses appear on either side of her nose pad—the nose wrinkles—her smile.

Wendy's smile was not the grin of a mischievous imp like Alice's Cheshire cat. Nor was it the simper of the cartoon's Felix. No—her smile carried with it a cool peace of mind and satisfaction not of a cat but more like the Mona Lisa. I had never seen the wrinky nose, Wendy's expression of affection, on any of my other cats, not even my dear Willie. Sure, they curled in my lap, gazed lovingly into my eyes, and slinked between my legs, but none of them had ever crinkled their nose when they gazed into my eyes. That was Wendy's idiosyncratic sign of adoration. When the skin puckered around her nose, she was expressing calm and acceptance with gladness, pure contentment with and appreciation of my company.

With her nose wrinkles hilled tightly around the end of her nose, she leaned to starboard and out of her throat bleated a tiny squeak. *"M-ya. M-ya. M-ya."*

"Oh, really? Well, as a matter of fact, I do remember seeing you on that fallen tree this afternoon. You conquered that tree like a pro, Wendy. It's fun climbing trees, isn't it—winding in and out of the branches. I used to do it, too, when I was much younger, just like you. It's wonderful sitting there in the canopy, especially in summer, with the birds and bugs whispering in your ears. Kitties and kids all like to sit in the treetops."

The side of her nose had relaxed for a few seconds, but at the sound of my voice, it drew up again into tiny hillocks. Her eyes never left mine as she twisted sideways, relaxed. My own smile-wrinkles curled up, too, and I stroked her wide moon belly. Then Wendy pawed the air in front of my face. *"M-ya. M-ya."*

I rubbed the thin webbing between her toes. "Uh-huh. Good thing that tree fell down last winter, since it's become your favorite spot in the woods. It's just your size—only five feet from the ground. You can scout squirrels, birds, and other stuff like an expert from your tree, can't you? And you can watch me pass when I run."

"M-ya, m-ya, m-ya."

"And you look so beautiful in your safety collar." It was the only lie I ever told her.

Her eyes went to slits. *"Re-ow."* I knew she didn't like wearing her rather cumbersome radio collar, a device that contained her within the boundaries of the underground fence. Wearing it, though, amounted to a lot less agony for me. At least she wouldn't be killed on the road.

"You don't mind the collar too much?"

"Re-ow." She disliked it, but she was going to

wear it so that nothing would happen as it did a year ago.

****

How I acquired the underground fence was precipitated by a rather emotionally traumatic event. I had been out weeding my garden about five hundred feet from the busy road when my eye caught a white flicker under one of the thirty-foot pine trees—a mere ten feet from the road. I squinted and then started to run—my heart bounding. From a distance it was hard to tell Wendy from a discarded plastic bag, but when the white thing leaped into the air after something, I knew it was my alter ego—dangerously close to the road. Running as though the devils of hell were clawing my heels, I flew down the driveway. Then, with no traffic in sight, I slowed, stood between her and the road in case she darted there, and called to my cat in a soft, unthreatening voice.

I summoned my nicest, most cloying voice. "Sweet heart." My heart pounded. I smiled and held out my arms as she looked up with a large moth in her mouth. "Sweet heart—you little shit. What are you doing down here so far from the house? Mommy's very angry. You're going to give Mommy a freakin' heart attack." I talked in such a nice quiet voice I'm sure she couldn't detect the hysteria in it. "Let's go back to the house now. Mommy would be very upset to see you smashed all over the road, now, wouldn't she?"

From under the pine tree Wendy looked up, her quarry forgotten, and she smiled. *"M-ya, m-ya, m-ya."*

I smiled, still panic-stricken, as the cars whizzed just feet away. I was scared silly she might turn and run toward the road. But I was counting on her undying devotion to me to distract her from the road. A tractor trailer roared past. In my nicest, most indulgent voice, I coaxed her. "That's right, Wendy. You come to Mommy, and she'll take you back home where you'll be grounded for the rest of the summer." Then I slowly walked over, bent down, and scooped her into my arms. Relaxed, she lay in my arm hammock, the appreciative parentheses curling around the sides of her nose. My heart relaxed. My Wrinky Nose was safe.

The moment after I deposited Wendy in the house, I had the underground fence guy on the phone. "As soon as possible."

In a few weeks the cats had grown used to donning their safety collars each morning. Throughout the day I saw them chasing insects and watching birds and relaxing in the sun. Though playing close to the house didn't offer the same thrill as hunting for wild things a stone's throw from a busy road, they tolerated it. When late afternoon came, they had had their fill of dragonfly and bird watching. Then they came back to the house where, once inside, I freed them from their collars.

****

So as I had done every day since that fateful moment by the busy road, I attached Wendy's collar and let her outside. That evening after Wendy's hard day playing outdoors, I scooped my white Mona Lisa into my arms, snapped off her collar, walked into the kitchen, and set her on the counter. Ricky and the others came running, too—dinnertime. My eight house cats were dancing around my legs in a grand chorus of yelps, meows, and growls, and I had to be careful not to step on any of the hungry throng.

Wendy was our only house cat allowed to dine on

the same counter where I prepared our human dinners. Even as a kitten she was the least aggressive of my cats, so at mealtime, after gobbling up their own food, they pushed her out of the way before she had eaten more than a few mouthfuls. So in order to insure her peace and her share of the rations, I let her eat on the kitchen counter.

Soon Wendy learned to jump onto the counter where she'd wait patiently for her meals. When I bent down to take cat food from a drawer, she developed a quirky and endearing habit, spurred by anticipation. Each time I bent down, the gesture was imminent. I relished it.

As usual, that evening I bent down, opened the cabinet door, and then Wendy went into action on the kitchen counter above me. As I took a few cans into my hands, I glanced up, and there she was, as usual, pacing and strolling along the countertop, her eyes staring down into mine. *"M-ya,"* she squeaked. I laughed. *"M-ya, m-ya, m-ya."*

Then I slowly stood up, and as my head became level with the counter, I saw it coming and then felt it— a tiny head butt to my forehead.

I closed my eyes, and while the rest of the house cats were milling around my ankles, anxious for me to get on with the feeding ritual, I reveled in the head-butting that had become my best friend's daily term of endearment.

Bump...bump...bump. I stayed slightly bent, head up, as Wendy bopped her head into mine. With each butt she let out a tiny squeak. *"Mi-ya, mi-ya, mi-ya."* I felt *bump...bump...bump* again. I opened my eyes and smiled. Wendy was definitely on a mission. She butted me, let out a *"mi-ya,"* and began to pace. Then she reversed, came toward my face again, and I saw it way before she bumped me again—the wrinky nose, as I affectionately came to call her wrinkled nose. On her reversal and as she was gearing up for yet another bang into my forehead, I saw the nose wrinkles pucker. Then, with the two parentheses encircling her nose, she strolled toward me, dipped her chin, and hit me with her forehead. She yipped in triumph and turned away for another go 'round.

I giggled, and goose bumps erupted on my skin. If this wasn't acceptance and affection from an animal, then I'd never be able to tell what was. Sure, she was excited that she was being fed, but I'm sure that if a stranger were fixing her meal, she wouldn't have given her the ultimate compliment by butting that person's head. I let her head-bumping continue for several seconds before the other cats howled me to attention.

****

In four years Wendy had become my feline playmate and child companion. All my inside cats, and even my outside cats, were my children, and I didn't much care if mothers of human babies resented my equating my cats to children and my affording my cats affection usually restricted to the human species. The feelings were relative and personal, and I allowed myself that luxury. Other people didn't have to regard their pets as their children if they didn't want to, but my cats were the loves of my life—particularly Wendy.

In return, Wendy surely must have regarded me like a mother or a sister or, at the very least, one of her own kind. She greeted me when I came home, running in long glad strides to the door and walking beside me to the closet where I threw down my keys and purse. She lay with me nightly in the crook of my arm, and we watched The Travel Channel together and dreamed of riding the gondolas of Venice and climbing the Arenal Volcano in Costa Rica. When we watched the show's best ten beaches of the world, I whispered in her ear that my favorite beach was on Little Cayman where no other footprints but hers and mine would be visible. I told her how she would love to chase the crabs and iguanas in Little Cayman and that I would protect her from any barracuda that might be lurking in the calm waters off the beach. And as The Travel Channel geared up to its final first pick of beautiful beaches, we fell asleep together, true pals.

Wendy was my favorite child, not only because she conversed with me, laughed with me, played with me, but also because she loved affection. At any moment and no matter what each of us was doing—whether I was on my knees cleaning grout lines or whether she was relaxing poolside in the sun—I could depend on Wendy for a friendly kitty kiss.

While others may scoff at Wendy and me making kissy faces at each other, it was our "thing" and no one else need approve. Sure, Wendy never puckered her lips the way humans do when they kiss. No, her kiss was one that her physical limitations could accommodate. And she reserved her kisses for me only. She didn't offer kisses to anyone else.

Whenever I wanted a Wendy kiss, regardless if I were passing her on her fallen tree or if she were relaxing in a sunny window, I stuck my pursed lips out and muttered through them, "Gimme kiss. Gimme kiss." Then, with a prolonged, loud smooching sound, I sucked air into the caricature of a kiss. With that, no matter if she were hunting or relaxing, she'd march right up to me and bop her forehead into my lips. Though she couldn't pucker her thin kitty lips, she could wrinkle her nose and meet my kiss with her face. She butted my lips and backed up to see my reaction. "Yes, that was a lovely kiss, Wendell. Gimme 'nother kiss, Wend." Then she backed up, walked forward, and bopped my protruding lips again.

Wendy and I could have auditioned for vaudeville had it been fashionable in the new millennia. Instead, we kept each other company and played in the carefree way of children playing with each other.

Wendy died unexpectedly June 3, 2003.

****

Wendy's Memorial

None of my other cats came as any comfort when Wendy died. I had lost my best friend, and I was devastated.

I hung out with the scrapbook which, because she was only four years old when she died, had only a few pictures of her—one climbing her fallen tree in the woods, another, her sunbathing on the warm rocks around the pool, and her best shot, her sitting under the decorated Christmas tree.

I visited her daily in the cat cemetery behind our house, and I talked to her and gave her smoochy kisses above ground, hoping, somehow, she could hear me. And I cried and cried until I was sapped dry.

Searching the internet for a pet portrait artist, I happened upon the artwork of Pat Saunders-White. I loved her colorful, happy renditions of all sorts of animals. So I contacted Pat, sent Wendy's Christmas tree photo, and in a few months received the package in the mail.

That Christmas as I unwrapped the usual muck boots, winter barn coats, slippers, and other stuff, I kept Wendy's picture wrapped. Wendy's original painting would be my Christmas's pièce de résistance.

Then, when nothing was left to open, I took the package in my lap and began to peel back the paper. Then there was the bubble wrap to undo. I bit my lip and turned it around to face me.

Tears welled. "My Wendy. If only I could have my real Wendy back for Christmas."

I took her unwrapped painting in my hands, looked at it, and held it to my chest. "It's my Wendy—just as she always looked sitting under the Christmas tree." Tears streamed down my face. Then I looked at the tree I had put up weeks ago. Without Wendy under it enjoying its pine smell and twinkling lights, it looked unfinished, almost undecorated.

"She's beautiful. I know just where I'm going to hang it—where I can see it every day."

****

Each day when I write about animals—farm animals and pets—I see Wendy vigilant under the Christmas tree. She hangs in the office directly across from my desk. At any moment I can look up and imagine her and me walking through the woods and head-butting each other in the kitchen. And I can imagine her on her back, feet in the air, gazing into my eyes with those crinkly "parentheses" around her nose—her signature gesture of love for me.

Wendy lives on in Pat's work of art and in the memories painted indelibly in my mind.

****

In America many, many people love their animal companions as much if not more than their closest family members or friends. Their animal friends have demonstrated unquestionable loyalty and have taught their human companions so much. They teach us to live in the moment and to serve each other with the goodness and selflessness of the other's presence.

Because animals neither live in the past nor devise for the future, they live purely in the moment, in the present, in the spirit of the minute with their human friends. They find their happiness totally within the singular moment—eating a dish of food, chewing a carrot, slaking their thirst, relieving themselves, being rubbed and touched and talked with by their humans.

Pets also offer us their presence. Since they cannot speak our language, pets ease our worst fears and nightmares by just staying close. Their time is ours, our disappointments and tragedies theirs as well. They attend by simply allowing us to run a tense hand through their fur, to cry alongside without fear of mockery. Our pets' presence gives us relief from the human world and its trials. And in everyday life, the pet offers his or her presence, eager to accompany us to the store, the park, the state game lands, to be with us in front of the television and in bed.

The pet, too, looks to his human mate as a source of comfort. When a thunderstorm approaches, the scared dog calms in the presence of his human soul mate. While a nervous horse under saddle fears the loud blatting of an oncoming motorcycle, he absorbs his courage from his reassuring rider. The two protect each other.

The animal companion remains always loyal, trusting, uncritical, and nonjudgmental. He or she supplies his human with implicit love, demanding no qualifications, no limits, and no conditions through which he tempers his affections. Illustrative of this fact, is a quote valued by England's Queen Victoria (1837-1901), a proponent of humane treatment for animals. The queen used the observation on her dog's tombstone because it so fittingly defined Dash's lack of subversion. "His attachment was without selfishness, his playfulness without malice, his fidelity without deceit."

When a friend, an animal friend, we deeply love and have lived with dies, the most natural thing in the world is to prepare a fitting memorial, no matter the gesture be simple or grand. Our pets, individuals so unique, irreplaceable, and so loved, earn memorials because of the profound respect we have for them.

****

A quiet revolution born from the relationships nurtured between man and beast is rising from the depths of America's underground. Grieving pet owners want their friends, their neighbors, and funerary professionals to accept that their pets deserve the respect and care given humans after they die—thus, the trend for pet funerals, cemeteries, and crematoriums. Currently, over five hundred pet cemeteries exist in the United States, and, daily, directors of funeral homes are being asked to perform funerals for people's pets as well.

One cemetery in the United States, however, has taken pet funerals and pet cemeteries a step higher. Recently the Hillcrest Memorial Park in Hermitage,

Pennsylvania, received licensure to bury pets alongside their human companions.

The Hillcrest Memorial Park, established in 1935, first offered a cemetery garden for humans. Later they sectioned off land for an all-pet cemetery. Now, within the Hillcrest Memorial Park, a six-acre section of peaceful landscaping called Hillcrest Memorial Park People and Pet Gardens is devoted to burying pets alongside their human companions. A person can be buried in one plot with up to three pets, and more pets can occupy adjoining lots.

The Hillcrest-Flynn Pet Funeral Home and Crematory directors provide funerary services for pets, complete with viewings, cremations, and memorial services. After the funeral ceremony, the pet can be buried in either the Pet Garden or the People & Pet Garden. In addition, if a human companion chooses to be buried alongside his or her pet, that pet's name will be etched alongside his or her human companion's, into the same bronze marker.

Not only can a person be buried together with his or her pet or pets, but the Hillcrest-Flynn Pet Funeral Home & Crematory preserves a keepsake of the pet's fur, as well as a footprint stamped in clay. Not only do the director, Matt Record, and owner, John Flynn, offer grief counseling and pre-burial needs for pets, they also offer grief-stricken animal-parents the opportunity to meet and possibly adopt another pet through animal rescue organizations. Adopting a needy animal right after one's pet has passed on is one of the nicest memorials a person can make for his pet. Mr. Record truly believes what he advises. "The greatest honor [to one's passed pet] is to love another pet."

The Hillcrest Memorial Park People and Pet Gardens has just begun to sign up interested parties, so no one person or pet is buried there yet. The first person will be Mr. Tom Flynn, who wishes to be buried alongside his dog, Derek. Tom Flynn currently owns and presides over all eighty-eight acres of cemetery that is, together, called Hillcrest Memorial Park and the People and Pet Gardens. Mr. Flynn's dog, Derek, a Golden Retriever and the first Canine Companion for Independence dog to serve in a funeral home and provide families, particularly children, relief from grief, functions as a grief management animal, both in the human funeral home and in the pet funeral home.

Together Tom Flynn and Derek not only help people feel better during times of human and pet death, but they also donate their time and services to schools and hospitals. Though both man and his dog are very much alive, Tom and Derek will be buried together, partners in time and eternity, their names etched into the same bronze plaque, in the People and Pet Gardens.

****

People interested in contacting the pet funeral home and receiving more information about being buried alongside their pets can contact the Hillcrest Memorial Park by going to www.hillcrestflynn.com. Their address is 2619 East State St., Hermitage, PA 16148. Their email is mrecord@hillcrestflynn.com. Their phone number is 724-347-5100.

To the Reader

Memorializing pets has been popular since Egyptian times. Memorializing your pet in any way, so long as that way provides you with comfort and fulfillment, whether it be in a fantastic mummy case, a shadowbox holding a paw print and a shank of fur, a plain tombstone bearing the animal's name and photo, a gem made from cremains, a simple burial in the back yard, a "memory spot" in a corner of a living room, or a piece of art, will always remain an individual and very intimate choice.

In today's world, you need not feel foolish mourning and celebrating your animal family member's memory, no matter the extent or simplicity of the memorial. Any memorial, small or fantastic, is borne upon the wings of love.

A word about the author…

With a Ph.D. in English from Lehigh University, Gay Balliet-Perkins has been compared by reviewers to James Herriot. Her animal books detail life doctoring animals in the Pennsylvania Dutch country: *Touched By All Creatures: Doctoring Animals in the Pennsylvania Dutch Country* (1999); *Lowell: The True Story of an Existential Pig* (2000); *Lions & Tigers & Mares—Oh, My!* (2004); *There's a Bear in the Basement* (2016). *Next!* by Virginie Snow (2018) is her first work of women's fiction.

Her greatest literary accomplishment so far, she feels, is *The Celebrated Pet: How Americans Memorialize Their Animal Friends* (2020). Of this book she says, "I feel so close to the quirky, wonderful, courageous animals in this book. I feel as though I have come to appreciate and love them as much as their human companions have. This book has become the closest to my heart."

Thank you for purchasing
this publication of The Wild Rose Press, Inc.

For questions or more information
contact us at
info@thewildrosepress.com.

The Wild Rose Press, Inc.
www.thewildrosepress.com

www.ingramcontent.com/pod-product-compliance
Lightning Source LLC
Chambersburg PA
CBHW060454090426
42735CB00011B/1977